Primary Teaching Assistants

Teaching assistants are uniquely placed to support children's involvement with learning. The role of those who work alongside teachers in the classroom has changed dramatically in recent years and teaching assistants are increasingly involved in planning, teaching and assessing all aspects of the curriculum.

This second edition has been thoroughly updated and includes new chapters on learning in gardens, children's play in virtual environments, specialist approaches for children with communication difficulties, the nature of learning at home, the place of poetry, child abuse, learning in a breakfast club, children's spelling, and the importance of playtime. Exploring the issues that are central to fostering children's learning, the book examines:

- strategies for supporting learning and assessment in English, maths and science
- inclusive and imaginative practices in all areas of learning
- home and community contexts for learning
- working practices which support professional development.

Written for teaching assistants and also teachers, the book aims to enrich the contribution that teaching assistants, as team members, can make to children's learning.

Carrie Cable is an Educational Consultant and Researcher.

Ian Eyres is Senior Lecturer in Education at The Open University.

Roger Hancock is an Educational Consultant and Researcher.

Mary Stacey is a Writer and an Educational Consultant.

Primary Teaching Assistants:
Curriculum in context

This Reader, and the companion volume *Primary Teaching Assistants: Learners and learning* edited by Carrie Cable, Ian Eyres, Roger Hancock and Mary Stacey, form part of the Open University materials for modules about primary education.

Details of Open University modules can be obtained from the Student Registration and Enquiry Service, The Open University, PO Box 197, Milton Keynes MK7 6BJ, United Kingdom (tel. +44 (0)845 300 60 90, e-mail general-enquiries@open.ac.uk). www.open.ac.uk

Primary Teaching Assistants

Curriculum in context
Second edition

Edited by
Carrie Cable, Ian Eyres,
Roger Hancock
and Mary Stacey

Routledge
Taylor & Francis Group
LONDON AND NEW YORK

The Open University

First published in 2005
by Routledge

This edition published in 2013
by Routledge
2 Park Square, Milton Park, Abingdon, Oxon OX14 4RN

Simultaneously published in the USA and Canada
by Routledge
711 Third Avenue, New York, NY 10017

Routledge is an imprint of the Taylor & Francis Group, an informa business

Published in association with The Open University, Walton Hall, Milton Keynes,
MK7 6AA, UK

British Library Cataloguing in Publication Data
A catalogue record for this book is available from the British Library

Library of Congress Cataloging in Publication Data
Primary teaching assistants : curriculum in context /
edited by Carrie Cable . . . [et al.].—2nd ed.
        p. cm.
    1. Teachers' assistants—Great Britain.   2. Education, Elementary—Great Britain.
    I. Hancock, Roger.
    LB2844.1.A8P75 2013
    371.14'1240941—dc23   2012018597

ISBN: 978–0–415–50432–4 (hbk)
ISBN: 978–0–415–50433–1 (pbk)
ISBN: 978–0–203–12836–7 (ebk)

Typeset in Bembo
by RefineCatch Limited, Bungay, Suffolk

Printed and bound by Bell and Bain Ltd, Glasgow

Contents

Acknowledgements

We wish to thank those who have written chapters for this Reader or who have given their permission for us to edit and reprint writing from other publications. A special thanks to Kathy Simms for her invaluable secretarial support, and to Bharti Mistry and Gill Gowans for their ongoing involvement and preparation of the final manuscript for handover to the publishers.

Grateful acknowledgement is made to the following sources for permission to reproduce material in this book. Those chapters not listed below have been specially commissioned.

Lester, S., Jones, O. and Russell, W. (2011) 'Play, playtime and playgrounds', in *Supporting School Improvement Through Play: An Evaluation of South Gloucestershire's Outdoor Play and Learning (OPAL) Programme, Final Report* (London: National Children's Bureau/Play England) pp. 19–25.

Ryan, J. and Williams, J. (2010) 'Children's mathematical understanding as a work in progress: Learning from errors and misconceptions', in I. Thompson (ed.) *Issues in Teaching Numeracy in Primary Schools* 2nd ed. (Maidenhead: Open University Press) pp. 144–157.

English, R. (2010) 'The role of ICT' (subsection 'Why use ICT'), in I. Thompson (ed.) *Issues in Teaching Numeracy in Primary Schools* 2nd ed. (Maidenhead: Open University Press) pp. 98–101.

Stone, L. and Gillen, J. (2008) 'Poetry: an everyday activity' from 'White cars like mice with little legs', in J. Marsh and E. Hallet (eds.) *Desirable Literacies: Approaches to Language and Literacy in the Early Years* 2nd edn. (London: Sage Publications in association with the UK Literacy Association) pp. 37–60.

Bills, C. (2003) 'What can teachers learn from the language that children use?' *Education*, *31*(1), 3–13. Reprinted by permission of Taylor & Francis Ltd (http://www.tandf.co.uk/journals).

Nutbrown, C. (2001) 'Watching and learning: The tools of assessment', in G. Pugh *Contemporary Issues in the Early Years* (London: Sage Publications) pp. 66–73.

Hussein, H. (2010) 'Using the sensory garden as a tool to enhance the educational development and social interaction of children with special needs' *Support for Learning*, *25*(1), 25–31.

Murphy, P. (1997) 'Constructivism and primary science' *Primary Science Review*, *49*, 27–29.

Turner, J. (2010) 'Primary science: Are there any reasons to be cheerful?' *Forum*, *52*(3), 381–394. http://dx.doi.org/10.2304/forum.2010.52.3.381 Reprinted with permission of the author and Symposium Journals.

Moss, E. (1977) 'What is a "good" book?', in Meek et al. *The Cool Web: The Pattern of Children's Reading* (London: The Bodley Head) pp. 140–142.

Menzinger, B. and Jackson, R. (2009) 'The effect of light intensity and noise on the classroom behaviour of pupils with Asperger syndrome' *Support for Learning*, *24*(4), 170–175. Reprinted with permission from Blackwell Publishing.

Burke, C. and Grosvenor, I. (2003) 'School buildings: "A safe haven, not a prison . . ." ', in *The School I'd Like*. Reprinted by permission of Taylor & Francis Ltd.

Kenner, C., Arju, T., Gregory, E., Jessel, J. and Ruby, M. (2004) 'The role of grandparents in children's learning' *Primary Practice*, *38* (Autumn), National Primary Trust.

Thomas, A. and Lowe, J. (2007) *Educating Your Child at Home* (London: Continuum) pp. 8–19.

Marsh, J. (2010) 'Young children's play in online virtual worlds' *Journal of Early Childhood Research*, *8*(23), 23–39.

Feiler, A. (2010) 'Successful projects in the United Kingdom', in A. Feiler *Engaging 'Hard to Reach' Parents* (Chichester: Wiley-Blackwell) pp. 81–99.

Dann, R. (1996) 'Developing pupils' skills in self-assessment in the primary classroom' *Primary Practice: The Journal of the National Primary Trust*, *5*(June).

Eyres, I., Cable, C., Hancock, R. and Turner, J. (2004) 'Whoops, I forgot David': Children's perceptions of the adults who work in their classroom. *Early Years*, *24*(2). London: Taylor & Francis Ltd.

Lewis, A., Newton, H. and Vials, S. (2008) 'Realising child voice: the development of cue cards' *Support for Learning*, *23*(1), 26–31. Reprinted with permission from Blackwell Publishing.

Rix, J. (2006) 'From one professional to another', in B. Rix *All About Us: The Story of People with a Learning Disability and MENCAP* (London: MENCAP).

Blackledge, A. (1999) 'Literacy, power and social justice: Bangladeshi women and their children's reading' *Primary Practice: The Journal of the National Primary Trust*, *21* (September).

Pullman, P. (2005) 'Common sense has much to learn from moonshine', *Guardian* 22 January. Copyright Guardian Newspapers Limited 2005.

Bell, M. (2010) 'Supporting children with spelling problems', in *Special Children*, August, 34–38.

Introduction

As with this book's companion volume, *Primary Teaching Assistants: Learners and Learning*, two principles have played a role in the selection of all the chapters included: their relevance to the understandings and practices of teaching assistants in primary schools and their capacity to meet the needs of students registered on Open University modules about primary education.

The role of those who work alongside teachers in the classroom has changed enormously over the past decade or so. Where there was once a clearly defined (and often vigorously defended) line between the duties of those whose job is to teach and those who 'just assist', now the working relationship is much more likely to be characterised by shared responsibility, partnership, and a degree of overlap in the roles of teacher and teaching assistant. Several of the chapters that follow reflect this relationship, sometimes explicitly, often implicitly.

Perhaps the most remarkable feature of the development of the teaching assistant role has been their increasingly active involvement in planning, teaching, and assessing all aspects of the curriculum. Although 'supporting learning' continues to be used to describe what teaching assistants do, they are, of course, involved in teaching interactions with children. Teaching assistants often find themselves teaching 'the basics' related to English and maths. Increasingly, however, they also work with children across a full range of curriculum subjects and contexts. The contexts in which children learn, and the curriculum (in all its senses), are the focus of this volume.

We should stress that we do not conceptualise 'curriculum' simply as a set of 'things to be taught', still less as a set of subjects. We have found it useful to think of the curriculum in terms of three distinctive aspects (Robitaille and Dirks 1982):

- the curriculum as intended
- the curriculum as implemented
- the curriculum as attained.

Working in the context of primary mathematics, Askew (1998) sees the intended curriculum as something to be found in published and official documents. In each of the four countries of the United Kingdom, the intended curriculum for primary schools is expressed in guidance documents and frameworks. It is worth noting that while these 'intentions' usually come from outside the learning context, it is a matter for teachers and teaching assistants to convert them into action, so creating the implemented curriculum. Everything teachers and teaching assistants offer children to support or influence their learning, from choosing learning objectives through creating a physical environment to ways of speaking to children, contribute to the implemented curriculum. Finally, what each individual child actually learns will be a different set of things again, and this is the 'attained curriculum'. Some of the chapters that follow will focus mainly on just one of these aspects: Cathy Nutbrown's treatment of assessment (Chapter 6), for example, is concerned with the attained curriculum, while in their account of a 'willow garden' (Chapter 11), Sue Hadfield and Sam Burns give us a sense of how they implement a meaningful curriculum away from the classroom.

In choosing a title for this book, we felt very strongly that the word 'context' should occur alongside 'curriculum'. Of course, context is an important part of the view of curriculum outlined above, but we wanted to stress that learning always has a context, not least because of the crucial role played by teaching assistants in creating that context. An essential part of the context for learning – the reason why no two children will ever learn exactly the same thing from the same experience – is the knowledge and understandings that children bring with them from home, family, culture, and elsewhere. Many of these contexts may be more familiar to teaching assistants than they are to teachers and headteachers. The situation of bilingual teaching assistants, as outlined by Carrie Cable (Chapter 21), is an obvious illustration of this, but there are many others. Additionally, teaching assistants are often in the best position to really know the children they are working with.

In the UK, for some time now, the history of the primary curriculum has been a changing one. As we write, the coalition government is in the throes of yet another review of the primary curriculum. It seems to us, however, that, at a deep level of thought and practice, there is some stability for those who teach children. In our selection of chapters for this book, we have therefore sought to include authors who have lasting things to say about education. We believe that demands for a rigidly subject-based curriculum is giving way to encouragement for a way of working that is more contextualised and enjoyable and that allows for the fact that the same classroom experience can support a range of cross-curricular aims. We include many chapters where this is the case, in particular in respect of the use of language, ICT, and out-of-classroom learning. We also include several examples of teachers and teaching assistants taking an avowedly creative approach to teaching and learning across the curriculum.

When it comes to offering opinions about education, some voices are very loud. Loudest of all, in recent years, has been central government, but Her Majesty's Inspectorate, the press (often claiming to represent parents and the public), and employers have also been clearly heard. While some of these voices are (as is almost inevitable) included here, we have given prominence to a number of others we think are just as deserving of an audience: teaching assistants, teachers, parents, grandparents, and, most importantly, children. And who better to talk about the process of writing, in Chapter 31, than a highly respected writer?

Organising the chapters of this book into four sections has not been an easy task but it has served to extend our creative thinking about what a chapter can contribute. The section headings we settled on reflect the major themes outlined above, but most chapters could easily fall under two, three, or even four of the headings, and two chapters that might sit beside each other very comfortably may be found quite far apart in the list of contents. We feel this reflects the reality of teaching and learning and could only be avoided by choosing chapters that focused so tightly on particular themes that we felt they would not reflect the diversity of children's and teaching assistants' experiences. As we have argued above, for example, curriculum and context are largely indivisible, so the difference between these two sections is one of emphasis rather than substance. Students of E111, 'Supporting learning in primary schools', will find the module will provide a structure to their reading; readers wishing to research particular topics (e.g., mathematics or creativity) are advised to use the contents pages judiciously and not seek to find everything they want in the same place.

We hope that you will find words in this book to encourage you to think further about your practice, to even inspire you in your teaching and to support you as professionals.

A note on titles

We are aware of the many titles that are used to describe adults who now work alongside qualified teachers in schools. As the UK government has expressed its preference for the term 'teaching assistants' we have used this in the book's title. (We note that this could be interpreted as 'assistants to the teacher's teaching' or 'assistants who themselves teach'. From our experience of talking to teaching assistants, observing them in classrooms, and our involvement in training, both interpretations ring true.) Within the 34 selected chapters, however, a variety of assistant titles will be found and this is important because it reflects the diversity of roles that can be found throughout the UK.

References

Askew, M. (1998) *Teaching Primary Mathematics: A Guide for Newly Qualified and Student Teachers*. London: Hodder & Stoughton.

Robitaille, D., and Dirks, M. (1982) 'Models for the mathematics curriculum'. *For the Learning of Mathematics*, 2(3), 3–21.

Section 1

Children and the curriculum

For this opening section we have selected chapters that both illustrate and raise questions about important aspects of the primary curriculum. In Chapter 1, Stuart Lester and colleagues review the relationship between play, learning, and health and apply this to school playtimes and playground design. There is much here that helps adults understand why providing time for children's free play within the context of the school day is so important to children – whatever their age.

Awareness of the significance of 'errors' and 'miscues' in children's reading and writing gained momentum in the 1970s, giving rise to insights into the way children seek to work things out for themselves. In Chapter 2, Julie Ryan and Julian Williams highlight the significance of errors in children's mathematical learning and the importance of discussion in order that learning can stem from misconceptions.

In Chapter 3, Richard English argues for an 'ICT-rich curriculum' in learning, and specifically mathematical learning. One only has to visit an Apple Store to note how many children are confidently using and learning from quite sophisticated new technology – almost irrespective of the extent to which schools are incorporating ICT in classroom learning.

'Poetry draws on innate capacities for language' argue Liz Stone and Julia Gillen in Chapter 4. Taking a close look at practice in Liz's classroom, they argue for the integration of poetry and poetic approaches to learning throughout the teaching day. Both Chris Bills (Chapter 5) and Cathy Nutbrown (Chapter 6) consider the importance of what teachers and teaching assistants can learn from watching and listening to the children for whose learning they are responsible. Nutbrown, in particular, is putting the case for placing children at the centre of the curriculum, offering learning opportunities that match their existing level of knowledge and understanding. This is essentially a *social constructivist* approach. Many of the contributors to this book adopt a similar theory of knowledge. This view of learning, where children are seen as constructing their own knowledge through interactions with peers and with adults not only capitalises on children's enthusiasm, argues Patricia Murphy (Chapter 8), but also leads to more secure scientific understandings. Chapter 7, by Hazreena Hussein, reports on a study of sensory gardens and the ways in which they provide valuable social and educational experiences for users, and particularly for children with special needs.

The two remaining chapters in this section continue to explore scientific understanding. Given that science has long experienced insecurity with the primary curriculum, Jane Turner (Chapter 9) presents a heartfelt case for it having a strong presence in children's learning. Finally, Joan Solomon and Stephen Lunn (Chapter 10) emphasise the value of children's curiosity and excitement, with the former also outlining some of the subject knowledge essential for teachers and teaching assistants and the latter stressing the important role played by adults in helping children shape their scientific concepts.

Chapter 1

Play, playtime and playgrounds

Stuart Lester, Owain Jones and Wendy Russell

This chapter is taken from an evaluation report, by the same authors, on South Gloucester's 'Outdoor Play and Learning Programme'. Owain Jones is a research fellow at the Countryside and Community Research Institute and Stuart Lester and Wendy Russell both senior lecturers in play and playwork at the University of Gloucestershire. Although many schools have improved their playground spaces playtime tends to be given a low priority compared to what happens in classrooms. Stuart Lester and colleagues have things to say that will cause us to think more deeply about this time honoured school day event.

The nature and benefits of play

Play has been studied across a wide range of academic disciplines, each with its own perspective. Analysis of recent and historic policy initiatives (Powell and Wellard, 2008) shows that although there is no coherent understanding of play, and policies largely take an instrumental view of its nature and benefits. Direct causal links are assumed between particular forms of playing and the acquisition of particular skills (social, emotional and cognitive) or the amelioration of social problems (for example, obesity or antisocial behaviour), with adults directing children's play towards those specific forms of playing and therefore the desired outcomes (Lester and Russell, 2008). This approach pays attention to the content of children's play, its outward expressions, reading these literally as practising skills for adulthood. But what much of the research shows is that play's value lies in children's subjective emotional experiences of playing (for example, Burghardt, 2005). Rather than rehearsing skills, children appropriate aspects of their daily lives into their play and turn them upside down in an

Source: An edited version of Lester, S., Jones, O. and Russell, W. (2011) 'Play, playtime and playgrounds', in *Supporting School Improvement Through Play: An Evaluation of South Gloucestershire's Outdoor Play and Learning (OPAL) Programme, Final Report* (London: National Children's Bureau/Play England) pp. 19–25.

attempt to gain some control over the world by rendering it either less scary or less boring (Sutton-Smith, 1999). The enjoyment that this process affords is what provides the motivation for playing; these emotional experiences support the development of resilience across a number of areas such as emotion regulation, stress response systems, attachment (to people and places) and to a flexibility of responses to what children encounter (Lester and Russell, 2008).

Play and learning

Varying conceptualisations of play give rise to considerable and diverse research which links play activities to a range of developmental benefits. Studies, largely from the discipline of developmental psychology, converge to establish a common 'play-learning belief':

> Play, in its many forms, represents a natural age–appropriate method for children to explore and learn about the world around them . . . Through play children acquire knowledge and practise new skills, providing a foundation for more complex processes and academic success.
>
> (Fisher et al., 2008)

There are a wealth of texts that propose a relationship between outdoor play and learning (see for example Perry and Branum, 2009). This also finds expression in a range of policy guidance for schools and beyond: for example, the Early Years Foundation Stage (EYFS) places strong emphasis on the value of children's opportunity to play outdoors to support learning and all aspects of children's development, noting that being outdoors has a positive impact on children's well-being, as it provides the opportunity for doing things in different ways and on different scales from being indoors.

Research studies suggest that playtime, and opportunities to be playful in an unstructured environment, play a role in children's adjustment to school, classroom behaviour and approaches to learning (for example, Barros and others, 2009) Pellegrini (2009), drawing on a cognitive immaturity hypothesis, notes that for children, breaks during the school day, which provide the time, materials and space to interact with peers, should maximise the attention they pay to subsequent tasks. This is supported by results of controlled field experiments, and has led to a call for frequent breaks throughout the school day. This is also supported by the Attention

Restoration Theory (Kaplan and Kaplan, 2005) which proposes that time spent in 'effortless' pursuits and contexts is an important factor in recovering from mental fatigue.

Scott and Panksepp (2003) suggest that children's rough–and–tumble play offers them the opportunity to engage in bouts of high energy activity, reaching a peak of satiety, at which point children may be more receptive to participating in less vigorous social and learning opportunities. Other studies (for example, Pellis and Pellis, 2009) show how rough–and–tumble play makes a significant contribution to the development of social competence and friendships.

The benefits of play arise from its unique qualities of being spontaneous and unpredictable, and these qualities manifest themselves when children can find the time and space to play away from direct adult gaze and surveillance; the more natural and unstructured the environment, the 'richer children's play is as an educational activity' (Farné 2005, p. 173). Santer and others' (2007) literature review cites research which found that if play is allowed to develop, it becomes more complex. Appreciating this perspective suggests that effective play environments provide the space and time for children to create moments of their own design and intention, rather than being directed into adult desired and designated spaces and activity. It is somewhat inevitable that there will be tension between this reading of play and the nature and context (including historical) of educational provision, as recognised in much of the literature discussing play in schools and early years setting (for example, Adams and others, 2004). Understandings and applications of play in contemporary educational policy place great value on the importance of identifying 'what counts' in terms of good quality play, and then apply these methods and activities as a means to support children's educational progress and achievement. While policy documents may espouse the value of children's 'free play', they are often couched in terms and practices that reify the instrumental value of this behaviour (Lester, 2010). School spaces and time are highly regulated, with the need for adults to keep 'control', raising questions about the ways in which schools acknowledge and seek to manage these tensions.

Play and health

The state of children's health in the UK is a cause for considerable concern, in particular the dramatic increase in overweight and obese children (BMA, 2005) as recognised in the Conservatives' (2008) *Childhood Review*.

There is irrefutable evidence that regular physical exercise is effective in primary and secondary prevention of chronic disease (cardiovascular disease, diabetes, obesity and depression) and that healthy activity patterns are established in childhood.

Children spend a significant amount of their daily lives in school, and as such schools have a central role in promoting and supporting children's activity and health. Considerable research pays attention to the relationship between children's play, health and physical activity (e.g. Ramstetter and others, 2010), Mota and others (2005) suggest that school playtime is an important setting in which to promote moderate-to-vigorous activity. Research studies into the relationship between playground design and health suggest that sites which have 'advanced landscape features' have a higher degree of satisfaction for children and lead to more physical forms of play and associated health benefits of lower Body Mass Index (BMI) (Ozdemir and Yilmaz, 2008). Pupils' perception of the school environment appears to be directly related to their satisfaction with the playground, and greater satisfaction promotes more active behaviour (Fjortoft and Sageie, 2000).

Yun and others (2005) indicate that environments that have a dynamic range of variables are likely to have significant health benefits, and Fjortoft's (2004) study highlights the benefits associated with playing in a natural playground compared with more traditional play environments. Numerous studies highlight the benefit of children having playful access to natural space (e.g. Lester and Maudsley, 2007) and there are suggested links between children's opportunity to play with natural elements and their care and concern about environmental issues as adults (e.g. Wells and Leckies, 2006; Ward Thompson and others, 2008).

Studies from the field of environmental psychology also intimate that playful contact with natural space offers moments of fascination and a chance to 'be away', and may support the restoration of attention, necessary for concentrated and task-directed effort in the classroom (e.g. Taylor and Kuo, 2006). Play, in particular social forms of rough-and-tumble play, may also have considerable benefits for the reduction of impulse control disorders such as ADHD (Panksepp, 2007).

Given the relationship between play and health, and the increasing concerns over children's fitness and activity levels, there is a tendency to see playtime as a period for promoting structured physical exercises and games, yet as Ramstetter and others' (2010) review indicates, such moves undermine many of the social, emotional, cognitive and even physical benefits of unstructured play.

School attitudes to playtime

While there has been increasing attention given to play and outdoor environments in the early years, the notion of 'playtime' in school has attracted mixed opinions. In an educational culture that has seen an increasing emphasis on outcomes and achievement, playtime has been given lesser value and, as a consequence, school playtime allocation is reported to have been considerably reduced (e.g. Blatchford and Baines, 2006). Pellegrini and Bohn (2005) suggest that by curtailing playtime, schools may be reducing one of the few times during the day when children have the opportunity to interact with their peers in a generally unsupervised manner.

Playtimes are often a source of concern for teachers who perceive this unstructured period of the school day as a time when children become aggressive and unruly (Armitage, 2005). Pearce and Bailey's (2011) study of playtime in a south-west London primary school tellingly notes that 'risk' was a serious concern among the teaching staff, particularly around the impact of bullying, yet the authors' observations and discussions with the children offered no support for this concern.

Of equal concern is risk anxiety among staff about injury in the school playgrounds, leading to the removal of play equipment, the reduction in playtime and the implementation of constraining rules designed to restrict children's use of school playgrounds and force 'teachers into a policing, litigation-conscious role' (Bundy and others, 2009, p. 33). From their study of the introduction of loose parts into a primary school playground in western Sydney, Bundy and others (2009) note that while the staff saw a considerable and beneficial change in children's play patterns, they also perceived that risks to children's safety had been increased through the introduction of these materials. This promoted some interesting comments about their unease:

> 'I suppose at times I was noticing (risk) because it was there and it was so different. I don't know whether there was more risk or whether I was just noticing it more' and 'I suppose because it seems like grown-up equipment with little pieces of wood and tyres and everything, you're a little more tentative to start with'. Given that the incidence of injuries did not increase during the study period, it seems fair to say that concerns arose more from perceptions of what might have happened rather than from what had actually been observed. One teacher summed up her concerns by saying, 'something could happen

to somebody – I think that's a teacher's natural instinct to be worried
that something could happen'.

(Bundy and others, 2009, p. 40)

In response to this general unease, which is underpinned by the fear of
litigation, staff adopt a range of strategies. These include direct requests to
stop a particular activity, to remove materials that they perceived were
dangerous, to reduce numbers of children in certain areas, and to intervene
to discuss the situation with children to raise awareness of the consequences
of their actions and to encourage reflection. Staff also acknowledged that
children themselves were good at responding to possible risks. But overall
there was a degree of tension in relation to the use of the new materials
and, as Bundy and others comment, 'sometimes it seemed that teachers
were managing their own anxieties rather than the risk itself – for example,
"the majority of the time, while I was nervous, I'd still sort of let them go
through whatever" ' (2009, p. 41).

Another issue of concern highlighted by research relates to adult
perceptions of children's rough-and-tumble play. Children, in particular
boys, view this as an attractive form of play and report that they can readily
distinguish between play and real fighting (Smith and others, 2004),
However, despite evidence to show the contribution this form of play
makes to friendships and social competence, for teachers and playground
supervisors this form of behaviour is problematic, with many believing it
always 'gets out of control, leads to bullying, feeds aggression, and would
open them up to risk of legal prosecution if a child were to be injured'
(Freeman and Brown, 2004, p. 224). Smith and others (2004) suggest that
play fighting may result in real fighting in about 1 per cent of cases
(although this may be higher for those with poor social skills), yet teachers
make a considerable overestimation of this, citing a figure of 29 per cent. In
looking at possible causes of this overestimation Smith and others suggest
that some teachers find play fighting noisy and intrusive and prefer quieter
and more orderly forms of play; have concerns about accidental injury; and
generalise experiences of play fighting turning into real fighting to present
universal accounts of this form of behaviour.

Thomson (2003) refers to primary school playgrounds as 'well-equipped
hamster cages' in which the rationalisation of playgrounds through design
processes that encourage specific use of space exclude opportunities for
freedom of expression. In response to adult concerns over playtimes,
increasing control has been introduced by the 'teaching' of traditional
games as a means of productively engaging children in 'play' in a manner

deemed worthwhile by the adults involved (Armitage, 2005; Smith, 2007). Thomson's (2007) small-scale review of three primary school playgrounds notes that the outdoor space exerts a significant influence on the child's everyday life at school, yet this space is designed, produced and governed by adults. Studies have shown that within the playground, children's ability to play is severely restricted by adult promotion of what is expected and by sanctions imposed against children when they contravene this promotion (McKendrick, 2005; Thomson, 2007).

These promotions and constraints are underpinned by concerns around children's safety (and fear of litigation) and management of children's peer interactions to promote adult expectations of sharing, cooperation and a general 'play nicely' approach. Children perceive the adult negativity about their activities and generally accept that this represents the norms of behaviour in this space, and attempt to fit in with the general adult remit of the playground. Yet by 'limiting children's natural and spontaneous interaction with their environment we stunt their environmental knowledge, expertise and aesthetic pleasure' (Thomson, 2007, p. 498).

Despite the fact that children's playtime accounts for a significant portion of the school day, there is limited appreciation by adults of the importance of this time for children's health and well-being (Blatchford and Baines, 2006).

Playground design

Alongside this are issues related to the nature of playground design. Frost (2006), commenting on playground design in US schools, notes that while they tend to cater for motor play, they fall short in any features that integrate garden and nature areas, constructive play materials and props for imaginative and creative play. Rasmussen's (2004) research with children highlights the limited value that children place on school playgrounds, and playground designers should acknowledge this and plan for children's multiple possibilities rather than adult-determined notions of how space should be used. 'However, to most adults connected with the modern primary school what actually happens at playtimes remains a complete mystery' (Armitage, 2005, p. 552). Factor (2004) notes children will incorporate and adapt the physical elements of the environment to their own needs and purposes in play: 'youngsters create an intricate network of usage, play-lines invisible but known to every child at the school' (p. 142).

There is a significant research base that addresses the key features of attractive play spaces (e.g. Lester and Maudsley, 2007) which now

permeates much of the discussion around design of outdoor play
environments. The significant elements of this may be summarised as:

- In some way spaces need to be physically defined and enclosed but offer
  the possibility of variety and movement. This resonates with Ward's
  (1978) and Sobel's (2002) discussions on the role of dens, secret spaces
  and private spaces in children's play landscapes. Armitage's (2005) study
  of playground design reveals that regular and open playgrounds appear
  to promote one specific form of play (running games) rather than a
  variety of play possibilities. Spaces, although bounded, are not done so
  in too inflexible a way and children can find space at the margins as
  well as the middle.
- The form and material of spaces can be manipulated and be made
  'polymorphic' rather than 'monomorphic'; that is, space can be put to
  differing uses at differing times (and even differing uses in parallel).
  Play spaces are liminal and remain open for future possibilities for play
  (Matthews and others, 2000).
- Spaces should contain a range of malleable materials that are
  non-specific, 'ordinary' and 'polymorphic' (eg sand, mud, sticks) for
  use by children, rather than 'commercially' designed play products
  which are often overburdened with adult prescription (see, for example,
  Powell, 2007). Bundy and others' (2009) study of the introduction of
  loose parts into a primary school playground clearly establishes the
  impact on children's play patterns, noting the increase in more
  physically active play, not only in terms of aerobic exercise (running,
  jumping) but also in resistive activity (pushing, lifting, carrying, rolling
  materials around the playground).
- Children have a particular attraction to natural environments.
  Numerous studies have found that they often prefer to play in natural
  or wild spaces (e.g. Lester and Maudsley, 2007). The need for elements
  of nature is particularly important in three respects: natural spaces and
  substances often tend to be polymorphic and infinitely malleable
  (Powell, 2007); natural spaces are freer from adult prescription and
  therefore lend themselves to children's imaginative appropriation
  (Lester and Maudsley, 2007). Research also suggests that contact with
  natural space and elements supports children's fascination with the
  world and affords the opportunity for the restoration of attention
  (Taylor and Kuo, 2006).
- The wider landscape of the school should be taken into account as well
  as specific existing or proposed play areas. This includes opening up the

possibility of making differing routes through the school landscape and between play areas. This likens to notions such as Moore's (1986) 'flowing terrain' and Jones' (2008) discussion of how the geographies of children's lives and play need to be able to permeate through dominant adult-designed, scaled, ordered and controlled landscapes in order that they can in effect develop a parallel other world of spatial imagination and practice in the same physical spaces. Such a perspective also suggests that the world of the playground may remain hidden from adult understandings, by the very nature of children's play (Factor, 2004).

References

Adams, S. and others (2004) *Inside the Foundation Stage: recreating the Reception year.* London: Association of Teachers and Lecturers.

Armitage, M. (2005) 'The influence of school architecture and design on the outdoor play experience within the primary school', *Paedagogica Historica*, 41, 4, 535–53.

Barros, R., Silver, E. and Stein, R. (2009) 'School recess and group classroom behaviour', *Pediatrics*, 123, 2, 431–36.

Blatchford, P. and Baines, E. (2006) *A follow up national survey of breaktimes in primary and secondary schools.* Report to the Nuffield Foundation. London: Institute of Education, University of London.

British Medical Association (BMA) (2005) *Preventing childhood obesity.* London: BMA.

Bundy, A.C. and others (2009) 'The risk is that there is "no risk": a simple, innovative intervention to increase children's activity levels', *International Journal of Early Years Education*, 17, 1, 33–45.

Burghardt, G.M. (2005) *The genesis of animal play: testing the limits.* Cambridge, MA: MIT Press.

The Conservatives (2008) *Childhood review: more ball games.* Available at: www.davidwilletts.co.uk/wp/wp-content/uploads/2008/02/childhood-review.pdf (Accessed 26 June 2011).

Factor, J. (2004) 'Tree stumps, manhole covers and rubbish tins. The invisible play lines of a primary school playground', *Childhood*, 11, 2, 142–54.

Farné, R. (2005) 'Pedagogy of play', *Topoi*, 24, 169–81.

Fisher, K. and others (2008) 'Conceptual split? Parents' and experts' perceptions of play in the 21st century', *Journal of Applied Developmental Psychology*, 29, 305–16.

Fjortoft, I. (2004) 'Landscape and play: the effects of natural environments on children's play and motor development', *Children, Youth and Environments*, 14, 2, 21–44.

Fjortoft, I. and Sageie, J. (2000) 'The natural environment as a playground for children', *Landscape and Urban Planning*, 48, 83–97.

Freeman, N. and Brown, B. (2004) 'Reconceptualizing rough and tumble play', *Advances in Early Education and Day Care*, 13, 219–34.

Frost, J. (2006) 'The dissolution of outdoor play: cause and consequences'. Conference paper delivered at The Value of Play: A forum on risk, recreation and children's health, Washington, DC.

Jones, O. (2008) 'True geography quickly forgotten, giving away to an adult-imagined universe. Approaching the otherness of childhood', *Children's Geographies*, 6, 2, 195–212.

Kaplan, R. and Kaplan, S. (1989) *The experience of nature: A psychological perspective*. New York: Cambridge University Press.

Lester, S. (2011) Pedagogy play and space. In Pihlgren, A. (ed.) *Fritidshemmet*. Lund: Studentlitteratur.

Lester, S. and Maudsley, M. (2007) *Play, naturally*. London: Children's Play Council.

Lester, S. and Russell, W. (2008) *Play for a change: play, policy and practice – a review of contemporary perspectives*. London: NCB.

Matthews, H., Limb, M. and Taylor, M. (2000) 'The "street" as thirdspace', in Holloway, S. and Valentine, G. (eds) *Children's geographies*. London: Routledge.

McKendrick, J. (2005) *School grounds in Scotland research report summary*. Edinburgh: SportScotland.

Moore, R. (1986) *Childhood's domain*. London: Croom Helm.

Mota, J. and others (2005) 'Physical activity and school recess time: differences between the sexes and the relationship between children's playground physical activity and habitual physical activity', *Journal of Sports Sciences*, 23, 3, 269–75.

Ozdemir, A. and Yilmaz, O. (2008) 'Assessment of outdoor school environments and physical activity in Ankara's primary schools', *Journal of Environmental Psychology*, 28, 3, 287–300.

Panksepp, J. (2007) 'Can play diminish ADHD and facilitate the construction of the social brain?', *Journal of the Canadian Academy of Child and Adolescent Psychiatry*, 16, 2, 57–66.

Pearce, G. and Bailey, R. (2011) 'Football pitches and Barbie dolls: young children's perceptions of their school playgrounds', *Early Child Development and Care*, iFirst Article, 1, 19, 1–19.

Pellegrini, A. (2009) *The role of play in human development*. Oxford: Oxford University Press.

Pellegrini, A.D. and Bohn, C. (2005) 'The role of recess in children's cognitive performance and school adjustment', *Research News and Comment, AERA*, Jan/Feb 2005, 13–19.

Pellis, S. and Pellis, V. (2009) *The playful brain*. Oxford: Oneworld.

Perry, J. and Branum, L. (2009) ' "Sometimes I pounce on twigs because I'm a meat eater". Supporting physically active play and outdoor learning', *American Journal of Play*, 2, 2, 195–214.

Powell, M. (2007) 'The hidden curriculum of recess', *Children, Youth and Environments*, 17, 4, 86–106.

Powell, S. and Wellard, I. (2008) *Policies and play: the impact of national policies on children's opportunities for play*. London: NCB.

Ramstetter, C.L., Murray, R. and Garner, A.S. (2010) 'The crucial role of recess in schools', *Journal of School Health*, 80, 11, 517–26.

Rasmussen, K. (2004) 'Places for children–children's places', *Childhood*, 11, 2, 155–73.

Santer, J., Griffiths, C. and Goodall, D. (2007) *Free play in early childhood: a literature review*. London: Play England.

Scott, E. and Panksepp, J. (2003) 'Rough-and-tumble play in human children', *Aggressive Behaviour*, 29, 539–51.

Smith, A. (2007) 'Fit for play?', *Education 3–13*, 35, 1, 17–27.

Sobel, D. (2002) *Children's special places*. Detroit: Wayne State University Press.

Sutton-Smith, B. (1999) 'Evolving a consilience of play definitions: playfully', in Reifel, S. (ed.) *Play contexts revisited, play and culture studies, Vol. 2*. Stamford: Ablex.

Taylor, A. and Kuo, F. (2006) 'Is contact with nature important for healthy child development? State of the evidence', in Spencer, C. and Blades, M. (eds) *Children and their environments*. Cambridge: Cambridge University Press.

Thomson, S. (2003) 'A well-equipped hamster cage: the rationalisation of primary school playtime', *Education 3–13*, 31, 2, 54–59.

Ward, C. (1978) *The child in the city*. London: Penguin Books.

Wells, N. and Leckies, K. (2006) 'Nature and the life course: pathways from childhood nature experiences to adult environmentalism', *Children, Youth and Environments*, 16, 1, 1–24.

Yun, A. and others (2005) 'The dynamic range of biological functions and variations of many environmental cues may be declining in the modern age: implications for diseases and therapeutics', *Medical Hypotheses*, 65, 173–78.

Chapter 2

Learning from errors and misconceptions

Julie Ryan and Julian Williams

Julie Ryan is a senior lecturer in mathematics education at Manchester Metropolitan University and Julian Williams is professor of mathematics education, and director of graduate research students at the University of Manchester. In this chapter they review current thinking about the place of errors and misconceptions in children's mathematical learning and, arising from their research, they classify these into four main categories – modelling, prototyping, over-generalising, process-object thinking. Where these are tentatively observed in children's reasoning, it is suggested that they should be taken into account in the teaching of mathematics.

Introduction

Classrooms can be places where children see themselves as mathematical beings rather than simply receivers of pre-digested knowledge. The most wonderful moments for us as teachers have been when a learner exclaims, 'Ah, I get it now!' and when they then go on to explain their mathematics with clarity and confidence. Before these moments of clarity, the learner has *necessarily* made false starts or faulty connections. We may simplistically term these 'mistakes' or 'errors', but there is thinking behind these errors and much for teachers to interpret and understand as we support the learner in making the next steps. Dialogues provoked by 'mistakes and misconceptions' involve mutual learning by the teacher as well as the learner.

Source: An edited version of Ryan, J. and Williams, J. (2010) 'Children's mathematical understanding as a work in progress: Learning from errors and misconceptions', in I. Thompson (ed.) *Issues in Teaching Numeracy in Primary Schools* 2nd ed. (Maidenhead: Open University Press) pp. 144–157.

Errors and misconceptions as starting points for learning

When we as teachers first recognize a child's 'mistake', we may be tempted in the highly paced classroom flow to simply label the response as incorrect and resort to a teaching strategy to 'fix it' *and quickly*. But there can be more thoughtful and engaging reactions: we could identify the response, for example, as partially correct, partially misconceived, stumbling or tentative. Such labels might suggest that a particular pedagogical view is at work here: that here is a teacher who is trying to *make sense of the response* in order to create a learning experience that works *with* the child's ideas and helps to build on them.

So you can see that our professional vocabulary may be useful because it can guide our teaching response to learning. We must use some vocabulary to communicate, and words take on all sorts of meanings of course, so we state here that in our use of the terms 'errors and misconceptions' we are promoting a positive view of errors and misconceptions as productive starting points for learning. The word 'error' describes an incorrect response that you hear or see, while the word 'misconception' describes incomplete conceptions, or partial reasoning, usually hidden behind the error, and which may 'explain' the error: this may not be immediately accessible to the teacher. Questions such as 'Why has the child made this response?' and 'What is their reason for it?' help us to consider the current understanding of the learner. We believe that when children are learning mathematics they are trying to make sense of difficult ideas. They are usually trying to enter a world of thinking that is often quite puzzling and alien to their everyday experience. We, as teachers, can support them as they express their own ideas, their own explanations and, importantly, their own identity as independent learners, if we have a teaching strategy that explicitly values errors and seeks articulation of (mis)conceptions. This approach is usually called diagnostic teaching, because it involves a process of 'diagnosis', that is, the revealing of the underlying causes or explanations for errors (in this view errors are only symptoms, and we do not just 'treat' symptoms).

Learners' responses are not usually thoughtless or random – we are all thinking beings trying to make sense of the world. But there are several forces at play when we respond erroneously and the public classroom itself introduces a special dynamic to learning. We may be panicked to respond when we are not ready or confident; we may have been distracted, troubled or be day-dreaming; we may have misheard or misread; we may have made a slip; or we may have dismissed ourselves already with negative beliefs, thinking 'I'm one of those people who can't do maths'.

Teachers can be sensitive to all these possibilities, both social and cognitive. We remember one story where a child wrote that the mathematical drawings presented to her were 'angels'. The sensitive teacher thought the child had made a spelling mistake and *did* know that the drawings represented 'angles'. On checking with the child, however, she found that she actually thought the drawings were flying angels. So teachers' first thoughtful responses can be erroneous, partial and misconceived too! We can all jump to the wrong conclusions.

Perhaps the challenge of discovering what a child is really thinking is what makes our profession so special – it is ongoing 'detective' work. Investigation starts with building up our knowledge base by reading, researching and developing on-the-job experience about children's likely responses. A useful plan is to anticipate children's responses to mathematical tasks; create opportunities for the children to articulate their reasoning; keep an open mind about their understanding; and be prepared to change your mind based on the evidence.

We are promoting a pedagogy where teachers and teaching assistants anticipate and identify likely errors and work with them; lesson design where children have opportunities to consider their own conceptions and work towards strengthening, refining or reorganizing their understanding, themselves. We call this approach diagnostic teaching.

Classifying errors and misconceptions

When we studied children's erroneous responses to test questions, we tried to classify different types of response in terms of the thinking that (perhaps) lay behind them. There were, naturally, careless slips of memory or attention; jumping to conclusions; only dealing with one of the two conditions or steps in a task; and there were some errors that we could not diagnose. Many of these may be due to the assessment conditions – lack of motivation or high test anxiety. But there were several categories which we thought were significant in terms of cognitive development: they suggested there were underlying (mis)conceptions or conceptual limitations behind the errors. We explained these types of errors as due to modelling, prototyping, overgeneralizing or process-object linking. We concluded 'that the latter four types of errors are the result of intelligent constructions that should be valued by learners and teachers alike' (Ryan and Williams 2007: 13).

Modelling

We use the word modelling to refer to the way mathematics is connected with a 'real' everyday world – the everyday world being then represented by the mathematics. 'One can say perhaps when a child has a "modelling error" that the child has their own "model" of the situation, in conflict with the "mathematical model" expected in the academic context of school' (Ryan and Williams 2007: 16).

The representations and contexts we use in classrooms to model the mathematics – such as fractions of cakes, number lines, hundred squares, the context of money for decimals – ideally bring meaning by providing connections with what is already known intuitively by the learner and the mathematics under consideration. But such representations have their limitations: one model or context will not represent all of the mathematics and the learner will need to experience several models and be able to move flexibly between them to successfully build the mathematics.

Prototyping

We use the phrase 'prototype of a concept' to mean a culturally typical example of the concept. For example, we will perhaps all share an image of a 'triangle' as an equilateral triangle oriented on its 'base'; think of a hexagon as always regular; read scales as marked in units; make a half-turn for 'turn'; or think of fractions as unit fractions. As a consequence, an error may result, for example, in not recognizing some triangular shapes because they are in untypical orientations; or a scale may be incorrectly read '1, 2, 3, . . .' because the unitary prototype is intuitively so powerful for the child.

Prototyping is an intelligent – even essential – element of concept learning and draws on early first experiences of concepts. Questions that challenge prototyping include:

- What makes this or that a triangle (or a hexagon)?
- Where is the whole unit on this scale?
- How much should I turn?
- What do the numerators and denominators in a fraction represent?

From the prototype we refine and broaden our conceptual understanding.

Overgeneralizing

Overgeneralizing is also an intelligent response to earlier experience and is closely related to prototyping – it involves an active attempt to build on previous learning. One of the most common overgeneralizations is that 'multiplication makes bigger' or 'division makes smaller'. These statements were correct for previous classroom situations and experiences but outside the domain of whole numbers they are no longer always true.

Almost all the overgeneralizations we have found in our research sprang from generalizing rules that worked for the whole numbers into domains like fractions, decimals and negative numbers. Consider these paired statements: $4 \times 2 > 4$ but $4 \times \frac{1}{2} < 4$ (the effect of multiplication by a whole number or a fraction); $42 > 5$ but $0.42 < 0.5$ and $2 > 1$ but $-2 < -1$ (ordering numbers). Clearly, generalizations of rules for whole numbers do not always hold in the new number domains of fractions and negative numbers. Mathematics is largely about generalizing, so an important focus in classrooms is testing a generalization and drawing attention to the domain in which it 'works'. Again, this involves refinement and development of mathematical understanding, in which the formulation and testing of false conjectures is an essential element.

We also found quite sophisticated overgeneralizations for decimals. Some children (and trainee teachers) read a decimal number as a pair of whole numbers separated by a point. This leads to a 'separation strategy'. This strategy works well for additions like $2.4 + 5.1$ where you add the two numbers to the left of the decimal point and then the numbers to the right giving 7.5. However, it no longer works in the case $2.4 + 5.8 = 7.12$. Similarly, $2.3 + 1.47$ does not equal 3.50.

Another overgeneralization occurs with the overuse of the 'additive strategy' when a multiplicative strategy is required. For example, children using an additive strategy for completing a fraction question like '$3/12 = 6/?$', may write 15 as the missing denominator. They see that 3 has been added to the numerator ($3 + 3 = 6$) so they add 3 to the denominator ($12 + 3 = 15$) rather than multiply by 2 ($3 \times 2 = 6$, and $12 \times 2 = 24$) to establish equivalence. This strategy is very resistant to change and is found across many mathematical contexts up to the age of 16 years for many children.

A key question we suggest for challenging generalizations in classrooms is: 'When does a particular generalization *not* apply?' For example, when does multiplication *not* make numbers bigger? Such questions foreground attention to *over*generalization and thus foster metacognition.

Process-object linking

Concept formation often requires that processes be made into new mathematical objects. If we ask young children 'How many toys are here?' the question may signal a response of counting, for example '1, 2, 3, 4, 5, 6'. What *we* are interested in is the 6–ness of the set of toys, that is, the cardinality of the set. We are hoping the child will make the link between the counting from 1 to 6 and the cardinality of the set of toys (6) by realizing that the last number name spoken answers the question we posed. Thus there is a need for a link between the process of counting and its object, the last number in the sequence.

Questions that teachers ask children may prompt process or object conceptions, and eventually require flexible switching between both conceptions. For example, in a sum such as 8 + 3 = ?, the equal sign prompts the *process* of addition and the child perhaps says '8 plus 3 *makes* 11'. But a task like 8 + ? = 13 requires a more sophisticated understanding of the equals sign and a conception of a number sentence recognizing there are relationships between the numbers. The processing or action needs to be 'extracted' from the number sentence object. Similarly, more difficult number sentences, like 9 + 3 = 6 + ?, require a conception of equality that appreciates that the outcomes on both sides of the equals sign must be the same.

Here are three 10–year-old children discussing a number sentence task '? × 6 = 9×4' called 'missing numbers' in conversation with the teacher. They had earlier written their different answers to the task. Sonia had been correct and she moves flexibly between object and process in justifying her answer, Gareth had used a process conception and had answered '36', but with support from the teacher, and because he had listened to Sonia, he was moving towards an object conception of the number sentence. Robin has also reconsidered his earlier response and additionally shows mental flexibility with the arithmetic structure of multiplication facts.

Sonia: I did 9 times 4 to get my answer of 36 and then saw there was 6 there so I thought to myself *what* times 6 equals 36 and then I thought of my 6 times table in my head and got 6.

Gareth: Well, to be honest I didn't know 9 times 4 quickly, so I just changed it round and took 4 off 40, because 10 times 4 is 40, and it came out as 36. Then I thought 5 times 6 is 30 so I just added on a 6 to get 36.

Teacher: So 36 is the answer to what?

Gareth: 9 times 4.

Teacher: 9 times 4, right.

Gareth: And then I thought 36, and half of 10 times 6 is 30, so 5 times 6, then I added another 6. 6 times 6.

Teacher: Robin, how did you do this one?

Robin: I knew that 8 times 4 was 32. I added another 4 because it's the 4 times table. If you were changing it around as well, it would be the 9 times 4 – er, the 9 times table. 9 times 4 is 36. And then that would be *something* times 6 would be 36. And I 'looked' through my tables and then 6 times 6 equals 36.

Teacher: So you've got a different way of getting that 36 from Gareth – he went up to the 40 and you started at the 32, you said you knew the 8 times 4 one. How did you know that one?

Robin: Erm – just know it.

Process-object linking and understanding of mathematical structure is often a significant step. We think that if this step is not made confidently many children resort to formal manipulations or 'rules without reason'. The consequence may be withdrawal from mathematics that does not make sense to them and a loss of identity as a competent learner.

The patterns and structure of early arithmetic lay a strong foundation for algebra in the secondary school. For example, the counting numbers 1, 2, 3, 4 . . . go 'odd, even, odd, even . . .'. What can we say about the number after an odd number? Is it always the case? Are there images which can convince us that 'even + odd must be odd'? What about 'odd × odd'? Can such investigations of structure develop a 'feel' or confidence for number? For example, confidence in stating that 7×5 could not possibly be 32 because the answer should be an odd number, or being sure that the answer could not be 32 because multiples of 5 end in 0 or 5, or knowing that since $6 \times 5 = 30$ the answer should be 5 more. This is pre-algebraic number pattern awareness and everyday language is a powerful tool for describing it.

The four categories we have identified above have several features: they diagnose a learner's current understanding (tentative diagnosis); they demonstrate the learner's natural intelligent engagement with mathematical processes and concepts; and they signal a learning opportunity or potential for further development. Since the existing understanding is based on thoughtful construction and motivation, it is sensible to design teaching and learning opportunities that further engage children's reasoning. We will now discuss what we call a dialogic pedagogy.

Children reorganizing their thinking through argument-in-discussion

The test questions we used in our research were crafted as *diagnostic* questions, in the sense that they were written to uncover children's thinking in order to determine the next steps in their learning. We make a first guess (inference) about why a child responded in a particular way; but we then have an opportunity to check that inference by either *asking* the child to justify their response or, we think more productively, by setting up peer discussion and *listening* to children's reasoning. In such peer discussions children are asked to justify their response in order to persuade another child of their view or to consider changing their own mind. At the heart of our method is the child reorganizing or strengthening their understanding through *articulation* or through what we call argument-in-discussion. It is intended that persuasion through reasoning is required (Ryan and Williams 2007: 31–52).

Productive dialogue starts with a shared problem and different points of view – we call this a problematic. Our diagnostic questions can be a source of problematics if they provoke different responses from children. A discussion proceeds when all children have an opportunity to communicate, listen and consider different points of view. Children also need to have some criteria to decide what makes a good mathematical argument and some social rules to foster collaboration and respect. Finally, a reflection step should summarize or bring the discussion to some conclusion or temporary closure. We think it is useful to make these four steps explicit as the conventions for classroom discussion. Children of all ages are capable of reasoned discussion with appropriate support, but this does require teachers' attention.

Teachers we have worked with have organized groups for discussion in a range of different ways (see Ryan and Williams 2007: 45–7). One teacher set up peer discussion by forming groups of children who had given *different* answers to diagnostic test questions (that is, 'conflict groups'). She gave the children clear rules about social and mathematical interaction so that thinking and listening were maintained. Another teacher formed groups of children who had given the *same* response to the diagnostic questions. This gave the children an opportunity to articulate their positions first. She then regrouped the children into mixed–response 'conflict' groups so they could consider and argue with different views. Both teachers moved from small–group discussion to plenary whole–class discussion which reflected on the reasoning that helped children to change their minds (or not).

Summary

A dialogic pedagogy shifts attention from mathematical content to argumentation and consideration of changing one's mind. We do not say that this method should be used all the time or that it is the only way to address errors and misconceptions, but we suggest that there is much for teachers to learn from giving voice to children's errors and misconceptions and from providing more time for them to reason in order to establish secure understanding.

   Teachers and teaching assistants have roles to play in not just setting up classroom discussion but also has an active role in deciding what interventions and directions sustain discussion and move it forward: for example, what questions to ask and when to ask them; which models to suggest and at what particular stage; when to be silent; and when to reinforce. These are considerable professional decisions. A child's belief in their ability to reason mathematically will grow from thoughtfully designed opportunities provided in classrooms.

Reference

Ryan, J. and Williams, J. (2007) *Children's Mathematics 4–15: Learning from Errors and Misconceptions*. Maidenhead: Open University Press.

Chapter 3

Why use ICT?

Richard English

Richard English is a senior lecturer at the University of Hull, Centre for Educational Studies. In this chapter he argues for the place of ICT in education, and specifically in children's mathematical learning. ICT, he argues, can serve to motivate children, can encourage them to take productive risks, and to employ skills such as trial and improvement, estimations and reasoning. All of course, are central to mathematic and scientific thinking.

Why use ICT?

If you want to argue the case for an ICT-rich primary curriculum then you need look no further than your own lifestyle, starting with what is in your jacket pocket or handbag. Many of us carry around a single, compact device that combines the capabilities of a mobile phone, a high-resolution digital video camera, a CD-quality music player, and a high-specification computer with email and Internet access. Looking beyond our pockets and handbags there is the wider high-technology world in which we live, for example, the wealth of electronic gadgetry that we have in our homes, as well as the technology we encounter when we go through the self-service supermarket checkout, fill the car with petrol, withdraw money from the bank, make a hotel or restaurant reservation online, borrow a book from the library, and so on.

Our working lives provide further evidence of the vital role of technology, with very few occupations not utilizing it in some form or another. We therefore owe it to pupils to prepare them to be citizens in a technology-rich world and this should start in the earliest stages of their schooling. Aubrey and Dahl (2008: 4) provide evidence to suggest this is

Source: An edited version of English, R. (2010) 'The role of ICT' (subsection 'Why use ICT'), in I. Thompson (ed.) *Issues in Teaching Numeracy in Primary Schools* 2nd ed. (Maidenhead: Open University Press) pp. 98–101.

already happening, when they state that 'most young children aged from birth to five years are growing up in media-rich digital environments in which they engage actively from a very early age'. So preparation for the realities of their future adult world should be sufficient justification for ensuring that all children see and experience the full potential offered by ICT, not just in mathematics but in all areas of the curriculum.

The availability of ICT in primary schools allows purely mechanical tasks to be carried out very quickly and efficiently, thus freeing the user to concentrate on higher-level things such as analysis, interpretation, reasoning and problem solving. One example of this is pupils' use of data-handling software to sort, search and graph data that they have collected. The speed of a computer also allows real-life situations to be modelled effectively. For example, random numbers on a spreadsheet can be used to simulate the rolling of dice, hundreds or even thousands of times. If two dice are involved, then the spreadsheet can add the scores, produce a graph of the outcomes and calculate the average score, all in a matter of seconds. As well as being fast and powerful, computers can also store and retrieve huge quantities of information, both locally, for example, using hard disks, DVD-ROMs and memory sticks, and remotely via wireless networks, intranets and the Internet. Teachers, pupils and parents therefore have access to a wealth of resources that were simply not available a few years ago. Technology also allows the information to be presented more accurately and more attractively than by traditional means, thus engaging the target audience. Why rely on a hand-drawn pie chart on the white board when you can produce a far superior visual aid with a computer? Technology is also inclusive in that the information can be presented in a variety of ways according to the size of the audience and the particular needs of individuals. One can also combine various media such as text, graphics, sounds, animations and video in an interactive way, to capture the interest of the user and motivate them to want to learn.

It is not possible within the constraints of this chapter to conduct a discussion of the many theories about learning that have been put forward over the years, so instead one simple observation will be offered: children learn what they choose to learn. We cannot force pupils to learn and it is this optional feature of learning that requires us to inspire, to motivate, to encourage and to make them want to learn. ICT can play a key part in achieving this. Many teachers will have anecdotal evidence of how children are motivated by ICT, but there is a growing body of research literature to support these beliefs. This evidence suggests that ICT can have a positive impact on pupils' levels of concentration, self-confidence, self-esteem, independence and behaviour. This applies to all pupils, but there are particular benefits for those who are reluctant learners or have special educational needs. One reason for this is that the ICT-based approach requires pupils to employ different sorts of skills from those needed when using traditional tools such as pens, pencils, rulers, protractors, graph paper, and so on. These pupils adapt to the ICT-based approach more readily than the traditional approach and so have an opportunity to savour some much needed success, thus raising their self-esteem. Similarly, ICT also provides access to the curriculum for those with a special educational need of a physical nature, for example, those with poor motor-control who find it difficult to produce legible work by hand, or those with a visual impairment.

ICT can also benefit pupils with special educational needs in other ways, particularly when they are using computer-based learning materials. First, such materials often break down the skills and content being taught into small, achievable steps, thus allowing the learner to demonstrate measurable progress and enjoy the praise that results from it. Second, there are advantages in terms of the learning taking place 'in private', particularly at a time when whole-class teaching approaches continue to be encouraged. The child can work at their own pace without fear of appearing slow or holding back the rest of the class. If a mistake is made then the child does not have to worry about looking foolish in front of everyone else and they can simply have another go, usually after being given additional hints or clues by the computer. The computer is no substitute for good quality interaction with an effective teacher but the instant, impartial feedback it offers is something that the teacher is not always able to provide.

When engaging in computer-based activities, pupils are also more likely to experiment and take risks, which is precisely what we want them to do, particularly when carrying out investigative, open-ended, problem-solving activities which encourage the pupils to make decisions, predictions and generalizations, and to employ skills such as trial and improvement, estimation and reasoning. A spreadsheet can be used by the pupils or the teacher to model particular mathematical situations, for example, how the volume of a box changes as its dimensions are altered, or how a bank deposit appreciates in value over time depending on the interest rate. ICT also enables pupils to get to grips with tricky mathematical concepts quickly, for example, the use of a programmable floor robot makes the concept of angle as an amount of turning accessible to young children. Another example, involving older children, is the use of data-logging equipment which opens up complex scientific and mathematical concepts such as the warming and cooling of liquids and the graphical representation of these changes over a period of time.

ICT enables teachers and teaching assistants to access or create stimulating resources; to distribute or display them attractively to individuals, groups and whole classes of pupils; to capture the interest of their pupils and motivate them; to address the issue of inclusion by providing all pupils with access to the curriculum; to share resources with colleagues; and to carry out the many administrative demands more effectively and efficiently. Essentially, there are many things that are done better with ICT than without it.

Reference

Aubrey, C. and Dahl, S. (2008) *A Review of the Evidence on the Use of ICT in the Early Years Foundation Stage*. Coventry: Becta.

Chapter 4

Poetry: an everyday activity

Liz Stone and Julia Gillen

Liz Stone is a senior teacher at St John Southworth Primary School, Nelson, Lancashire and Julia Gillen is a senior lecturer in digital literacies in the Department of Linguistics and English Language, Lancaster University. In this chapter they write of their collaborative study of how poetry is creatively embedded in one Reception classroom. They provide ideas, suggestions and justifications for the use of poetry and describe an approach which offers rich, multimodal experiences for children's language and literacy development.

To introduce ourselves: the first author, Liz, is an experienced practising teacher; the second author, Julia, a supportive researcher. I (Liz) would describe myself as having a love for poetry in my professional and personal life. When I think back to my childhood, as one of seven children, I remember my parents, perhaps unconsciously, fostering within us a love of wordplay, poetry and rhyme in the games they played with us and the rhymes and songs they sang to us.

The second author (Julia) has drawn on understandings of poetry in her research into child language development (Gillen, 1997; 2006; 2007). The first of those was inspired in part by reflections on sharing nursery rhymes with young children on a car journey – clearly a rite of passage for many of us! The task is to either begin or continue that nurturing process by 'immersing' children in words, rhymes and poems with which they can play and enjoy. Ultimately, they in turn will use them to extend and enrich their vocabulary and enhance their ability to describe their experiences of the world around them.

Source: An edited version of Stone, L. and Gillen, J. (2008) 'Poetry: an everyday activity' from 'White cars like mice with little legs', in J. Marsh and E. Hallet (eds.) *Desirable Literacies: Approaches to Language and Literacy in the Early Years* 2nd edn. (London: Sage Publications in association with the UK Literacy Association) pp. 37–60.

Why poetry?

Poetry draws on innate capacities for language. Even before language as such develops, babies have innate capacities for distinguishing between all the phonemes of language; their capacities to discriminate between sounds are in some sense even more fundamental than sight, which on the contrary remains blurred and restricted for the first few months. Nevertheless they are, in this very early stage, very capable of interacting with others in interactions that may be termed 'protoconversations', as explained below:

> In the gentle, intimate, affectionate, and rhythmically regulated playful exchanges of protoconversation, 2-month-old infants look at the eyes and mouth of the person addressing them while listening to the voice. In measured and predictable cycles of response to regular time patterns in the adult's behaviour, the infant moves its face, which it cannot see or hear, and reacts with movements of face, hands or vocal system to modified patterns of adult vocal expression that it is incapable of mimicking, and that have not been available in that form *in utero* [. . .] Evidently the responses of the infant are made expressive by internally generated motives and emotions that resemble those carried in the adult expressions. Infant and adult can, for a time, sympathise closely and apparently equally with one another's motive states, using similar melodic or prosodic forms of utterance and similar rhythms of gesture.
>
> (Trevarthen and Aitken 2001: 6)

There is a number of interesting points in this explanation by Trevarthen and Aitken:

* Human infants are innately disposed, sometimes people say by analogy 'programmed', to communicate in a dyadic situation (that is, with one other) when extremely young, before much motor control is developed.
* This communication is nonetheless multimodal, especially once the baby is around three months, old with gestures (especially gaze and smiles) as well as vocalisations.
* Interactions are rhythmic, in terms of exchanges between the two parties and within those turns.
* These communications are primarily playful, and clearly bring pleasure to each party.

Wonderful sources for examples of delightful protoconversations can be found in the book and video/DVD from The Social Baby Project (Murray and Andrews [2000] and NSPCC [2004]). You can also read explanations of young children's language development in Peccei (1999) and Gillen (2003).

Research on protoconversations and playful interactions in early language provide support for an argument that it is the exchange of patterned sounds, not the transmission of propositional knowledge, that is at the heart of communication, and that language is intrinsically multimodal and created in dialogue. Vygotsky, the influential Russian psychologist, wrote: 'In the home environment [. . .] the process through which the child learns speech is social from start to finish' (Vygotsky, 1987: 90). Obviously, discussion of this process is beyond the scope of this chapter, but we can note that for many children listening to and then participating in songs, rhymes and other language routines (that is, where repetition features strongly) is an important element of their language learning (Gillen, 1997).

Liz's granddaughter, Ruby, was quite slow to begin talking. Her family knew the value of songs and rhymes in developing speech and language, and read and sang to her regularly. At a very early age, Ruby showed pleasure at hearing familiar songs and rhymes and, though reluctant to join in at first, Ruby began prompting the reader/singer to repeat them, with phrases such as 'gain, gain' (meaning 'Sing/say it again'). At about 20 months Ruby could 'fill in the gaps' at the end of each line of the 'potty poem' (see page 50). By 27 months she was singing whole songs or rhymes, making up the words and using some known words as she wandered happily around the place; for example, she would sing "Twinkle twinkle ittle tar oh why under what ee are' (Twinkle twinkle little star, how I wonder what you are). Ruby also used familiar tunes and sang parts of rhymes to them, for example:

> Humpty Dumpty sat on a wall
> Humpty Dumpty sat on a wall
> Humpty Dumpty sat on a wall
> Humpty Dumpty sat on a wall (All sung to the tune of 'Twinkle
>   twinkle little star'!)

Ruby has also attended nursery school for two half-days per week from the age of four months. Her nursery operates within recommendations for good practice in the Early Years Foundation Stage and its guidance on communication, language and literacy states that 'music, dance, rhymes and songs play a key role in language development' (DfES, 2007: 39). Ruby's mother talked to her key worker to find out songs and rhymes they used regularly and which ones Ruby particularly enjoyed so that she could say and sing them at home. As soon as Ruby was able to sit up, and before she had any formal vocabulary, she would smile and giggle and make 'rowing and rocking' movements to the song, 'Row, row, row your boat', which they had sung regularly at nursery.

Recent developments in Liz's school and classroom have been in tune with Alexander's (2003) observation that despite policy claims around the end of the twentieth century to prioritise orality in the curriculum, the basics of pedagogy were identified (with various terms) as what has traditionally been known as the '3 Rs' (reading, writing and arithmetic). Drawing on his extensive research abroad, Alexander argued that 'from an international standpoint the educational place of talk in our primary schools seems ambivalent' (Alexander, 2003: 23). More recently, policy in England seems to have taken this view seriously: 'Far more attention needs to be given, right from the start, to promoting speaking and listening skills to make sure that children build a good stock of words, learn to listen attentively and speak clearly and confidently' (DFES, 2006: 3).

Poetry also helps children develop phonological awareness by listening to the sounds in words and phrases. 'Children need first to hear the constituent sounds in words and phrases, and then begin to map out the graphic symbol for them' (Goswami, 1993, cited by Jeni Riley 1996: 10). Poetry facilitates the gradual awakening of phonological awareness through its patterning, its frequent devices of employing repetitions in syntactic structures and sounds, with carefully employed variation. So content is 'cast in verbal forms designed to assist the memory by conferring pleasure' (Havelock, 1986, cited by Luce-Kapler, 2003: 85).

Speaking and listening skills can be developed by simple reciting of familiar rhymes and poems. We have found that many children are reluctant to speak in group or class situations, but will happily recite a familiar rhyme or listen to another child reciting a rhyme, and help them with sequence and order if they need it.

In Liz's role play theatre, we provided costumes and written versions of familiar nursery rhymes, such as 'Miss Polly had a dolly', 'How much is that doggy in the window?', 'Little Miss Muffet' and so on. Acting with a considerable degree of independence, the children dressed themselves up, allocated roles and assisted each other in reciting the rhymes and acting out roles.

Other pupils bought tickets for the theatre and sat with ice creams and popcorn as they watched the show. The main objectives and outcomes linked to this activity consisted of showing an awareness of rhyme and speaking clearly, and showing awareness of the listener. On the second time this activity took place, Liz decided that the children were so busy 'reading the texts' that it impaired their ability to speak with volume and expression. As an intervention strategy, staff removed the written versions of the poem and put them in the book corner: this was more effective.

At the early, emergently literate stage, children benefit much more from hearing poems than reading them. When the teacher reads, the children are able to access rich and wide-ranging vocabulary. New vocabulary can be explained first, and then the text is heard in its purest form, uninterrupted, there to become immersed in and to enjoy: 'The dissection of the reading process should never be allowed to diminish the pleasure of the text' (Riley, 1996: 86).

Children can also experiment with changing words (led by the teacher) in poems and rhymes, and thinking about how this changes the meaning. Liz led the way with the following example:

> Hickory Dickory dock the mouse ran up the clock,
> Hickory Dickory din, the mouse is very thin.

The children retorted:

> Hickory dickory doo, the mouse went to the loo.
> Hickory dickory doo, the mouse just lost his shoe.
> Hickory dickory doo, the mouse just had a poo!
> Hickory dickory dee, the mouse just came for tea,
> Hickory dickory dee, the mouse sat on my knee.
> Hickory dickory dee, the mouse just had a wee!

Prediction skills using context and syntax can be developed by learning poems and rhymes by heart. The same skills can be developed by using rhyming poems, read by the teacher, the children using 'oral' cloze procedure to put in rhyming words. The repetition and patterns of poetry make it an excellent resource for the development of early reading skills

(Riley, 1996). The patterns can be used as models for children's own writing.

How can we make poetry and rhyme an integral part of the early years curriculum?

In Liz's classroom, poetry is part of the everyday routines and Liz does not limit words and their constituent sounds to a short phonics session. For example, as the children come in, they start the day with a song. Most songs are basically musical poems and the usual prediction skills can be used to help the children to learn the words. Liz does not limit the songs to the usual ones for the very young, but prefers to be relatively ambitious. The repertoire is broadened to include songs from other cultures, pop music, musicals and so on. Julia was charmed to be welcomed on her first visit to the classroom by a rousing rendition of 'Getting to know you' (Rodgers and Hammerstein) from the classic musical *The King and I*. This enables the children access a range of vocabulary, music and styles.

In this Roman Catholic school (which welcomes other faiths, especially Muslims), the morning begins with a sung prayer, sometimes composed by the class, or the teacher. The class sings a 'days of the week' song, an alphabet song and chants the months of the year. The children look at the clock and play a 'What time is it Mr Wolf?' reading time game. They look at the weather and include the day's weather in the 'What is the weather today?' song.

In this short space of time, approximately 20 minutes, the children have experienced a range of music. They have used poetry and song in prayer, used vocabulary related to the weather, experienced vocabulary related to the passing of time (days, months, numbers), read the time on a clock and had a great deal of fun in the process! Liz is part of a job-share, and there are two other members of staff. Both teachers share the same philosophy on the importance of using poetry and rhyme, and support staff are fully informed as to why it is used and are enthusiastic in their own use of it.

Teachers and teaching assistants should try to be a poetry role model and we strongly recommend 'having a go' at writing your own poems. Read them to the class and ask children to be your critical friend, or ask them to help you with the last line. The poems can be very simple, for example:

You and Me

You're cold, I'm hot
You're good, I'm not
You're tall, I'm small
You stand, I fall.

You're young, I'm old
You're hairy, I'm bold
You're thin, I'm fat
You're bumpy, I'm flat.

You're generous, I'm mean
You're dirty, I'm clean
You're smooth, I'm rough
You're tender, I'm tough.

But I like you!
          Liz Stone, 2005

In Liz's classroom this poem has been recited several times and made into a game. Liz can now start it off, say the first line, then pause after 'You're' and 'I'm' and the children collectively supply the missing words. Their memories have clearly been stimulated through use of the regular structure. Peters and Boggs (1986) emphasise how useful to language development this 'slot and fill' pattern can be.

Teaching staff may play two different versions of the same song and ask children what is similar different about them and which one is their favourite and why. This can also draw their attention to the fact that poetry is not just about what is written, but how it is read. Staff can make taking the register an opportunity for word-play through alliterative names, changing first phoneme in names, rhyming names, saying 'Good Morning' in some of the children's home languages (such as Urdu, Polish, and so on). Initially, these are mostly modelled by the teacher but as the children become more familiar with the activities, they will begin to try them out themselves.

Number songs and rhymes are familiar to the children and can be used in a cross-curricular way or simply composed for use in mathematical activities. For example, in a subtraction activity the class had a teddy bear shop (linked to the text *We're Going on a Bear Hunt* by Michael Rosen and

Helen Oxenbury, 1993), and changed the words to the number rhyme 'Five currant buns in a baker's shop' to:

> Five teddy bears in a teddy bear shop
> Soft and cuddly with fur on the top
> Along came a girl/boy with some money one day
> Bought a teddy bear and took it away.

The poem below was written to use in a dance session where the children used ribbon sticks to represent the movements of the wind as described in the poem:

The Wind

> Warm, gentle, soothing wind,
> Brushing, stroking, cooling wind.
> Whirling, whipping,
> swirling wind.
> Curling high,
> Sweeping low.
> Buzz off wind!
> It's time to go.
>
> Liz Stone, 2006

Action rhymes are used as warm-ups and cool-downs to physical education lessons. If the same rhyme is used over a number of weeks, the children are able to recite it as they move.

Staff try to read at least one poem a day, followed by a discussion of the poem when they have read it, and asking questions such as: 'What did we say this word meant?'; 'Talk to your partner and try to think of another word you could put here which has the same meaning'; 'Can you think of a better word to use here?' In all everyday activities and routines, teachers draw the children's attention to interesting words: 'I think this word sounds really exciting'; 'This word sounds like what it is describing' (onomatopoeia); 'What do you think this word means?'; 'This word makes me laugh'. It is sometimes useful to model using a thesaurus if you are writing together.

Children and staff often learn a new short poem together, preferably one which requires good expression when reading; for example 'Potty'. Over a period of, say, a week, the children take turns in performing the poem, commenting on expression and delivery so as to improve performance as a whole. It is rewarding for staff and children because 'To be able to say a favourite poem to yourself, or quote passages which have meaning to you, can so often bring comfort and satisfaction' (Brownjohn, 1994: 350).

Potty

Don't put that potty on your head, Tim
Don't put that potty on your head
It's not very clean
And you don't know where it's been, so
Don't put that potty on your head!!

In Liz's classroom, just a few readings of this poem (using the obvious prop of a potty!) led to unsuspecting visitors (in this case Mrs Gillen!) having a 'hat' placed on their head whilst the children recited the poem with wonderful expression and intonation.

There then followed a barrage of volunteers wanting to stand with a friend in front of the class and recite the poem alone.

Planning poetry activities

When writing poems, Liz always uses a model, keeping it simple and repetitive. Rhythms and routines have a strong place in which to anchor language development, aiding processes of segmentation, analysis as well as providing the 'gaps' pregnant with possibilities in which creativity occurs (Gillen, 1997, 2007). In the classroom, staff guide the children through the process, 'feeding' them with words and ideas as necessary to keep them engaged. If they cannot think of their own words, they are given choices and use their word choice so that they have ownership of the finished poem. Pride in the finished result often means that confidence is enhanced, and the degree of scaffolding they have actually received may be forgotten. Then, their expectations as to what they can do next time are actually strengthened, with heartening results.

In the Foundation Stage in particular, it is almost impossible for the teacher alone to present planned sessions, therefore detailed plans and enthusiastic and willing support staff are an invaluable resource. Some of Liz's plans are used elsewhere in the school, and adapted as required. Figure 4.1 is an example of the plan used to support the children in the writing of a poem about a boat trip.

The Boat Trip

Objectives

- to use language to imagine and recreate roles and experiences
- to expand vocabulary, exploring the meaning and sound of new words
- to use talk to organise and clarify thinking, ideas, feelings and events
- to use all their senses to help them describe what they experience

Activities

Tell the children that they are going to go on an imaginary boat trip (explain that imaginary means pretend or not real).

Tell them that together, you are going to write a poem about what you can see on our boat trip and that you are going to ask them some questions which will help them to think of what to include in the poem.

Explain that you will write the words for them, but that it will be their poem and you will be reading it to the rest of the class.

Questions

- How do you feel?
- What is the weather like?
- What is the weather doing to you?
- What does that remind you of?
- What can you see?
- What can you hear?
- What does that remind you of?

Ask each question, listening to or recording children's answers, giving them choices of words if they cannot think of them themselves, and write each line of the poem as it develops, reading it back to the children as you add each new line.

Inside, the children draw a picture of themselves on the boat trip and something that they saw or experienced.

Differentiation by outcome and teacher support

- prompt as necessary
- model multisensory experience, reflection and the selection of appropriate words
- encourage use of similes – accept the unexpected comparison

---

Figure 4.1 An example of planning: guided poetry writing.

Incorporating words and pictures in authored texts

Pictorial poetry writing using a multimodal approach is entirely appropriate for, and yet should not be restricted to, the early years. Children's drawings, particularly post-Foundation Stage are too rarely valued as 'texts'. Dyson

(2004: x) notes that 'drawing, for example, is often dubbed as "planning for writing" even though it may not have been so intended by the child.' We agree strongly with her declaration:

> Given time, materials and space young composers quite readily interweave whatever symbolic tools are at their disposal – drawing, singing, gesturing, talking, and, yes, writing.
>
> (ibid)

In one class activity, the teacher models a simple poem by manipulating a small set of objects on an interactive whiteboard. The pupils select from the set of images and repeat the basic template of the poem, while introducing their own adjectives or modifying phrases. One boy said:

> I like crunchy apples,
> I like wobbly jellies.
> I like popping out peas.
> I like soft strawberries.

Liz and colleagues try to make poetry authoring multisensory, authentic and active. The same poetry-writing activity may involve the child painting simple pictures, drawing, collecting objects from the classroom or outdoors, using a digital camera to take pictures and so on. Young children can 'write' poems based on first-hand experience, so if, for example, the poem is about a tree, a multisensory approach is needed. They need to see, touch, hear and smell the tree before and during the writing process. Asking questions such as 'How does it feel?'; 'What does that remind you of?' are useful teacher prompts.

It is not necessary for children to scribe at all during the writing process; taking the physical act of writing away will enable them to concentrate on visual, oral and tactile elements. Research (for example, as discussed by Medwell and Wray, 2007) has demonstrated that giving opportunities to children to dictate texts to adults leads to an increase in quality of their composition. When the poem has been scribed by the teacher, the children can then make a pictorial representation of the poem, sometimes changing the order or sequence of the poem to make it their own and indeed sometimes voluntarily deciding to add some written words to it.

From this activity the children 'wrote' the following poem and presented it pictorially:

I see a huge, rough tree
I see swishy, swashy grass
I see a speeding train
I see a black, spotty gate.

Another poem read:

I see green grass
I see speeding cars
I see the wet boat
I see the circled logs
I see the willow tree.

Conclusions

Current national curriculum documents for the UK and beyond make relatively few direct references to poetry. The discerning teacher, recognising the importance and value of poetry within the school curriculum, will find many objectives which can be met through listening to, reading, writing and experiencing a range of poetry and rhyme.

It is important that teachers and teaching assistants are aware that not all children are introduced to nursery rhymes, poetry and songs from birth, and that parents should be informed of the value of these in developing children's early language and communication skills. One stance to take with poetry is that it is one of the arts that marks high culture; that it may be at best, pleasant to read with children, at worst irrelevant. This can lead to an ambiguous attitude as to its value:

> Poetry is a pleasure in itself. It can be read for no other reason than its intrinsic value as an art form. As such, it could be regarded as something of a luxury in a busy classroom, intent on raising standards.
> (Lancashire Schools Effectiveness Service, 2005)

We propose that poetry in the home, nursery and classroom, as we describe it here, offers particular potential for what we assert to be a key aim in education, not just across the Early Years Foundation Stage (as useful as it is) but also a continuing priority. This aim is the fostering of the ability to *discriminate* – that is, to make meaningful distinctions. The word 'discriminate' can be rescued from its sometimes negative connotations to the expression of a powerfully positive human ability. Acts of discerning differences, of defining them, of communicating these differences to others, are those in which we increase our own abilities to comprehend phenomena in the world, and indeed therefore our ability to act effectively. Improving our abilities to discriminate – to perceive similarities and differences, and to express and communicate these – surely is a conceptual thread of education from the early years through to advanced endeavours; whether in the sciences, arts or elsewhere and throughout life. The penultimate word then, to Anthony Wilson in his introduction to *The Poetry Book for Primary Schools*, who suggests that, 'poetry is uniquely placed in allowing children to say what they really want to say in the way they want to say it' (1998: 4). The final word to a reception age pupil from Liz's class, who independently read their own shape poem about a spider as:

> *Spider*
>
> Climbing, climbing walls,
> Climbing the ceiling,
> Tickly.
> Creepy, creeping,
> Spider in the web!

Acknowledgement

With thanks to St John Southworth Primary, Nelson, Lancashire, for permission to use the case study material.

References

Alexander, R. (2003) 'Oracy, literacy and pedagogy: international perspectives', in E. Bearne, H. Dombey and T. Grainger (eds) *Classroom Interactions in Literacy*. Buckingham: Open University Press.

Brownjohn, S. (1994) *To Rhyme Or Not to Rhyme*. London: Hodder and Stoughton.

DfES (Department for Education and Skills) (2006) *The Rose Report: Independent Review of the Teaching of Reading*. London: HMSO.

DfES (Department for Education and Skills) (2007) *Practice Guidance for the Early Years Foundation Stage*. London: HMSO. Available online at http://www.teachernet.gov.uk (accessed 16 August 2007).

Gillen, J. (1997) ' "Couldn't put Dumpy together again": the significance of repetition and routine in young children's language development', in L. Abbott and H. Moylett (eds) *Working with the Under-Threes: Responding to Children's Needs. Volume 2*. Buckingham: Open University Press, pp. 90–101.

Gillen, J. (2003) *The Language of Children*. London: Routledge.

Luce-Kapler, R. (2003) 'Orality and the poetics of curriculum', *Journal of the Canadian Association for Curriculum Studies* 1 (2) 79–93.

Murray, L. and Andrews, L. (2000) *The Social Baby*. The Children's Project/NSPCC.

NSPCC (with Lynn Murray) (2004) *The Social Baby DVD/Video*. The Children's Project/NSPCC. Available online at http://www.socialbaby.com (accessed 16 August 2007).

Peccei, J.S. (1999) *Child Language. Second edition*. London: Routledge.

Riley, J. (1996) *The Teaching of Reading*. London: Paul Chapman.

Trevarthen, C. and Aitken, K.J. (2001) 'Infant intersubjectivity: research, theory and clinical applications', *Journal of Child Psychology and Psychiatry* 4(1): 3–48.

Vygotsky, L.S. (1987) 'Thinking and speech', trans, by N. Minick in R. Rieber and A. Carton (eds) *The Collected Works of L.S. Vygotsky. Vol. I Problems of General Psychology*. New York: Plenum Press, pp. 43–287.

Chapter 5

Learning from the language that children use

Chris Bills

How can we tell whether children have really understood the concepts we ask them to work with? Chris Bills's research into the teaching and learning of primary mathematics led him to conclude that the words and metaphors children use can be a strong indicator of the depth and nature of their understanding. His findings have implications for the way teachers and teaching assistants talk to children about mathematics and underline the need to listen carefully when making assessments.

As a teacher of mathematics I am concerned to know what children have learned as a result of my teaching. I also need to know what they have learned from their previous teachers if I am to build upon their existing conceptualisations.

When I asked children to perform mental calculations and to tell me 'What was in your head when you were thinking of that?' I found that the words they used related to classroom activities I had previously observed. This leads me to suggest that the metaphoric language used in children's descriptions of how they have performed mental calculations can give teachers an indication of the experiences which have influenced the thinking of their pupils.

In addition to these echoes of previous classroom activities my study indicates that different modes of language use are associated with achievement. I discovered that the use of present tense, use of the pronoun 'you' and use of causal connectives are all most commonly associated with correct answers to mental calculations. These 'linguistic pointers' may help teachers gauge children's confidence in their mental calculation procedures.

Source: An edited version of Bills, C. (2003) 'What can teachers learn from the language that children use?' *Education, 31* (1), 3–13. Reprinted by permission of Taylor & Francis Ltd (http://www.tandf.co.uk/journals).

Indications of previous learning

On my first visit to Bright Cross, a primary school near Birmingham, England, I watched a lesson with six- to seven-year-old children. The teacher, Mr. K used Dienes Blocks to demonstrate addition of two two-digit numbers. First he balanced ten 'ones' on his hand, one on top of another, to show that they were the same height as a 'ten'. When the tower collapsed the 'ones' were laid along the 'ten' to show again that ten 'ones' made a 'ten'.

Two pupils were selected to help Mr. K give Mandy two 'tens'.

Mr. K: Another way of putting it?
Mandy: Twenty.

Mandy was then given four 'ones'.

Mr. K: How many altogether?
Mandy: Twenty-four.

Mr. K gave Nina one 'ten' and two 'ones'.

Mr. K: How many altogether?
Nina: Twelve.
Mr. K: Now put them together in my hands.

Mandy and Nina put their 'tens' in one of his hands and the 'ones' in the other hand. He then held out both hands for the pupils to see.

Mr. K: How many altogether?
Pupils: Thirty-six.
Mr. K: Look how easy it is to add them instead of all individual cubes.

One week later I interviewed several of the children and asked them to calculate 24 add 53, which I had printed on paper but asked them to work out in their heads. They had no materials or pencil and paper. The influence of the previous lesson seemed clear in the response of one girl, Elspeth:

I: How would you do it?
Elspeth: Put those together. (Points at numbers)

I: Why would you put those together?

Elspeth: Well you add the tens together then you add the units because it's like in one hand you have the tens and in the other you have the units.

Elspeth made explicit the connection with the physical handling of objects by her use of 'like' but the metaphoric language of manipulation is also apparent in 'put those together'. This is a metaphor because we cannot 'put together' symbols yet use of these words may indicate that she was thinking about the manipulation of the symbols in terms of the manipulation of the physical objects.

Elspeth's response gives some indication of the way in which the language associated with manipulating physical apparatus may subsequently be used when talking about operations on number. In my subsequent observations of lessons and pupil interviews, I found that the language children used often related to previous classroom activities when talking about how they had performed mental calculations. Another example occurred a few months later, when Mrs. J gave this lesson about three-digit numbers to the Year 2 class. Some language that was subsequently used by children is in ordinary type for emphasis:

Mrs. J: You have been throwing dice and all sorts of things. You also looked at rolls of raffle tickets like this:

Mrs. J drew on the white board: | |186| |

Mrs. J: What comes next?

Pupil: 187.

Mrs. J: What comes before?

Pupil: 185.

Mrs. J: Why wasn't the one or the eight changed?

Pupil: Because you are not adding tens or hundreds.

Mrs. J then replaced 186 on the white board with 199.

Pupil: What comes before?

Pupil: 198.

Mrs. J: What comes after?

Pupil: 200.

Mrs. J: But that means I'm altering the tens and hundreds. That's because I can't have more than nine in any column.

To illustrate *going to* the next number she held up three single-digit cards and then changed the units digit card for a different one. She indicated that only the units digit changed except *when the nine is changed for a naught* and then the ten digit is changed as well. She showed three-digit numbers by holding up three cards and suggested keeping two *the same* and only *changing the end digit* to add-on one. In this context 'change' means the physical exchange of one card for another.

In a subsequent interview I asked, 'When you are counting what comes next after 379?' The children's responses gave indications of their previous classroom activities:

Elaine: I just put away the three um 300–79 – after that comes 80 and then – I do 380.

Hazel: We have to change the – seven to an eight and we take nine to an oh.

Others used similar language but did not give the correct answer to the calculation:

John: 389 . . . I changed the ten to the next.

Christine: 550 – I added one more on to the units makes ten and then I added it on so it was four made five.

The language used by these children was sufficiently different to suggest that they had conceptualised from their own experiences, yet sufficiently similar to suggest that they had been influenced by their classroom experiences.

More metaphors

As the children learned more about written calculation procedures the language they used to describe mental calculations showed the influence of the algorithms. The expressions 'the units', 'put the five', 'carry the one', 'the tens' are all appropriate in the context of the written calculation. These expressions also, however, occurred in the language of children when they described how they had performed a mental calculation. This again suggests that the classroom experiences had influenced the way they communicate. These expressions are also metaphoric in the sense that the language of one context (written algorithm) is used in describing another context (mental calculation).

Expressions related to written calculation were common when children were asked to calculate mentally questions such as '48 add 23'. For instance these were typical responses when, having given the answer, 44 children were asked. 'What was in your head?':

Dennis: I was adding the eight and the three, which makes 11, and then I was adding the two and four and that equals six. But then it needs to be carried by one.

Irene: Well I added eight and three, which makes 11, then I added the four and two which makes six but the 11 is over 10 so I added another one, another ten to the six to make 70.

The use of the language of the algorithm indicates that the pupils conceptualisations for calculation seem to have been influenced by these experiences.

It is important to realise that not all the children used this language. Others seemed to have been less influenced in their thinking by these written procedures. Some simply counted and one seemed to have been influenced by numberline activities:

Myles: It was like a ruler. I counted along it, I think it was in fives. And when I got to 70, I counted another one.

Notice the metaphors of movement and position apparent in 'when I got to'. Language related to numberlines was relatively uncommon in this classroom and this may reflect the low proportion of time given to these activities. Other pupils used mental calculation strategies:

Bobby: I added 20 which makes 60 and then you add two to make 70 and added one more which makes 71.

Bobby's response is also interesting because of his use of tense and pronouns. Notice that 'I' and past tense were used initially but then he changed to 'you' and the present tense when he seemed to be giving the rule he was following. This aspect of the children's language will now be explored.

Pronouns and tense in descriptions of mental calculations

The use of 'you' and the present tense is common in rule-giving in everyday life and in the classroom. Rowland (1999) noted that children may also start to use 'you' when they discover a generalisation. In his study children used 'you' to distance themselves from a statement and thus indicate that it was not peculiar to them but was in general true. He suggested that pronouns are 'linguistic pointers' which indicate a mode of thought.

In the classroom teachers and pupils frequently use 'you' instead of the more formal 'one'. The present tense is also appropriate in the classroom when a rule is being described when a calculation is being performed. Here is an excerpt from a typical Year 3 lesson in which Miss P reminded pupils of the method she had shown them to halve an odd number. A pupil described what to do as Miss P drew on the board:

Miss P: How to half an odd number equally? Do you remember what to do?

Pupil: 11 is made out of 10 and one and you put . . .

Miss P: Carry on 'you put . . .'

Pupil: You put half of 10 is five and half of one is half so it's five and a half.

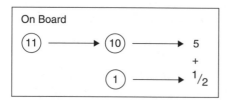

In a subsequent interview I asked, 'What is nine split in two?' and then 'What was in your head?' My past-tense question was frequently answered in the present tense when a rule seemed to have been used. Similarly instead of the expected 'I' to describe what the individual had done, the use of 'you' indicated the influence of the classroom activities and language:

Nora: Well – you get nine is made out of eight add one, and half of eight, is, four, and half of one is half, – so you add eight and a half together and you get – four and a half.

My analysis indicates that use of 'you' was more frequently associated with correct answers. When 'you' was used exclusively, 79 per cent of the answers were correct. When 'I' was used, 65 per cent were correct. This seems to indicate that when the pupils have mastered the rule it tends to be expressed in the general 'you' mode. Similarly the use of tense indicated differences. When the past tense was used exclusively 62 per cent of the responses were correct. In comparison 71 per cent of the responses using present tense accompanied correct answers to the calculations.

When the children had difficulty performing the mental calculation their responses to 'What was in your head?' were often descriptions of what they had done in that particular instance. When they had given the answer easily they more frequently gave the rule using the classroom mode of description (i.e. present tense and use of 'you').

Language associated with explanations

Since the use of 'you' for descriptions of procedures is common in everyday life it is not surprising that it is also common in the mathematics classroom. Its use, as we have seen above, is also actively encouraged in the classroom discourse. There were other examples in my observations that illustrate the similarities in language used by teachers and pupils. There was evidence that pupils were being encouraged to adopt the speech styles common in mathematics. For instance, explanations involving 'because' were used both by teachers and pupils. Again this is not uncommon in everyday life but pupils frequently followed the teacher's lead in the use of the word. For example in a lesson on 'adding and subtracting near-multiples of ten' Mrs. F first talked to the Year 4 children about 36 add 19. She used a hundred square:

Mrs. F: *What is 19 nearly?*

Lynne: *20.*

Mrs. F: *If you wanted to add 20 to 36 how would you do it?*

Lynne: *Go down.*

Mrs. F: *So 36 go down two is 56 but we have to take one because we are only adding 19 not 20.*

More examples of addition were worked through with the class, then subtraction was described in a similar way. Mrs. F wrote 55–19 on the board.

Mrs. F: See if you can do it in your head but using that strategy.

Peter: 36.

Mrs. F: Tell us how you did it.

Peter: 'Cause 19 is near 20 so I just took two tens from 55 and added one.

In this example 'because' was used by the teacher and the pupils immediately followed suit. The use of 'because' is part of the speech style of mathematicians. Since deduction is an essential element of mathematics the use of 'if', 'then', 'so' and 'because' are inevitably common in the mathematics classroom. Children's use of these words can be an indication of their adoption of a mathematical style of reasoning.

In my interviews, many children spontaneously used causal connectives. Having given an answer to a mental calculation there was no necessity to give explanations in reply to 'What was in your head?' yet many children did so:

17+8	*You add three on because five add three is eight*
97+10	*I can't add a ten so I put the one in front of it.*
17+9	*If you take off one, because it was the nine, it would be 26.*
Round 239	*If it's 30 then it's under 50.*

Use of causal connectives was associated more frequently with correct answers to the mental calculations. This seems to suggest that children who are secure enough in their calculation strategies to give correct answers are more likely to describe their methods in the language associated with explanation. They do not simply describe what they did. They explain why they do it that way.

What can we learn from children's language?

I have given three examples where the language children use to describe their mental calculations can inform teachers of the ways in which the children may be thinking.

- When children use words associated with particular classroom activities such as the manipulation of blocks or cards there is an indication that experiences with these materials have influenced their thinking.
- When children adopt a classroom speech style involving use of 'you' and the present tense there is an indication that they have internalised the rules and follow them when making their own calculations.

Children in my survey seldom adopted this mode of expression when they used their own idiosyncratic methods.

- Children also spontaneously used causal connectives in an explanatory mode of expression even though they had been asked simply 'What was in your head?' There was an indication that this style of language was associated with correct answers. This seems to suggest that this mode of language use points to the use of a familiar routine that is well understood.

Listening to children's language can assist teachers in identifying the differences in their conceptualisations. An understanding of the significance of the words that are used can thus be an aid to formative assessment.

My study suggests that the 'image like' nature of children's language (Bills 1999) is indicative of the influences on their thinking. This may only confirm what we have always known: teachers and teaching assistants need to listen to what children say if they wish to find out what is going on in the children's heads. I hope, however, that I have also given some pointers to help interpret the words that they use.

References

Bills, C.J. (1999) 'What was in your head when you were thinking of that?' *Mathematics Teaching*, 168, 39–41.

Rowland, T. (1999) 'Pronouns in Mathematics Talk: Power, Vagueness and Generalisation' *For the Learning of Mathematics*, 19 (2), 19–26.

Chapter 6

Watching and learning: the tools of assessment

Cathy Nutbrown

Assessment is a key feature of the work of teachers and many teaching assistants. However, all too often, external demands and considerations can mean that the focus is on outcomes and measurable achievement – assessment *of* learning rather than assessment *for* learning. Cathy Nutbrown, professor of education, The University of Sheffield, argues that we need to reconsider why we assess young children's learning and to develop assessment practices that begin with and respect the learner, and that will provide us with information to engage with and support children's learning and understanding. She suggests that observation is an essential tool in achieving this. Although the focus here is on young children, the conclusions have implications for those working with older children as well.

This chapter focuses on how early childhood educators can understand the capabilities of the children they teach. It begins by asking why assessment is important, discussing why educators need a broad picture of children's capabilities, and considers observation as one of the best 'tools of the trade'.

Why assess young children's learning?

To ask 'Why assess children's learning?' is to question one of the most fundamental components of teaching young children. Children's learning is so complex, rich, fascinating, varied and variable, surprising, enthusiastic and stimulating, that to see it taking place, every day, before one's very eyes is one of the greatest privileges of any early childhood educator. The very process of observing and assessing children's learning is, in a sense, its own justification. Watching children learn can open our eyes to the astonishing

Source: Nutbrown, C. (2001) 'Watching and learning: The tools of assessment', in G. Pugh *Contemporary Issues in the Early Years* (London: Sage Publications) pp. 66–73.

capacity of young children to learn, and shows us the crucial importance of these first few years in children's lives. But there is much more to say about assessing children's learning. There is much more to be gained from watching children learn than to make us marvel at children's powers to think, do, communicate and create, for there is an important piece of work for educators to do to help them to understand – really understand – what they see.

The legacy of some of the pioneers of early education (such as Froebel, Piaget, Vygotsky and Isaacs) and of those whose work in the latter half of the twentieth century has illuminated children's learning (such as Donaldson 1983; Athey 1990; Abbott and Rodger 1994) helps educators to consider their own observations of children in the light of a rich literature which opens up the meaning of children's words, representations and actions. Educators' personal experiences of individual children's learning can help them to see more clearly the general principles that other researchers and educators have established as characteristic of that learning.

Some of the pioneers of early childhood education learnt about children's learning by watching and learning themselves, by observing children and thinking about what they saw. Those published observations can be useful to educators now as tools for reflection on children's processes of learning and as a means of moving from the specifics of personal experiences to general understandings about children's thinking. Susan Isaacs, for example, ran an experimental school, The Malting House, in Cambridge from 1924 to 1927. Her compelling accounts of the day-to-day doings of the children in the school show clearly how her analysis of children's intellectual development is the product of a mass of detailed anecdotal insights. For example, she describes the development of the basic concepts of biology, change, growth, life and death, illustrating this process with a wealth of evidence:

18.6.25
The children let the rabbit out to run about the garden for the first time, to their great delight. They followed him about, stroked him and talked about his fur, his shape and his ways.

13.7.25
Some of the children called out that the rabbit was dying. They found it in the summerhouse, hardly able to move. They were very sorry and talked much about it. They shut it up in the hutch and gave it warm milk.

14.7.25

The rabbit had died in the night. Dan found it and said: 'It's dead – its tummy does not move up and down now.' Paul said, 'My daddy says that if we put it into water it will get alive again.' Mrs. I said 'shall we do so and see?' They put it into a bath of water. Some of them said, 'It is alive.' Duncan said, 'If it floats, it's dead, and if it sinks, it's alive.' It floated on the surface. One of them said, 'It's alive, because it's moving.' This was a circular motion, due to the currents in the water. Mrs. I therefore put in a small stick which also moved round and round, and they agreed that the stick was not alive. They then suggested that they should bury the rabbit, and all helped to dig a hole and bury it.

15.7.25

Frank and Duncan talked of digging the rabbit up – but Frank said, 'It's not there – it's gone up to the sky.' They began to dig, but tired of it and ran off to something else. Later they came back and dug again. Duncan, however, said, 'Don't bother – it's gone – it's up in the sky' and gave up digging. Mrs. I therefore said, 'Shall we see if it's there?' and also dug. They found the rabbit, and were very interested to see it still there.

The diary entries by Isaacs and her colleagues were more than entertaining anecdotes: they formed the basis for her analysis of children's scientific thinking. Isaacs was able to learn about learning by intently studying her own detailed observations. Thus, assessment of children's learning through the tools of observation is not at all new, though for some who have not had the opportunities to continue to practise their skills of observing and reflecting upon their observations, those tools may well have become somewhat rusty. However, many have followed Isaacs' observational practice; indeed, much of my own earlier work on children's learning has been informed by my diary jottings (made while teaching) of children's words, actions and graphic representations (Nutbrown 1999). Similarly, the pioneering practice of Reggio Emilia in northern Italy is developed largely through careful observation, documentation and reflection upon the children's work (Filippini and Vecchi 1996; Abbott and Nutbrown 2001).

The 1990s saw a proliferation of criteria for high-quality provision for young children's learning. Such statements represented attempts to identify and specify necessary conditions for this learning and development but, as

Woodhead (1996) illustrates, quality is often culture and community specific and it is difficult to agree universal statements of quality. What might suit the discussion of quality in the UK may well be quite unsuitable in, say, the Caribbean. That said, it is true that – whatever their setting and whatever their international location – where educators observe children and use their observations to generate understandings of their learning and their needs, they are contributing to the development of a quality environment in which those children might thrive. The evaluative purpose of assessment is central for early childhood educators, for they cannot know if the environments they create and the support they provide for children as they work are effective unless they watch and learn from what they see.

Observation can provide starting points for reviewing the effectiveness of provision, and such observational assessments of children's learning can be used to identify strengths, weaknesses, gaps and inconsistencies in the curriculum provided for all children.

Assessment can be used to plan and review the provision and teaching as well as to identify those significant moments in each child's learning which educators can build upon to shape a curriculum that matches each child's pressing cognitive and affective concerns.

Observation and assessment can illuminate the future, as well as provide information with which to improve the quality of the present. This forward-looking dimension of assessment is the means by which early childhood educators can explore the possible outcomes of the provision they offer; the curriculum, pedagogy, interactions and relationships. Increasingly, formal assessments are being used to diagnose children's abilities. There is a danger that formal assessment of four-year-olds on entry to school limits the opportunities they are offered rather than opening up a broad canvas of learning. It is important, however, to use the active process of assessment to identify for each individual the next teaching steps so that learning opportunities in the immediate future are well matched to the children they are designed for.

This focus on the next steps in teaching (and learning) takes us into the area of development Vygotsky called 'the zone of proximal development'. He used this concept to argue passionately that assessment does not end with a description of a pupil's present state of knowing, but only begins there. He wrote: 'I do not terminate my study at this point, but only begin it' (Vygotsky 1978:85). Effective assessment is dynamic, not static, and can identify for the educator what the learner's next steps might be; assessment reveals learning potential as well as learning achievements. Vygotsky's arguments show how 'learning which is oriented toward developmental levels that have already been reached is ineffective from the viewpoint of a child's overall development. It does not aim for a new stage of the developmental process but rather lags behind this process' (Vygotsky 1978:89).

Observation and assessment are the essential tools of watching and learning by which we can both establish the progress that has already been made and explore the future – the learning that is still embryonic. The role of the adult in paying careful and informed attention to children's learning and reflecting upon it is crucial to the enhancement of children's future learning.

Early assessment for the future

Children's early learning and development are exciting. It is stimulating and rewarding for teachers (as well as children and their parents) to see a child taking new steps in learning. But the prevailing conditions for effective teaching must include a fair breeze with a following wind. Everything must be heading in the same direction – charting the same course, running the same race. It will not do for those who teach and those who are responsible for teachers and education in terms of policy to be in opposition – a team effort is what children need. The status of assessment for teaching is essential to optimum early education experiences for young children. But there are other conditions that make up a fair breeze for early education: time for children (enough teachers to work with them), time for assessment, confidence in teachers' teaching and assessments, and recognition of the judgements teachers make about what they teach, how they teach and when. These together can make for teaching that enhances learning.

So what might the future hold for the improvement of assessment for learning in the early years of education? First, the elevation of the status of ongoing teacher assessment as the main tool for understanding children's learning needs and progress; second, professional development opportunities that challenge teachers and other early childhood educators to observe children's learning and understand what they see.

With due respect . . .

In this chapter I have discussed why educators should observe and assess young children. Future policies and practice must support the full involvement of parents and educators towards respectful understandings of children's learning.

The 'one-stop' summaries of children's abilities according to predetermined lists (that miss the true riches of children's minds) do nothing to truly focus the minds of educators on children's learning.

Time for teaching and assessment, *confidence* in teachers' teaching and assessments, and *recognition* of the judgements teachers make can create the important climate of *respectful* teaching. The concept of respect can underpin and inform the way adults work with children and the ways in which policies are developed and implemented, but the notion of respect in education can be misunderstood (Nutbrown 1996, 1997). What do I mean when I speak of *respect* in education? 'When advocates of respect for children are accused of being "idealistic", of "romanticising early childhood" – their meaning is misunderstood. Respect is not about "being nice" – it is about being clear, honest, courteous, diligent and consistent' (Nutbrown 1998).

The concept of respectful assessment and respectful teaching may still raise an eyebrow or two, and could be dismissed by some as an over-romanticising of work with and for young children. So the careful articulation of our terms is important, and it is worth examining here what the concept of respectfully working with children might include. Table 6.1 shows some aspects which I suggest might constitute respectful teaching, and it is worth noting that the opposite of respectful approaches is *dis*respectful. (I doubt that anyone would endorse such a term!)

Table 6.1 What is a respectful educator? What is respectful teaching? What is respectful assessment?

Respectful approaches	Disrespectful approaches
Taking account of the learner 'children as participants'	Ignoring the learner 'children as recipients'
Building on existing learning	Disregarding/unaware of existing learning
Based on tuning into learners' agendas	Based on predetermined curriculum
Responsive to learners' needs and interests	Unresponsive to learners' needs and interests
Informed by children's developmental needs	Informed by targets/key stages/ages
Curriculum based on children's identified needs	Curriculum based on external definitions of needs
Includes/embraces issues of children's rights	Ignores/disregards issues of children's rights
Clarity for learner	Lack of clarity for learner

(Continued overleaf)

Table 6.1 Cont'd

Respectful approaches	Disrespectful approaches
Authentic assessment to inform teaching	Inauthentic assessment used to track progress of cohort
Challenge	No challenge
Opportunity for extension and diversity	Closed to extension
Holistic	Compartmentalised
Involves parents	Excludes parents
Evaluation	'It works' – no evaluation
Revision in the light of experience	Carrying on regardless
Recognises all achievements	Values achievement of specific prespecified goals
Purposeful	Lack of purpose
Knowledgeable teachers	Teachers with limited knowledge
Professional development for teachers and other educators	Lack of professional development for teachers and other educators
Teachers and other educators with appropriate initial training and qualifications	Teachers and other educators with limited/inappropriate training qualifications
Each learner matters	The cohort/group/majority matter
Equality for all children	The 'same' for all
Includes all children	Excludes some children
Sufficient and appropriate equipment/resources	Insufficient and inappropriate equipment/resources
Appropriate ratio of adults to children	Too many children – too few adults
Sufficient/appropriate space and access to learning areas/experiences	Insufficient/inappropriate space and limited access to learning areas/experiences

Teaching young children needs those qualities of clarity, honesty, courtesy, diligence and consistency. It means identifying what children can do, what they might do and what their teachers need next to teach. This is indeed a task that – despite repeated attempts to make it simple – can never be other than complex. Watching children as they learn and understanding the significance of those learning moments are complex tasks that make high demands on all who attempt them.

References

Abbott, L. and Nutbrown, C. (2001) *Experiencing Reggio Emilia: Implications for Pre-school Provision*. Buckingham: Open University Press.

Abbott, L. and Rodger, R. (1994) *Quality Education in the Early Years*. Buckingham: Open University Press.

Athey, C. (1990) *Extending Thought in Young Children: A Parent–Teacher Partnership*. London: Paul Chapman Publishing.

Donaldson, M. (1983) *Children's Minds*. Glasgow: Fontana/Collins.

Filippini, T. and Vecchi, V. (eds.) (1996) *The Hundred Languages of Children: Exhibition Catalogue*. Reggio Emilia: Reggio Children.

Nutbrown, C. (ed.) (1996) *Respectful Educators – Capable Learners: Children's Rights in Early Education*. London: Paul Chapman Publishing.

Nutbrown, C. (1997) *Recognising Early Literacy Development – Assessing Children's Achievements*. London: Paul Chapman Publishing.

Nutbrown, C. (1998) *The Lore and Language of Early Education*. Sheffield: University of Sheffield Division of Education Publications.

Nutbrown, C. (1999) *Threads of Thinking: Young Children Learning and the Role of Early Education*, 2nd edition. London: Paul Chapman Publishing.

Vygotsky, L. (1978) *Mind in Society: The Development of Higher Level Psychological Processes*. Cambridge, MA: Harvard University Press.

Woodhead, M. (1996) *In Search of the Rainbow: Pathways to Quality in Large Scale Programmes for Young Disadvantaged Children*. The Hague: Bernard van Leer Foundation.

Chapter 7

The sensory garden

Hazreena Hussein

In this chapter, Hazreena Hussein, senior lecturer, Department of Architecture, University of Malaya, reports on her study of two sensory gardens in the UK. Her aim was to observe and record the users' experiences and behaviour when engaging with features within these gardens. The data collection included interviews with teachers and therapists, and photography. For children with special needs, amongst other benefits, the study highlights the way in which a sensory garden can stimulate their senses, increase their tactile sensitivities to support way-finding and mobility, and enable their social interaction.

Multi-sensory design, focusing on the garden as an outdoor environment, is becoming increasingly popular for educational purposes in special schools, for rehabilitation purposes in hospitals and for health benefits in nursing homes.

Robinson (2008), an Inclusive Designer with the Sensory Trust, defined 'sensory' as 'relating to the senses or the power of sensation'. The *Oxford American Dictionary* defined 'sense' as 'A faculty by which the body perceives an external stimulus: one of the faculties of sight, hearing, taste and touch, smell'. In this study, the term 'multi-sensory' describes the multiple bodily senses to which children with special educational needs, in the two sensory gardens selected, could be exposed; namely, to a stimulating environment that is designed to offer sensory stimulation using textures, colours, scents, sounds.

According to Pagliano (1998, p. 107),

> 'A multi–sensory environment is a dedicated space or room . . . where stimulation can be controlled, manipulated, intensified, reduced,

Source: An edited version of Hussein, H. (2010) 'Using the sensory garden as a tool to enhance the educational development and social interaction of children with special needs' *Support for Learning,* 25 (1), 25–31.

presented in isolation or combination, packaged for active or passive interaction and temporally matched to fit the perceived motivation, interests, leisure, relaxation, therapeutic and/or educational needs of the user. It can take a variety of physical, psychological and sociological forms'.

(p. 107)

'The multi-sensory environment is a "living environment" where a physical environment is determined by the needs of the user and shaped by the intelligence and sensitivity of the disciplinary team that manages it'.

(p. 14)

Evolution of the multi-sensory environment

The evolution of the construction of multi-sensory environments began in the 1970s. However, it was only in the late 1980s that they began to take account of visual and aural ambiences and to install equipment that could accommodate the needs especially of people with profound and multiple disabilities in special schools and nursing homes. Longhorn (1988) examined the development of auditory, physical and visual disabilities in people with profound and multiple disabilities, and they developed respective multi-sensory curricula. Longhorn (1988, quoted in Mount and Cavet, 1995, p. 52), suggested:

> 'without stimulation and an *awakening* of the senses, children with profound and multiple learning difficulties would find it almost impossible to make sense of their experiences and to begin to learn' (emphasis in original).

As a result, a multi-sensory curriculum was integrated into the special needs educational system to accommodate the United Kingdom's National Curriculum. Following on from the recognised positive multi-sensory indoor experiences, sensory gardens have literally developed out of this. The only difference is that the cost of having a sensory garden is considerably less and it is a truly natural multi-sensory environment compared to a manufactured multi-sensory or 'snoezelen' room.

In this study, a sensory garden could also be described as offering a variety of sensory stimuli to children with special educational needs, just as they are to be found in the 'snoezelen' rooms. The study summarises the findings based on two case study sensory gardens in the United Kingdom, in terms of the educational development and social interaction of children with special needs and the staff who care for them. The aim was to observe and record children's behaviour when engaging with features in the sensory garden. The data collection included interviews with teachers and therapists, and observation.

Play, outdoor education and disability

The *Building Bulletin 102* (2008) outlined what is necessary when designing for children with special educational needs. One of the requirements when designing a special school is to provide an accessible outdoor environment, which emphasises multi-sensory experiences for therapy, educational and recreational use.

Wolff (1979) categorised play into six types as follows:

1. *Solitary play* is defined as an activity that a child plays alone without interaction with others. This type of play offers no social skills but a sense of privacy.
2. *Parallel play* is when a child engages with a similar activity to his or her peers without interacting with them, verbally or physically.
3. *Positive interaction with peers* is a play behaviour between a child with another that sometimes involves verbal communication. This play category affords social skills, such as sharing: for example, climbing or sliding down the slope together while talking, etc.
4. *Negative interaction with peers* is a type of play that involves aggressive behaviour, such as fighting, refusing to share any play features, unwilling to help or work together with a peer, etc.
5. *Positive interaction with adults* is when a child is willing to work together with an adult by offering or receiving help. This play behaviour affords social skills, such as communication.
6. *Negative interaction with adults* is when a child is being non-co-operative with an adult, for example resisting interaction, kicking, screaming, etc.

Examples from the six types of play behaviour above showed that children understand the functional properties (affordances) of the environment by experiential involvement through perception and movement, that is, play. Thus, play should be recognised alongside education as a vital part of children's healthy and happy development.

Outdoor education

Having an accessible school ground, for example a playground or a sensory garden, is highly important for children to give them the opportunity for free play and choices for exploration and learning. They also value an environment that can provide them privacy. Titman (1994a, p. 58) identified four elements that children looked for in school grounds: *a place for doing* (opportunities for physical activities); *a place for thinking* (opportunities for intellectual stimulation); *a place for feeling* (to provoke a sense of belonging); and *a place for being* (to allow them to be themselves). Her research focused on the value of improved school grounds as an educational resource to demonstrate how children's attitudes, behaviours and learning skills could be enriched.

One of the ways to achieve an environmental education is to choose plants that are fast growing, able to provide shade and able to offer visual stimulation through the use of colour, texture and scent. Plant compositions must be carefully considered so that they provide mystery and the ability to hide and to create space. One example of a school that has built this kind of environment is Meldreth Manor School in Hertfordshire (Frank, 1996; Stoneham, 1996). The sensory garden there was designed with a series of ramps and raised pathways integrated and woven around the existing apple trees; while preserving the trees, it offers pupils a variety of sensory experiences.

Having a multi-sensory environment in special schools is beneficial for teachers, teaching assistants and pupils as it provides a two-way learning process.

Outdoor environmental learning can give children a stimulating experience as well as influence their behaviour and their development in terms of social relationships. Lucas (1996, p. 26) added that this notion has received further support from Barbara Dunne of the Royal School for the Deaf and Communication Disorders, Manchester: 'Pupils are most likely to succeed when they are involved in "doing" activities rather than academic learning. Environmental education is an ideal activity learning medium'.

Research by Jacobson (1998) found that it is easier for a visually impaired person to orientate and navigate in the outdoor setting when landmarks and walkways are distinguished through texture or other means as clues. Tyson (1998, p. 75) noted that 'the composition of selective plantings, strategic location and significant elements could orientate people with impairments around green spaces'. Kaplan *et al.* (1998, p. 50) supported this view: 'The distinctiveness of such elements, where they are placed, and the number of them are all key aspects of designing for way-finding'. For example, during one of the observation days at the case study sites, 'Eileen', who has special educational needs, was able to find her way back to her classroom after the literacy session through the use of plants.

McLinden and McCall (2002) differentiated between the close senses (touch and taste) and the distance senses (sight, smell and hearing). They further noted that 'when the distance sense of vision is impaired, young children may be able to compensate to some extent by making greater use of their other distance sense – hearing' (p. 54). For example, during the observation period at one of the case study sites, a teacher expressed her feeling that it was a pity that the water feature was not working because her visually impaired student loved to hear the sound of the water and when he did, he would remain near the water feature for a longer period.

Findings

The interviews with the teachers and therapists of both case study sites showed that, since the sensory gardens had been introduced, the children had benefited in terms of their educational development and social interaction. These benefits were as follows.

Walking under a row of shady trees on a sunny afternoon might be evaluated as a comfortable ambience in which to undertake such an activity. In contrast, a stormy day with heavy rainfall might be evaluated as an undesirable situation in which to be in the natural landscape. Cool temperatures in the morning and evening afford users the chance to enjoy the weather in comfort, whereas high noon temperatures sometimes need to be avoided. For example, a child with multiple disabilities became agitated because it was too sunny.

Although the willow tunnel is located towards the end of a sensory garden in one of the case study sites, some children liked to use this feature to hide in, to play with the artwork displays and to spread their arms wide while feeling the willow.

One teacher and one student played with some of the artwork displays while the other pair spread their arms wide while feeling the willow. The four of them finally walked towards the end of the willow tunnel and returned back to the pathway. Besides experiencing the features at the willow tunnel, it also increased the students' confidence.

Another example from one of the case study sites illustrates how a speech therapist used the images on the rubber walkway to encourage verbal communication. One afternoon in the observation period, a therapist and a child with speech difficulties were strolling in the sensory garden. When the therapist reached the rubber walkway, she jumped on to one of the images and said, '*Flower!*' Then she jumped from the 'flower' on to a blank space and let the child jump on to the flower image. The child copied what her therapist had done and responded very well. Seeing that the child had behaved positively, the therapist continued jumping on to a series of different images until the end of the walkway. The rubber walkway, therefore, afforded jumping and communication.

At the Lyndale School in Wirral, a number of teachers and children who were physically able enjoyed stamping on the boardwalk and making a noise. Teachers drew the children's attention to the vibration and sound of the boardwalk.

'As the teachers and children gathered in pairs around the conifer tree, with a plank as the floor surface, the teachers sang, "Here we go round the mulberry bush". As they chanted, the author thought it was a perfect song to sing as it invited many physical movements that generated sound and vibration for the children, such as stamping, jumping, skipping, clapping and cheering. The children responded positively by swinging their hands while turning their heads from one side to another. Some children opened their mouths and tried to mimic their teachers.

A young girl in a wheelchair was in the sensory garden with her teaching assistant. She was quiet and just sat still in her chair, feeling the rainwater running on her cheek. Her teaching assistant kept on wheeling her despite the weather. At one point, the teaching assistant stopped to tie her own shoelace. The girl opened her mouth and shouted out loud, shrill noises while jumping a little in the wheelchair. She was irritated! The teaching assistant knew that she disliked that they had stopped and explained to the girl in sign language why she had to do that. After a short while, the teaching assistant gently wheeled the girl on. Passing the water feature and the scented plants at the raised beds, the girl became silent. Now the only noises that could be heard were the wind in the leaves, the trickling water from the water feature and a little splashing on a puddle.

In both schools, staff and children liked to brush their legs and hands against the lavender while walking on the pathway. A few of them smelled their hands after touching this scented plant. In a preliminary interview I conducted with M. Gough, a teacher of the Royal School of Deaf and Communication Disorders in Cheshire, she mentioned a child with poor sight who trails very well, using the lavender and when she (the child) smells it, it reminds her of her mother at home, who had it planted in her garden. Children on specially adapted bicycles also liked to feel the soft texture of the moss against the rough texture of the raised brick beds.

One of the standard multi-sensory curriculum items, used by teachers in all special schools, is the Picture Exchange Communication System (PECS). PECS allows staff and children with autism and other communication difficulties to initiate communication. This involves showing photographs and finding objects in the sensory garden using touch, hearing, smell and sight. Literacy sessions are also conducted in the sensory garden. Both of these exercises are beneficial for way finding, mobility, speech therapy and identifying significant features in the garden.

Conclusions

Based on the results of the interviews, together with selected recorded evidence from observation, it is clear that the two sensory gardens were used in an educational context to stimulate the senses, to increase tactile qualities to support way finding and mobility, to encourage behavioural changes and social interaction as well as to support mental development, hence renewing children's functioning through engaging with and responding to the environment. These observed positive developments are important in outdoor environmental education; for example, plants found in both school settings encouraged a greater understanding of and exploration by users, afforded easy way finding and generated further activities. Thus, children with special educational needs recognised the functional properties of their outdoor environment. However, if their needs are not met, users may feel frustrated and even threatened; thus it will add to their fears and apprehension.

Climatic factors such as temperature, wind and rain also contribute to the sensory experiences that trigger users' senses and affordances. Thus, allowing users the opportunity to engage with natural features supported the link that has been established between personal experiences and developing environmental cognition; an individual learning process has to occur to allow people to understand the benefits or disadvantages of the natural elements. Their memories of familiar features and reflections on their past experiences at home were vivid, signifying positive behaviour. As a result, the users showed a strong sense of bonding, such as preference for and attachment to the garden by suggesting improvements to its content and showing their willingness to come back to the sensory garden. Finally, and perhaps most importantly, sensory gardens should be incorporated in the design of special schools as part of their sensory learning curriculum. Design of the sensory garden should be considered during the pre-planning stage of the special school development, which would allow the architect, teachers, parents and therapists to allocate space to the sensory garden and to see it as an extension of the school's indoor classroom rather than just as detached outdoor space.

References

Building Bulletin 102 (2008) *Designing for Disabled Children and Children with Special Educational Needs*. Norwich: The Stationery Office.

Jacobson, R. D. (1998) Cognitive mapping without sight: Four preliminary studies of spatial learning. *Journal of Environmental Psychology*, 18, 289–305.

Longhorn, F. (1988) *A Sensory Curriculum for Very Special People*. London: Souvenir Press.

Lucas, B. (1996) A feast for the senses. *Landscape Design: Journal of Landscape Institute*, 249, 26–28.

Mount, H. and Cavet, J. (1995) Multi-sensory environments: an exploration of their potential for young people with profound and multiple learning difficulties. *British Journal of Special Education*, 22, 2, 52–55.

Pagliano, P. J. (1998) The multi sensory environment: an open-minded space. *British Journal of Visual Impairment*, 16, 93, 105–109.

Robinson, L. (2008) *Sensory Garden: What's That Then?* [Online at http://www. sensorytrust.org.uk]. Accessed 03/03/08.

Titman, W. (1994a) *Special Places, Special People: The Hidden Curriculum of School Ground*. Cambridge: Learning through Landscapes/World Wide Fund for Nature UK.

Wolff, P. (1979) The adventure playground as a therapeutic environment. In D. Canter and C. Sandra (eds), *Designing for Therapeutic Environments: A Review of Research*, pp. 87–117. New York: John Wiley & Sons.

Chapter 8

Constructivism and primary science

Patricia Murphy

A curriculum that emphasises the teaching of content or subject knowledge can leave little space for children to develop their own ideas and feel in control of their learning. Patricia Murphy, professor of education (pedagogy and assessment) at The Open University, argues that how we teach children is as important as what we teach them and that this should include opportunities to think, question and make decisions. In this chapter she explores 'constructivist' approaches to teaching in science and suggests that these will encourage children's curiosity and enthusiasm and ultimately the quality of their scientific understanding.

Joan Solomon (1997:4) argues that 'no one who is without curiosity has a hope of understanding what science is about'. For this reason she believes that how we teach children is at least as important as what we teach them, if not more so. She identifies two ground rules for fostering children's curiosity:

- the *'locus of control'* must reside with the learner
- the *'instructional density'*, that is the amount of teaching, must not inhibit or get in the way of the child's thinking and decision-making so as to remove the activity completely from them.

The theory

Mike Watts, Brenda Barber and Steve Alsop (1997:6) highlight research into *'question-rich environments'*. Such an environment, they argue, nurtures learners' natural curiosity. The children in the classrooms observed were encouraged to formulate questions after having been given the means and

Source: An edited version of Murphy, P. (1997) 'Constructivism and primary science' *Primary Science Review*, 49, 27–29.

opportunities to *'speak their minds'* (Watts, Barber and Alsop: 7). This approach, like Joan Solomon's, places the locus of control with the children. However, there is also an important and demanding role for the teacher, that is to know what activities to select and when to give help and in what form. Children need to learn how to collaborate and be given tools to assist them in making their thinking explicit to themselves, other children and their teachers. They also need to be able to identify a 'good' question in science and, importantly as Mike Watts and colleagues point out, where and how they might find a 'good' answer.

Concerns about how to teach effectively in science have emerged as understanding about children and how they learn. Pamela Wadsworth (1997) refers to *a constructivist approach* to teaching and learning. Constructivism is a general term which is open to numerous interpretations. However, central to a constructivist view of learning is the notion of *agency*. Jerome Bruner described agency as one of the crucial ideas that educators have learned in the last decade (Bruner 1994).

Agency in learning means that knowledge is not passively received by learners, rather it is actively built up by them. It is the learner who makes sense of his or her experiences. In making sense of new experiences children draw on their pre-existing knowledge and beliefs. There is therefore an essential link between the ideas children bring to science and the sense they make of the experiences provided for them. In a constructivist approach to learning, as Pamela Wadsworth (1997) points out, children's ideas matter.

A teacher who adopts this view of learning has to pay attention to children's ideas but also, and importantly, has to help them to learn about their learning precisely because they are the ones in control of it. Learning about learning is another central idea in a constructivist approach. Bruner referred to it as *reflection*, 'not simply learning in the raw but making what you learn make sense, taking it inside you' (Bruner 1994). In a report into the effectiveness of existing teaching approaches used to introduce scientific ideas in Key Stage 2 classrooms (Sizmur and Ashby 1997:24), it was observed that 'for meaningful learning to take place there must, at some level, be a need for that learning'. An important way that the teachers observed in the study established 'a need to learn' was to use tasks that promote reflection and to provide tools to enable this. For example, children would be asked in a variety of ways to record their ideas and thinking and at various points in learning activities be given opportunities to reflect on and record any changes in them. The use of concept maps is a good example of an activity that elicits children's thinking and supports reflection.

The practice

Constructivism in its various forms is a major influence on research and curriculum development in science but what of teachers' practice? I decided to ask local teachers about their approach to learning in science. It was interesting but not surprising that some teachers were not convinced about a constructivist approach, in particular whether it was appropriate at all ages. Others had never heard of constructivism but were nevertheless committed to investigative learning where the children had 'freedom in the practical sense to decide what they wanted to find out and how to set about doing it'. Some described a constructivist approach as the children 'doing the doing'.

Those who had heard of the term were usually strong advocates of the approach and described it as 'children building on their previous experiences through practical investigation, learning through investigative, open learning situations within the classroom'.

An important element of the approach from the point of view of the teachers interviewed was that the classroom activities had to match the science learning objectives. 'If what we are wanting to do is to teach them about science they're not going to learn that just by watching and listening to somebody else. They only get that by being scientific themselves.' In the interviews I asked teachers if they tried to establish children's ideas about a topic: 'I would start a new session perhaps with a discussion about what they [the children] already know: Who can remember about . . .? What do you know about . . .? What do you think might happen . . .? So building on what they already know, not discussing it starting from where they are.'

For other teachers it was more problematic. For instance, one teacher said that she typically would find out what the children knew about a topic before any activity. However, when asked if that influenced what she did she said that it did not. The Sizmur and Ashby study (1997) found that few teachers elicited children's views in any systematic way. Furthermore, the lessons observed were structured in advance and were rarely reactive to children's pre-existing ideas. As one teacher I interviewed explained: 'There is so much that you have to pack into such a short time and the constraints are so rigid that they [the children] don't have an awful lot to say in what they're doing.' Another observed: 'It is so directed with the National Curriculum and we know they've got to understand this, this and this . . . it's as much a time constraint as anything else.'

The problem

If children have to make their own sense, then attempting to impart knowledge will either fail altogether or result in only superficial short-term learning. It would seem that for a constructivist approach to flourish in classrooms the curriculum structure and load in science need to change, and its assessment. Different kinds of understanding need to be valued and elicited by a wider range of assessment tasks and methods than is presently the case.

Guy Claxton (1990:29–31) has some useful images to apply to different views of the relationship between teacher and learner. For example, a belief that we can 'give' knowledge to children assumes a model of the teacher as 'a petrol pump attendant' and of the child as the passive recipient of knowledge. Teachers who want to 'fix' children's 'unscientific' ideas Claxton would label as 'watchmakers' tinkering with the children's brains. This approach, like the former, denies the learner's active role in learning and the essential requirement for the learner to perceive a need for learning. Although, as Claxton describes it, the children are involved in the construction of the watch they do not get to question the components or the objectives. A more constructivist-oriented image is that of teacher as 'gardener' where the 'growing' is done by the learner as she converts the nourishment she receives from the learning situation into her 'own fabric'. The gardener assists but cannot determine this process. Another useful image he offers is that of the 'sherpa' acting as a knowledgeable guide to an explorer of unfamiliar terrain.

One of the teachers interviewed described science as 'like teaching a foreign language', a language she had never learnt. Sutton (1996) uses a similar metaphor to make the point that science is a strange language and understanding how it is used by people to make sense is what teaching should focus on. This resonates with Claxton's image of the teacher as 'sherpa', helping children to negotiate a strange terrain.

Strategies

The Nuffield Primary Science materials offer a range of ways of eliciting children's ideas. I found that some teachers used these methods, such as annotated drawings, to elicit children's ideas about a concept and these informed the way they grouped children, usually on the basis of shared interests and questions. Sizmur and Ashby (1997) recommend an approach that is similar. They observed how in some classrooms children were given opportunities to discuss their ideas and to collaborate in the development of a set of shared questions or statements with which they could agree or disagree. The children then chose the best approach to address their chosen question. Their approach might be an investigation but it had to 'fit' the question. This strategy gives the locus of control to the children, both in deciding what is a good question and in identifying the approach to find a 'good' answer. It also requires the children to share their thinking with each other and with the teacher, and so promotes reflection on their own learning. Requiring children to organise their ideas into good questions is therefore an effective teaching and management strategy. It helps make manageable what some teachers fear, that is the potential range of children's interests and ideas.

This approach might help those teachers who expressed regret that prior to the National Curriculum there was more opportunity to explore children's ideas. This they saw as important because 'they [the children] see what they think is valued and what they are interested in as valued'.

Children's views

I also talked to children from Years 5 and 6 to see whether 'constructivist' approaches were affecting their view of the importance of their ideas. I asked them what they thought about the 'control' they had over their learning in science. The children liked science and identified two reasons for this: the opportunity for finding out, and the ability to have their own ideas explored. The children all agreed that their ideas were important in science, more so than in other subjects. They saw the teacher as the person who decides what is to be done, that is the topic selector, but it was they who decided the best way to find things out: 'We make up our own mind how to do it.' In explaining why they thought it was good to explore their own ideas, one child observed: 'Sometimes even though the teacher's ideas might be better we've got something to go on for ourselves.' Another child added wisely: 'It's also a way teachers can see what we think and know and that's important.'

It may well be that opportunities for working with children in the way described are difficult to find. Nevertheless, children welcome being the decision-makers and want their thinking and ideas to be valued. The pay-off for teachers is both in the enthusiasm for learning science that such an approach fosters and in the quality of children's scientific understanding that results.

Acknowledgement

My thanks to all the teachers whose views were drawn on, particularly the children and staff at Gifford Park County Combined School, Milton Keynes, who provided some of the information reported.

References

Bruner, J. (1994) 'Four ways to make meaning'. Invited address to the 1994 Annual Meeting of American Educational Research Association. New Orleans.

Claxton, G. (1990) *Teaching to Learn: A direction for education*. London: Cassell.

Sizmur, S. and Ashby, J. (1997) *Introducing Scientific Concepts to Children*. Slough: NFER.

Solomon, J. (1997) 'Is how we teach science more important than what we teach?' *Primary Science Review*, 49, 3–5.

Sutton, C. (1996) 'The scientific model as a form of speech', in: G. Welford, J. Osborn and P. Scott (eds.), *Research in Science Education in Europe*. London: Falmer Press.

Watts, M., Barber, B. and Alsop, S. (1997) 'Children's questions in the classroom'. *Primary Science Review*, 49, 6–8.

Wadsworth, P. (1997) 'When do I tell them the right answer?' *Primary Science Review*, 49, 23–4.

Chapter 9

The case for primary science

Jane Turner

Jane Turner is an associate director at the East of England Science Learning Centre. She is concerned that science in primary schools is at risk of being squeezed out of the curriculum. In this chapter, drawing on her own classroom experience and her involvement in teacher professional development, she builds a persuasive case for children's engagement with science. This, she says, is partly to do with business, industrial and economic imperatives – 'those spoken loudest in the science education community' – but, more importantly, to do with the way in which the learning of science can have an impact on children's enthusiasm for learning more generally.

To begin I must declare my position. As someone who works within the science education community as a curriculum developer and CPD provider, I acknowledge that I have a vested interest in science remaining a significant part of the primary curriculum. I do not enjoy being told, in schools and the wider community, about the 'downgrading' of primary science. I am committed to championing high quality science in primary schools.

The reasons for my personal and professional commitment to primary science are different from those spoken loudest in the science education community. The world of science in schools often appears to be dominated by business, industrial and economic imperatives. The connection between a scientifically successful population and a successful economy is loudly stated as if it is the only reason for wanting good science teaching and learning in schools and colleges. Nationwide scientific literacy, the ability to understand and engage in debate about contemporary scientific issues, comes a poor second. Much of my work is with the Science Learning

Source: An edited version of Turner, J. (2010) 'Primary science: Are there any reasons to be cheerful?' *Forum, 52* (3), 381–394. http://dx.doi.org/10.2304/forum.2010.52.3.381 Reprinted with permission of the author and Symposium Journals.

Centre (SLC) network, which was tasked by the previous government to improve the quality of science teaching in UK schools with the expectation that better science examination results would lead to a more successful economic future. This expectation is based on persuasive evidence (Roberts, 2002). And the value of primary science to this long-term aim is indicated by research that demonstrates the link between the quality of science that children experience at primary school and later attitudes towards science, specifically subject choices at GCSE (Royal Society, 2006).

I do not underestimate the importance of this argument about creating future scientists; but my own argument in favour of promoting quality science education in primary schools science stems from more immediate observations. Personal experiences in the primary classroom and CPD training room, combined with the testimony of many teachers and children, have persuaded me that there is strong link between high quality teaching and learning in science and an enthusiasm and capacity for learning in general. Science teaching that supports children in expressing and following their own ideas and curiosity, encourages practical involvement with the stuff of the real world, engages children as individuals and in collaboration with others in genuine enquiry and problem solving is motivating and stimulating for teacher and learner alike (Murphy et al, 2005). It is an engaging manipulative and mental activity. Science teaching that convinces children of the robustness and validity of evidence to answer questions, while at the same time encouraging them to value speculation and supposition, forms a vital foundation, not just to further scientific learning, but to learning in all fields (Harlen, 2008). And science need not be taught as a separate discrete subject for these benefits to be apparent. In many European countries science does not form a separate curriculum subject at primary level. Increasingly in England teachers are successfully linking science with other subject areas, planning for stimulating contexts for science learning that connect with children's wider experiences.

That is my position. I am a supporter of science in primary schools, and I know that at present its future is unsure. As I write the coalition government is promising more curriculum review and an overhauling of primary assessment regimes at the same time as stringent financial cuts in local government and the higher education sector. Teachers, advisory staff and initial teacher education colleagues are working in an atmosphere of uncertainty and for many, insecurity. So to return to my question: are concerns about science in primary schools justified or are there reasons to be cheerful? I offer no definite answers, nor a comprehensive review of all that has happened with science in primary schools in the last 30 years. Rather, I reflect on the challenges and opportunities that I see facing primary science at this time.

By the time I began teaching in 1986, it was accepted that there were good reasons based on argument, experience and research evidence, for claiming that science education at the primary level had a crucial role to play in preparing children for their future lives (Harlen, 2008). However science was then still new to most primary teachers at all career stages. As the National Curriculum took root many local authorities appointed science subject advisors and ran highly rated 20-day CPD courses to train new subject leaders. Recognition quickly grew that a nature table in the corner and some occasional poetry about pollution were no longer sufficient. The 17 attainment targets, detailing the scientific knowledge and skills that every 11-year-old should learn, embodied a curricular revolution. The introduction of the formal science SAT as an accountability measure was another clear indicator that science was a subject that counted in primary schools. Progress was fast, and despite on-going concerns about teacher subject knowledge, an over-emphasis on SAT preparation, and the dangers of dry, didactic teaching that was fact rather that enquiry driven, science in primary schools was generally agreed to be a success (Parliamentary Office of Science and Technology, 2003). This is now evident in both policy and practice. Science is recognised as an entitlement for all primary school children. There was nothing in any political party's 2010 manifesto to refute this. Science also forms a compulsory part of all initial primary teacher education. The importance of science in primary schools is now widely recognised in schools, and not just by enthusiasts.

> Of course there are still teachers who drag their feet on the way to the science cupboard, but the ranks of the converted are much larger than when I first became involved with the Association for Science Education 20 years ago. Many more teachers, for whom science will never be their first love, appreciate its unique contribution to primary education and teach it conscientiously.
>
> (Turner, 2010)

As enthusiasts, of course, it is easy to over simplify. There are still traditionalist secondary science teachers who claim that all primary science does is fill children's heads with conceptual inaccuracies and wild ideas that 'science is fun', or even more dangerously, that science is something to talk about. Primary to secondary transition remains a tricky issue, with many secondary schools unwilling to acknowledge children's prior experiences.

Classrooms where science is a 'copy-from-the-board' or 'complete-a-worksheet' experience rather than a practical or discursive one, are thankfully rare but not unknown. Unfortunately some schools rely on expensive, commercial, after-school science clubs to engage their children in practical science activities. Resources and courses that guarantee to put the 'wow factor' into science are regularly promoted by commercial and other organisations, implying that science itself is intrinsically dull unless there is an explosion to observe. Some schools assert that they are working in a cross-curricular way, planning to include science in catch-all topics such as 'chocolate' and 'houses and homes', but then failing to recognise the need to plan for progression in scientific skills and understanding.

These are flaws; but they are small parts of a bigger picture which also includes some excellent practice underpinned by a significant body of research. Wynne Harlen has identified the key areas of such research that have influenced the teaching of science in primary schools. These are: finding out about children's own ideas, advancing their ideas, developing enquiry skills and formative assessment (Harlen, 2010). My own experience, working with teachers in and out of schools, supports Harlen's summary, though like her, I recognise that the teachers may not realise that the approaches and strategies they use originated in research. For example, the impact of the outcomes of the Science Processes and Concept Exploration (SPACE) research project which took place in the 1990s (SPACE, 1990–1998), systematically recording children's ideas about, for example, what makes things move, grow, melt, dissolve, can be seen in lessons where children's own ideas are taken seriously. It is now widely accepted that children have already formed quite firm ideas about phenomena in the world around them before they encounter them at school; and that these ideas often conflict with the accepted scientific view. This understanding has led to the promotion of a more constructivist approach to science teaching in some primary schools, emphasising the importance of teachers firstly gaining access to children's thinking and then supporting a reorganisation of their ideas to accommodate more accepted explanations. Practical work has been seen as central to this 'active learning'.

This constructivist, hands-on approach has not been without its detractors. Critics have argued that primary teachers lack the personal scientific understanding and pedagogic skills required to identify a multiplicity of alternative frameworks and prior knowledge, then to support their conversion through classroom activity into accepted scientific ideas. Too often children have no input in planning the practical activities in which they engage and spend little or no time interpreting their findings. 'Hands-on' does not necessarily mean the 'minds-on' approach required to enable the children to make sense of a concept by relating it to their own experience (Keogh & Naylor, 1996).

Much of the focus of primary science CPD and classroom resource development in the last decade or so has been on addressing these concerns and developing teacher confidence in building on children's own ideas. For example *Concept Cartoons in Science Education* (Naylor & Keogh, 2000), which are widely used in initial teacher training and at all levels of school science education, present a scientific problem in a familiar setting. They propose various predictions and explanations, representing commonly held scientific misconceptions, and so can stimulate argument and practical experimentation.

The value of children encountering scientific ideas and developing an understanding of scientific concepts through practical enquiry is axiomatic. The message is relayed loudly and frequently to primary teachers particularly by the science subject associations and Ofsted (Ofsted, 2005).

It is widely acknowledged that enquiry based activity in science is a good thing, and most schools' policies and schemes of work reflect this belief. This is a reason to be cheerful, but certainly not complacent. School policies have a habit of being written, filed and forgotten: their impact on, or relationship to, practice is often minimal. Primary teachers can have very different kinds of activities in mind when they refer to science enquiry. Some view science enquiry as 'discovery' learning while others see working systematically as fundamental. Some assume that it's only about practical work while others feel that it should include children learning scientific concepts. The criticism levied at an incomplete or superficial understanding of the value of constructivism in primary science can equally be levied at much classroom activity that purports to be science enquiry. Just because children are using equipment, working in groups, collecting data or completing graphs, it does not automatically mean that they are developing skills in science enquiry. It is the conscious search for and use of evidence, be that from first or second sources, in order to challenge ideas and answer questions that identifies an activity as an educationally valuable science enquiry. My own personal experience is that this is rarely the identified objective of a science lesson.

However, when teachers spend time thinking about what they understand by science enquiry and how their practice can embody this, the results can be very encouraging. For example, this extract from a school policy was written by a group of teachers at a London school, and recommends the following synthesis of pedagogic, curricular and scientific thinking:

All lessons:

- start with a question
- encourage creative thinking
- involve all children using all their senses to investigate real things
- have a context that connects with children's own lives and experiences
- allow pupils to ask their own questions and discover science themselves through practical investigations and research
- emphasise the role of evidence to challenge or prove ideas and answer questions
- include discussion and debate
- make good use of resources that are exciting, high quality and are of a quantity that allow full participation
- take into account pupils' prior knowledge and understanding
- support children communicating their scientific findings and understanding in different ways including talking and writing in

different forms using science vocabulary, pictures, graphs and using ICT.

(William Tyndale Primary School, 2010)

Reading this and seeing it brought to life as a planning and evaluation tool has been, for me, an heartening example of the research, policy, practice dynamic. The policy represents principles of procedure (Stenhouse, 1975), based on evidenced good practice and research, which are shared, understood and enacted.

A major recent development regarding assessment in primary science was of course the removal of the Science SAT in 2009, in response to the proposal of the Expert Group on Assessment. The evidence that the 'high stakes' testing of science at the end of Key Stage 2 was having a detrimental effect on the process of teaching and learning in the primary phase, and children's long term attitude to science, was overwhelming. The removal of the SAT, and consequently of the preceding months of revision and repetition (Wellcome Trust, 2010), was welcomed by all sectors of the science education community (SCORE, 2009), but interestingly perhaps not by the majority of children, who although voicing concerns about the impact of the science SAT on them, were unhappy about the government's decision to abandon it (Wellcome Trust, 2010). I share some of the concerns that children expressed, chiefly that science, which most children enjoy, would become less of a priority in schools. When asked for my opinion on the proposed removal of the SAT I faced a real dilemma. If science was removed from the statutory testing regime, would the already damaging domination of numeracy and literacy simply grow even stronger? Would children be denied the chance of engaging regularly with one of the most popular subjects in the primary curriculum? In a climate of cutbacks in CPD expenditure, would the opportunity to work with teachers on improving the quality of science teaching and learning totally disappear?

In the face of this radical change I decided to adopt a positive approach. I knew firsthand the damage that the science SAT had done to science teaching and attitudes to science learning. I had read the cautiously optimistic reports of a change in attitude and practice since the removal of the science SAT in Wales (Collins et al, 2009). And I rejoiced that science attainment data were still to be an accountability measure for schools and that standards would be monitored by analysis of teacher assessment data and sample testing (DfE, 2009). Teachers couldn't abandon science; but they would have to become more skilful and confident at teacher assessment. I recognised that this transition would not be an easy one for many teachers, and the danger that statutory pen and paper tests would be replaced by the equivalent commercially produced ones. However, like the scientific bodies, I hoped that teachers would recognise the challenge that this transition presented and rise to it. I, perhaps naively, dreamed of schools investing in developing teachers' understanding of progression in scientific skills, concepts and understanding, and supporting the planning of purposeful learning opportunities which offered rich evidence of children's understanding and attitudes. I was even open-minded about APP (Assessing Pupil Progress) (DfE, 2009). In unskilled hands this threatens to be an overly complex and paper heavy process. However, I was fortunate enough to spend some time in APP pilot schools in Lincolnshire observing lessons and talking to teachers, and I was impressed. It was inspiring to work with teachers who were thinking of their pupils as scientists rather than as levels, to observe stimulating lessons and to meet children who were independent, confident and motivated. Therefore I was hopeful that the removal of the SAT could provide an opportunity to develop and share good practice in teaching and learning, In many schools this is happening. I am fortunate enough to work with some of them: but ask myself whether their practice is an encouraging trend or an isolated phenomenon?

As I write my hopes are subdued. Rumours abound about changes to curriculum and assessment for science. Subject knowledge is apparently the coalition government's holy grail and any weaknesses in science attainment can only be the result of an inadequate transfer of knowledge between teacher and pupil (Gibb, 2010). We are told that ministers don't want to hear about formative assessment strategies in science which inform teachers and pupils alike about progress and next steps. If that is true, then they will not be interested in developing pedagogies building on the research that I have outlined above.

The impact of actions undertaken as part of the Primary Science Quality Mark (PSQM) in the last year include:

- an increase in practical science
- more visits, visitors and links with outside organisations
- more opportunities for pupils to experience science outside of lessons
- increased understanding of the teaching and learning of science in the school
- greater awareness of science in the school by governors and parents
- development of the confidence and capacity of the science subject leader

- the more widespread appeal of science
- a growing confidence among teachers about teaching the subject
- progress has been made, but this is just the start: the year ahead looks very exciting.

In November last year the Wellcome Trust awarded the ASE, in partnership with the SLC network and Barnet LA, £200,000 to support the roll-out of the Primary Science Quality Mark across the UK. This is a meaningful commitment to primary science from the world's leading scientific funder. There are now 43 active PSQM hubs across England, which means that over 230 science subject leaders, supported by local PSQM hub leaders, have embarked on a year-long programme to champion science in their primary schools. Each school has had to commit not only professional time, skill and energy but also cash; though many have been generously supported by their local authority or Specialist Science College. The intention is for up 30% of primary schools to achieve a Primary Science Quality Mark by 2018 and at the moment recruitment figures are looking good.

What excites me most about the Primary Science Quality Mark is that is emphatically not a tick list of criteria to be accomplished in exchange for a certificate. The scheme's processes are designed to ensure that submission should not be a summative description of actions, but a truly evaluative statement of impact of actions on the quality of science across the school. The emphasis is on developing reflective leadership, using Stenhouse's definition of the critical characteristics of 'extended professionalism' (Stenhouse, 1975) as an underpinning methodology:

- the commitment to systematic questioning of one's own teaching as a basis for development
- the commitment and skills to study one's own teaching
- the concern to question and to test theory in practice.

Schools 'chasing awards' is not a reason to be cheerful; but schools seeking out a professional CPD programme to raise the profile of science, participate in a tested model for development and to share and extend good practice, just might be. New Schools' Minister Nick Gibbs has promised that 'we're going to place greater trust in professionals to give teachers more freedom to decide how to teach' (Gibb, 2010). Could it be that the Primary Science Quality Mark is an early example of this policy in practice?

We cannot accurately predict how government education policy will develop, and I recognise that my optimism may be naive. So in conclusion I return to the policy written by teachers at the North London School cited earlier. This exemplifics the possibilitics for high quality science teaching and learning when teachers and schools are given the flexibility to be accountable to their own shared principles and values, and when those principles and values are underpinned by research. Primary Science has come a long way in the last twenty years. I am hopeful that in the classrooms of reflective, enthusiastic teachers such a journey will continue.

Note

The 'snowman' illustration is reproduced with the kind permission of Millgate House Publishing Ltd from the book *Concept Cartoons in Science Education* by Brenda Keogh & Stuart Naylor, 1999 (www.millgatehouse.co.uk).

References

Collins, S., Reiss, M. & Stobart, G. (2009) *The Effects of National Testing in Science at KS2 in England and Wales.* London: Institute of Education.

Department for Education (2009) Assessing Pupil Progress. http://nationalstrategies. standards.dcsf.gov.uk/node/259801 accessed 15 July 2010.

Gibb, N. (2010) Speech to the Reform Club, 1 July 2010. http://www.education.gov.uk/ inthenews/speeches/a0061473/nick-gibb-to-the-reform-conference accessed 16 September 2010.

Harlen, W. (2008) Science as a key component of the primary curriculum: a rationale with policy implications, *Perspectives on Education 1 (Primary Science), 4–18.* London: Wellcome Trust.

Harlen, W. (2010) Teaching Primary Science: how research helps, *Primary Science,* 114, 5.

Murphy, C., Beggs, J., Russell, H. & Melton, L. (2005) *Primary Horizons: starting out in science.* London: Wellcome Trust.

Naylor, S. & Keogh, B. (2000) *Concept Cartoons in Science Education.* Sandbach: Millgate House.

Naylor, S., Keogh, B. & Goldsworthy, A. (2004) *Active Assessment: thinking, learning and assessment in science.* Sandbach: Millgate House.

Ofsted (2005) Science in primary schools http://live.ofsted.gov.uk/publications/ annualreport0405/4.1.12.html accessed 16 July 2009.

Parliamentary Office of Science and Technology (2003) *Postnote: primary science.* London: Parliament.

Royal Society (2006) *Taking a Leading Role.* London: The Royal Society

SCORE (2009) Press release 7th May 2009. http://www.score-education.org/5news/ page1c.htm accessed 16 September 2010.

SPACE (1990–1998) (Science Processes and Concept Exploration) Research reports. Liverpool University Press: Liverpool.

Stenhouse, L. (1975) *An Introduction to Curriculum Research and Development.* London: Heinemann.

Turner, J. (2010) Primary School Science: reasons to be cheerful, *Education in Science*, 238, 10.

Wellcome Trust (2010) *'Marks Tell You How You've Done . . . Comments Tell You Why'*: *attitudes of children and parents to science testing and assessment*. London: The Wellcome Trust.

William Tyndale Primary School (2010) *Policy for Science*.

Chapter 10

Learning science

Joan Solomon with Stephen Lunn

'Science should be everybody's favourite subject in primary school', said the distinguished academic and authority on science education, Joan Solomon, who sadly died in 2009. Here, in conversation with Stephen Lunn, for many years one of Joan's close colleagues at The Open University, she explained how a delight in using their senses, and a natural propensity to play, prepare children perfectly for the role of scientist. However, they also need adults to guide their learning, for example by offering vocabulary, asking questions, and helping to bridge the gap between what children can achieve by themselves, and what is needed for a 'successful' outcome. Teaching assistants, often working with small groups or individuals, are often best placed to take part in these scientific conversations.

Children learning science

I think we know very little about how children learn, in spite of years of looking at them. As far as teaching assistants are concerned, you need to know whether almost everybody in a class of thirty children, or the group of six, is really hanging on your every word, or simply very busy in some way. It doesn't do just to keep the pupils quiet, which is what I sometimes see happening. There are all sorts of 'withdrawal' things that children do which make a total barrier to any ideas coming in, like, for instance, chewing their nails and fiddling with bits of paper. So, making sure that children are absolutely quiet can be detrimental to learning. If on the other hand you have an idea that you genuinely believe will be of great interest, then don't try and get them quiet, try and get them excited, even if it's a bit noisy. You will of course have to say, 'You won't hear what I've got to say about baby

Source: A revised version of Solomon, J. with Lunn, S. (2004) 'Learning science', commissioned by The Open University for *Primary Teaching Assistants: Curriculum in Context* (London: Routledge). Reprinted by permission of The Open University and Taylor & Francis Ltd.

elephants or whatever unless you do keep really quiet', but I've seen so many lessons recently in which even well-established teachers have managed to keep the children quiet, but where they haven't really been listening at all.

I think science is the most wonderful context for learning. Children are fascinated by animals, we all know that, but not just small furry ones. I've seen children, even babies, pointing a chubby finger at an ant going across the table. You know, they are absolutely fascinated. Once, when the National Curriculum first came in, I went round lots of places on the edge of Oxford, asking the children what was their favourite subject. At First School they all said 'science', and in Middle School, quite a lot of them said 'science'. They didn't, however, in the upper schools. Children like science, because of the things that it deals with. When it's snowing, you can take them out to look at the snowflakes as they fall on their jerseys, and they're fascinated by that. If an animal is warm and furry they hold it and they feel this tiny heart going terribly fast, and it's astonishing to them. Then of course they will try and find out if their own hearts are going fast and you can try and introduce them to pulses and things like that.

I have no doubt that, with reasonably good teaching, science should be everybody's favourite subject in primary schools. One of the reasons is that it's closely connected with children's senses. Now if there's one thing small children excel in, it is the acuity of their senses. A tremendous number of little children can 'feel' tremendously well and so holding an animal is marvellous for them. They can actually hear much better than we can, much higher frequencies. When my grandchildren from London come to see me, the first thing they do when they come out of the car is look around. It's the first time they've met granny for a while, but they're not interested in granny at all, of course. I think what they are looking at is birds, and then I suddenly realise there are birds calling everywhere. It's like an orchestra for them. They're absolutely astonished. Much of this I cannot hear.

Mostly children have all five senses and they love using them. A little boy came out on our nature walk and he sniffed and said, 'I can smell nature already, Miss.' I'm sure a lot of their enjoyment of science is to do with the straight use of the senses, and they get a great joy out of this because it's natural to them. It doesn't need any effort. When they discover that grown-ups can't hear as well as they can, they get thrilled to bits because grown-ups are usually better at absolutely everything than they are. It was recently discovered that elephants have a mating call which is too low for most adults to hear. I'm actually frightfully fascinated by elephants, but then so are a lot of children. It was a woman who was exploring elephants somewhere in some national park in Africa who remembered that when she was little she used to sing in the church choir. She leant up against the organ and the low pipes of the organ gave a note so low that she could feel it in the air, rather than hear it – a sort of throbbing. I have a little CD which has got all the noises that elephants make. I got it from writing to the BBC because they'd done a programme about elephants. And there they were, the five different calls. But the interesting thing is that that was a discovery that could have been made by any eight-year-old child, and it was made by a woman remembering what it was like when she was eight, not by an adult, because adults can't really hear it. It is interesting, isn't it, because this is what we have to do if we're working with primary school children. We must know something about what life is like for them. You won't find many books on primary education which tell you anything like that.

Finding the words

When doing science children can find themselves at a loss for the right word. I saw a lesson once which started off with a piece of plastic, fairly thick plastic, and some drops of water on it, big ones and little ones. I've subsequently written about a lesson called 'gobbling drops' because when the two drops touch each other, they go 'woomph' and coalesce to form a big drop. This is a function of surface tension which I don't teach them anything about of course. They need words to describe it, so the teacher said, 'What are the drops like?' Various things came out: 'They're round', 'They're circles', 'They're drops', 'They are little balls'. Somebody said they're like an ice cream, which I thought was incredibly silly at first. But it wasn't really them being silly, it was me if you think about it. In a cornet, that's exactly what you have, that round bit, or almost exactly. So the teacher said: 'Those shapes, they aren't completely round, are they? They're flat underneath. That shape we call a dome.' And all these little children went round saying 'dome', because it's a particularly nice word to say because if you practice it in the corner with nobody looking, you'll find that you use your lips rather curiously. There was a little girl, who was a bit bumptious but very clever, and she said to her teacher, 'Well, they aren't all, they're flat on top.' And the teacher said 'Would you put your hand up if you've got something to say?' And I thought 'Oh dear', because the child had actually finished off the explanation. It was a communal discussion activity with the teacher coming in every now and then – 'Yes, it's not quite like a ball, yes, it's not actually a flat circle is it', and so on. Then this little girl, whose name I think was Anne, got it in the neck for saying they're flattened on top! But in fact she had brought it to a conclusion. So they now had new words and they had a new observation, and both of those went together.

When you're trying to describe things in science, you'll need more vocabulary, but it won't necessarily be the technical vocabulary that makes people say: 'Oh science has so many technical words.' The word 'dome' will be used again if you were looking at architecture, for example. If you watch children learning science, where they give answers to the teacher or teaching assistant who is carefully bringing out new vocabulary, you'll see that you couldn't tell whether it was an English lesson or a science lesson really. Of course, numeracy comes into science as well. People seem to see that numeracy comes in, but are not so good at seeing that vocabulary comes in all the time. Listening to elephants, you've got to be able to describe what you hear. You might say 'throb', and you have a little child who might say 'when I hurt myself, I can feel it sort of throbbing in my finger'. So, in this way, we can bring these words together and it's very important to talk it over.

Feelings about science

The first thing that teachers and teaching assistants have to do is to make sure that they never say, 'Now, we're going to do something about electricity. Now you pay attention because this is very difficult.' I've heard that so many times. If children find that adults find science very difficult, very shortly they will find science very difficult because they base themselves on what adults do. This country has always assumed that teachers (and teaching assistants) will teach with almost no training. At the beginning of the National Curriculum, there was the 'cascade' method of training people. America was giving a ten-year introductory period to introducing science into their elementary schools. It seemed we weren't giving any time at all. We were just saying, 'During your ordinary lesson times or after school or in your INSET days you will learn all these things.' So people had to learn them in a hurry, which reinforced them in their view that it was too difficult. 'It must be difficult because I don't understand it' – and that is dreadful. You really must feel that turning on an electric bulb is just play. Right at the beginning of the National Curriculum many primary teachers assumed that science and technology would be at the bottom of the things that they could teach, and about three years later they found it near the top, and that's the play part of it.

With regard to play, there are those who've written about this like Jerome Bruner and also Suzanne Miller who said one of the things about play is that there's a sort of 'moratorium on failure'. You can't fail if you're playing because in play there's no objective except the fun of finding out something. If it isn't fun, children discontinue the play and go on to something else. In most primary schools, all the way through Key Stage 1, there's quite a lot of activity which you could call play. For instance, nature walks are like play, and you can't go wrong. That's the difference between play and study. In study, there is a straight line and you're trying to achieve something, but in play children do a number of things, but can stop and change direction at any point – 'I'm just playing,' as they say.

Adults who didn't relate to science teaching at school are the ones who ought to be playing, the same as the children. They should take science home and do it on their kitchen table or on a windowsill. I learned all the things I know about transistors on a kitchen table, because I had very small children at that time. I hadn't got time to go to any courses and it was great fun actually. There I was, a physics graduate. I suppose it must have been in the 70s, so I suppose I was 40. I didn't know how you could make circuits and what sort of resistances we were talking about, and what were the most likely mistakes. The likely mistakes, of course, in all electrical experiments are that you haven't taken the insulation off something, you know, something absolutely simple like that.

People talk about feelings and values in relation to, for example, experiments on animals. I don't know, but I think children will feel very passionately about animals. When talking to children, it's important to bring out their values, find out what they actually think, and give them some credibility. Of course now there are so many people changing to being vegetarians – well that comes out too. Adults and children may have very strongly held beliefs that you shouldn't harm animals.

Supporting children's learning in science

I think that it would be a good idea, when the teaching assistant is in class supporting individuals, supporting groups, to get the children to talk. For example: 'I didn't understand about that. What did you think about those flowers? Have you seen them before?' I would have thought that it involved putting themselves on the conversational level of the children. Some children can engage in discussion at the whole class level, but a lot find speaking up in front of the whole class a big challenge, whereas in a small group around the table it's much easier to engage in a dialogue. And when you have 30 children, and there still are 30 children in classrooms I notice, often, it's awfully difficult to engage them all from the front, so obviously what you need to do is to have groups.

I think teaching assistants have a great deal to contribute to children's independent and collaborative working. If, as a teacher, you think that you'll be able to have everybody doing autonomous things in the classroom, the answer probably is that first of all you have five people on each table and try and get them to work in small groups. But if you're teaching from the front it's really quite difficult to do that if you've got a difficult group that insist on quarrelling with each other – and some do. But then if you're a teaching assistant, and you've got a group of six children, you have really a golden opportunity. You could come in a bit, and say, 'Gosh that was interesting', and then keeping the train of thought going, 'What would happen if . . .?' You're in a marvellous position, I would have thought, as a teaching assistant working with just one group to get them going, to get them engaged in the enquiry, thinking and talking, and wondering how to find out. If you're the teaching assistant, you could do very well by little self-effacing questions like: 'I wonder if it would be true in such and such a case?'

Looking to the future

My thoughts about a future science curriculum follow on from what I've been saying. I'd like to give children lots of things which stimulate them, their senses, their interest, and I would like to receive descriptions from them. I wouldn't want a massive amount of writing. Perhaps say to them: 'Just words that you could use if you were telling your mum about what you saw or felt.' So the science curriculum would be connected with the natural world and sometimes, as with electricity, not with the natural world. So there are a whole lot of things that can be linked to science, but I think I'd always go back to the senses. I think it's very valuable for primary aged children to do painting, music and dance. I don't believe that all experiment is about controlling variables and fair tests, and so there should be very little of that I think. Science should be in the child's lived world and also their imagined world.

Section 2

Contexts for learning

Where can children best engage with a school's curriculum? In Chapter 11, 'Tadpoles in the willow garden', Sam Burns and Sue Hadfield write of their enthusiasm for learning outside. Not only, they claim, do children learn effectively in the willow garden that they have designed and created but they themselves feel inspired to be enthusiastic teachers when there.

In Chapter 12, Sheilagh Crowther uses ICT and other resources to provide a supportive context for two children learning English as an additional language. Where context is so influential on learning we cannot escape the conclusion that it is an integral part of the curriculum.

What is it that attracts children to books and creates a wish to read them? Elaine Moss, in Chapter 13, gives us reason to think hard and wide about this time honoured question. To Elaine's surprise, her daughter, Alison, became very attached to a book with words and pictures that are 'totally without distinction' that did not appear, to her mother, to have very much literary merit at all. However, it was a book that was precious to Alison for reasons that her mother had not appreciated.

Classrooms are, inevitably, quite noisy and sometimes over lit environments. In Chapter 14 Bernhard Menzinger and Robin Jackson write about a school-based study looking into the effects of light and sound intensity on pupils with Asperger syndrome. Their research would appear to relevant to all children with sensory sensitivities and those who generally find it difficult to concentrate in classrooms. Linking with the classroom environment theme of Chapter 14, Catherine Burke and Ian Grosvenor in Chapter 15 highlight the importance of school buildings and the influence of architecture on children's learning experiences.

Finally the section considers some out-of-school learning contexts. The context for learning that Kayte Brimacombe has created for her son, and that she describes in Chapter 16 includes both a physical context and 'rules of engagement'. A child's family can be considered a learning context in a number of ways. For many children much of the period of their most rapid learning, their first 5 years, is largely experienced in their own home, and they take the knowledge and learning strategies they develop in that context into school with them, to become part of the context of their school learning. Parents are not the only family members who support children's learning, and in Chapter 17 Charmian Kenner and her colleagues examine the role played by grandparents in a number of families.

Some parents choose to educate their children at home. In Chapter 18, Jane Lowe and Alan Thomas compare home and school as contexts for learning. They argue that school staff stand to benefit professionally by having an understanding of the way in which home educating parents teach their children.

Chapter 11

Tadpoles in the willow garden

Sam Burns and Sue Hadfield with Roger Hancock

Forest Schools aim to offer a sustained approach to outdoor learning. Originating in Scandinavia, they provide a philosophy about the completeness of learning when it happens through direct experience of the natural environment. The approach recognises that many children are becoming more and more isolated from the natural world and that there is therefore a need to create additional opportunities to help rectify this. In this chapter, Sam Burns and Sue Hadfield provide an overview of a willow garden that they developed and that uses a forest schools approach and process where nature is the teacher. The garden enables them to realise a long held belief that outside learning is not only very special for children but for adults too.

The willow garden is a relaxed place where we find we can talk to children at their level. The children really respond to that. They seem to open up and be more receptive to what's going on. We can feel ourselves relaxing as it's so good to be in a place where there are trees, blossom, and birds, and the children probably feel this too.

What's been happening in Denmark has influenced us, especially in that children there don't start formal school until later, when they're six plus. Before that, Danish children appear to do almost all learning outside, which makes things very magical. We think it's hard for some teachers in Wales, especially in Key Stage 2, to engage with these ideas given the pressure that's on them to meet curriculum targets. Currently there's a huge push in Wales on language and literacy because we're seeing ourselves as being behind in performance tables. So, it's said, we've got to go back to the basics and children need to move sequentially through the milestones in their learning. But we think we are providing many basic skills through their learning in the willow garden.

Source: Commissioned by The Open University for this volume.

We respect what children want to do in the garden. They sometimes come to us to ask questions or for our help to do something but we try not to do things for them. We're there to support and to guide them, especially by talking about things. We find we do a lot of standing back and watching what's going on. We gently step in if we feel children are not involving themselves as much as they could.

We like to have times when we come together to share what they've been doing. We often do this in the willow hut that is made of rounded and interlaced willow stems with a circle of log seats on the inside. We always aim to make the children feel proud that they've achieved something. We have snack time in this little open hut and maths can come from that – sharing and counting, for instance. So we feel we are enriching the primary curriculum. We also want to make it a social time because we're all having a meal together. There's also independence because they're buttering rolls and pouring drinks.

We both enjoyed being outside when we were young – building dens and fishing – so our childhoods have left us remembering these times as adults. We were on a course a little while ago and the leader asked everyone to write down their best memory. Many people wrote about a memory that involved an outside experience. So, maybe we're wishing to pass some of these feelings on to children who come to the garden. The children, we believe, are more likely to remember real life experiences. The Welsh Foundation Phase too emphasises the importance of outdoor play which gives confirmation to what we're doing. Quite a number of the children don't seem to have the opportunities for outside experiences of the sort we're providing. Many live in flats so they haven't got easy access to a garden or even a park.

The idea for the willow garden began when the school's senior management team visited another school and saw their stimulating outdoor area. Our Foundation Stage manager then approached us and asked if we would be happy to develop an area in our school as a garden that the children could use. We had already been doing gardening with the children so she knew we would be very interested. The head teacher was keen to make the most of our expertise. We looked around the school to see where the garden could be. The area that attracted us was linked to the playground. It was actually a small field with some trees and the children weren't allowed to go up there because it was seen as waste ground. So we put our heads together and we drew up a plan as to how we wanted it to look (Figure 11.1). The design was related to things that had previously worked well in engaging children's interest and other ideas related to outside learning from the Foundation Phase guidance.

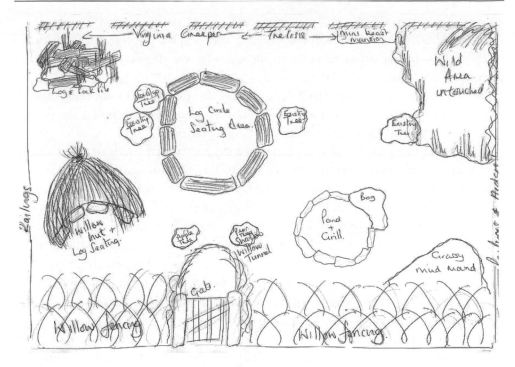

Figure 11.1 Plan of the Willow Garden.

In the beginning of January 2010 we stood in the cold with a landscape gardener, Richard Littlewood, and we thought with him about the kind of areas we would have. We decided upon a log and rock pile, a log circle near three existing trees, a wild area, a willow hut with log seating for quiet social times, singing, stories, and meals, a pond with a safety grill, and a grassy mound. A local tree surgeon, Tom Seymour, donated some logs at a small delivery cost and cut them to size for our sitting area. In our design we were always thinking of the need to encourage wild life including mini-beasts. The garden area would be enclosed by existing railings on three sides and, on the other, by a shaped, willow fencing with a gate leading onto the school playground. At first the thin willow fencing didn't look particularly special because it needed to grow and establish itself.

In terms of the time span, we were approached by the Foundation Stage manager in November 2009 and we progressed the garden over the period from January 2010 to the end of March 2010. We had to do a fair amount of Internet searching for ideas and people to help us and we had a budget of around £1,000 supplied by the school. When we were building the garden, we periodically took the children out to see what was happening and involved them in as many ways as possible. We kept a photographic record of the build so that other schools might see how we developed it and possibly make a garden for themselves.

We've had visitors from other schools and the teachers do say how nice it was. We are very proud of what we've achieved because we believe it is important to children's wellbeing and their learning.

When children first visit the garden we do introduce them to rules and boundaries and safety considerations. In the willow hut we all talk about what we can do and what it would not be right for us to do. Children are involved in tidying and looking after what is there and we hope they apply these skills to their own local environment. We tell them this is your garden and they can look surprised when we say that but it helps them to feel they should look after it. We have a cherry tree and when the fruit drops we mash it up with the children and make paint from it. The blossom is good too for making fairy crowns. A lot that comes from the plants and trees can be used for play and learning in this way.

We take out all the children in the nursery and Reception. The garden is a great means of support for children with a range of additional learning needs. The children who are confident serve as role models for others and help bring them out a little.

Recently we had a 3-year-old boy whose behaviour in the nursery was quite difficult so we took him out and the difference in him was quite phenomenal. He sat, he listened, and he concentrated on what we were doing. He thrived on the responsibility and the independence we gave him. After a while, we noticed the difference in him when he was back in the nursery. He still had difficulties at times but he was calmer and much happier than he was.

We take a resource trolley to the garden and this supports the children's learning. We stock it every week according to the planned activities but it also has things like paint brushes, paper and pencils, and water sprays all of which children use in an independent way. Often, our activities are geared towards the seasons. A while ago, some children brought tadpoles into school and we felt we wanted to show them how they live in their natural habitat. So, we introduced some frog spawn into the pond, but this year it's happened without us. It's as though the frogs have returned to help us with our tadpole activities. When we study the tadpoles we display factual books and stories about frogs with some toy frogs on a carpet area.

When we're in the garden, we do tend to feel very positive and seem to have more patience with children and their ways than we do when inside.

This seems to have a knock-on effect so that they in turn tend to behave well themselves. Our smaller outside groups mean that we can spend more time with individuals and be relaxed when talking with them. We make sure that the activities we set up are ones that all can do so they are unlikely to feel they're failing at any of them. We also don't make them feel they're being judged on what they're doing and you can see how comfortable this makes them. For some children, sitting quietly in the willow hut looking at a book is an achievement in itself.

We remember one nursery boy, Dylan, who just took to being outside. Later when he had moved on in the school he came bouncing in to tell us that he had been given an allotment as a Christmas present. His parents had picked up on his outside interest and acquired an allotment for the family. In fact, he features in one of the Welsh Foundation Phase publications as a case study of a child who develops his learning skills through being outside.

We evaluate what happens in the garden. We show the other staff the photographs that we take each time we have a session. We have our planning that we reflect on and have objectives but we make them realistic for us and the children. We also contribute to children's classroom portfolios by sharing with teachers what we have seen children do in the garden. Through their interests and questions, the children seem to stimulate us to learn more about outside things. The garden is a special place and we do feel privileged to spend time there every week with children.

Chapter 12

ICT and bilingual children

Sheilagh Crowther with Ian Eyres

Sheilagh Crowther is a teacher supporting children with English as an additional language in their own classrooms. Ian Eyres is a senior lecturer at The Open University. Sheilagh has developed particular expertise in the use of ICT and in this chapter she describes how she, a class teacher and a teaching assistant worked together to use technology to help two Polish children play a full part in the life of their class while developing their English.

Two Polish ten-year-old twins, Bartek and Wyktoria arrived in their new Year 6 class in Tring Primary School at the end of September. All newly arrived children, whatever their age or first language, need to feel welcome and they need to have their past achievements and experiences recognised. Bartek and Wyktoria had been confident, successful pupils in Poland and found a classroom environment in which they were unable to communicate easily with adults and children frustrating.

Although the long-term aim was for the two children to play a full part in every aspect of the life of the class, initially additional support strategies were essential. Without these, lessons would be difficult, if not impossible for the children to understand. The pace would often be too fast, and there would often be no visual or concrete material or action to support what teachers, teaching assistants and children were saying. Unfamiliar subjects and the style and format of the lesson itself could compound the problem. Children could also experience difficulties in following instructions and suggestions, and they may not be able to attempt set tasks on their own.

Source: An edited version of Crowther, S. with Eyres, I. (2004) 'Making sense of it all: using ICT to support older bilingual new arrivals', commissioned by The Open University for *Primary Teaching Assistants: Curriculum in Context* (London: Routledge). Reprinted by permission of The Open University and Taylor & Francis Ltd.

Making sense through ICT

Newly arrived children like Bartek and Wyktoria are seeking to make sense of the experiences, and especially the language they encounter in their new classroom environment. Many of the things ICT can do are of potential benefit to pupils who are learning English. Even in their first few days, pupils will be able to make some sense of what they are seeing and hearing, and computers, for instance, can help them gain additional information with which to build up a more comprehensible picture. A computer will allow them to work at their own pace, listening or reading as many times as they need to. Children can record and listen to their own voice, use on-line translation facilities and find pictures to explain words. ICT can enable children to work independently and initiate activity, and can also support interactive ways of working which promote children's communication skills.

Older new arrivals, like Bartek and Wyktoria, will be used to performing at a relatively high level in their first language, and a computer will permit them to continue to do this. ICT resources in many languages are readily available, as are websites in pupils' first languages. Email, which allows rapid and even instantaneous responses ('real time chat'), permits the setting up of links with overseas schools and pupils.

Besides being an essential continuing connection with family and culture, the use of their first language allows children to continue to develop a full range of concepts and thinking skills without the hindrance of having to do everything with the limited vocabulary and grammar of an unfamiliar language.

The maintenance of their first language will also benefit children's English development: oral and literacy skills are transferable, so that what pupils learn in their first language will assist them in learning in English.

Classroom interactions

When Bartek and Wyktoria started at Tring, the first concern of the teaching assistant based in their class was to make the pupils feel as welcome as possible. She used an internet translation site to produce labels for classroom equipment, and learn greetings, and useful nouns. The class were then able to say 'Hello' 'Welcome' and 'My name is . . .' 'What's your name?' in Polish. She taught the new arrivals to say these things in English.

Later, she worked with the pupils to translate key words for class topics, displaying this vocabulary around the classroom. Working together at the computer, the two children were able to practise English pronunciation of words. They also taught Polish words to the class, so that practising repetition was a purposeful two-way process. These initial activities encouraged monolingual English peers to use the translation tool collaboratively with the Polish pupils, which assisted communication and collaborative work.

A six-week 'study-buddy' scheme was set up for the class. During independent reading time, two children (different each day) took part in an interactive activity with the twins. Often pupils chose to use the computer to translate some words they needed. Turn-taking games tend to repeat certain phrases and Bartek and Wyktoria gradually began to use these.

The two children were introduced to a reading scheme – they were competent and fluent readers in Polish, and this presented a problem in finding age appropriate texts in English. They were quickly 'reading' (i.e. decoding) texts which were beyond their level of comprehension. Bartek and Wyktoria preferred not to read aloud. The difference between the ways Polish and English use the same alphabet to represent sounds – for example written 'w' in Polish is pronounced like an English 'v' – and the difficulty of pronouncing consonant blends not found in Polish made this a trial, even though they were able to interpret the gist of a text. Instead, they used the computer with headphones to listen to talking books related to their reading scheme. This provided modelling for pronunciation, and visual support for reading comprehension through the visual animations. The talking books also encouraged the children to use a variety of skills in their reading – for example using picture clues, and provided exercises to check comprehension, such as sequencing text and pictures.

ICT thus offered opportunities for Bartek and Wyktoria to become familiar with a topic before it was presented to the whole class. A talking book on 'The Solar System' supported their comprehension in the term's science topic on 'The earth and beyond'. The language of Macbeth was not accessible, but watching a video animation version beforehand allowed them to follow the story. The class worked in groups to present dramatisations, and this gave the children the opportunity (working in different groups) to participate with their peers. They were actively involved in making costumes and props, and they began to communicate using gestures and short two- or three- word utterances, e.g. 'Nathan hat big' with gesture to indicate that the hat was going to be too big.

Bartek and Wyktoria had good numeracy skills, which they could express well in their first language, but were not initially able to access much of the content of mathematics lessons. They were placed for an initial period in a different group where the class teacher used an interactive whiteboard. In this group, teaching concentrated on mathematical language, reinforced with visuals on the whiteboard. This helped the pupils gain some mathematical language in English, and they were given differentiated numeracy work which took account of their abilities.

Conclusion

Arriving in an established class which uses a different language is likely to be a bewildering experience, and Bartek and Wyktoria needed to find ways to communicate and make sense of their new environment as quickly as possible. Along with the support of the class teacher, teaching assistant and the children's new classmates, ICT through its interactive potential, its ability to support purposeful activity and help make meaning, offered many powerful resources to support Bartek and Wyktoria's learning.

Chapter 13

What is a 'good' book?

Elaine Moss

Elaine Moss, author and editor, wrote this short yet seminal chapter about reading in the late 1960s. It serves as a cautionary tale to adults when they feel they know best which books children should be reading. The ability to read and, indeed, the very desire to read are fundamentally based on our interest in what we read. The idea that children should sequentially progress through a graded scheme of reading books puts at risk this essential engagement precept. As Elaine Moss puts it, one can only really assess the value of a book 'by the light it brings to a child's eye'.

Don't go looking round the bookshops for *Peppermint*. Though this was probably the most important book in my younger daughter's early life, to your child it would probably mean very little: just another story and not a particularly good one at that.

Why, then, did mine clamour for it so often? Why, when it was falling to pieces, did I have to glue it together? Why was it never scribbled on, thrown out of bed, lent to a friend or given away with the jumble? I had no idea – for years and years.

Then one day, when Alison was about eleven, out of the blue came the revelation. How could I have been so blind – but yet, was it really so obvious? Before I give the game away I must describe *Peppermint* in some detail. If only you could see it – but you can't.

Peppermint is by an author whose name is Dorothy Grider. Dorothy Grider is also the illustrator. From the copyright matter I deduce that Miss Grider is an American and my guess is that she sold the story and pictures for an outright small sum (no royalty) to the Whitman Publishing Company, Racine, Wisconsin, who subsequently did a deal with Raphael Tuck and Sons, London, enabling them to put *Peppermint* on the market in

Source: An edited version of Moss, E. (1977) 'What is a "good" book?', in Meek et al. *The Cool Web: The Pattern of Children's Reading* (London: The Bodley Head) pp. 140–142.

the UK. It is a cheap book in every sense of the word, yet to one child it was, and still is in a way, pure gold.

Heaven knows how *Peppermint* got into our house – a visiting aunt must have given it to one of the children instead of a packet of jelly babies, I should think. For then, as now, I was knee-deep in review copies of new picture-books and storybooks from the 'good' publishing houses – the only books I bought were the great classic picture-books (early *Babars, Clever Bill, Little Tim*) 'without which', as blurbs are so fond of saying, 'no nursery bookshelf is complete'.

So of one thing I am certain. With the yardsticks I was already making for myself as standards by which to judge the steadily increasing flow of high quality picture-books for children in general (only the parent can tell whether a particular book 'takes' with her own child), I would never have forked out a penny for a book like *Peppermint*.

Peppermint has a shiny red cover from the front of which a white kitten face, sad-eyed, pink-eared and bewhiskered, looks soulfully (the adverb is important, as you'll see later) out. The word 'peppermint' is trick-printed in red and white twisty-candy-sticks above the pussy. On the back cover the series stamp (*Tell-a-Tale*) is surrounded by a cavorting pig, rabbit, lamb, goose, pony and squirrel – all loosely linked by a painted blue 'framing' ribbon. The spine, now merely desiccated sellotape, was probably once a thin strip of red paper.

The story of *Peppermint* is simply told in undistinguished (and un-Anglicized) flat American prose: Peppermint, the frail little white kitten, is the fourth of a litter of kittens born in a candy store. Is she sick? No, she's just thin and pale and nobody buys poor Peppermint – though Lollipop, Chocolate Drop and Caramel, her sisters, are all gleefully acquired by young customers. One day a little girl cries in the candy store because there is to be a Cat Show at school and she has no kitten – and no money to buy one. The candy store owner gives her Peppermint. Peppermint is taken home lovingly; she is bathed, 'blued', brushed and combed; she wins first prize in the Cat Show and she lives happily with the little girl for ever after.

Like the words, the pictures are totally without distinction. Comic-style kids and cats, blobby colours, accentuated sashes and splashes. Totally expendable, one would have thought: a watered-down, vulgarized *Ugly Duckling*. Where, oh where did *Peppermint's* special appeal to this one child lie hidden ?

I'm ashamed to say that its appeal was not hidden at all. It was as clear as daylight – but I was looking in the wrong direction. Alison is an adopted child; her hair is pale straw, her eyes are blue; she was taken home, like Peppermint, to be loved and cared for and treasured. It was a matter of identification not just for the duration of the story but at a deep, warm comforting and enduring level.

So we still have *Peppermint*. Its place on the family bookshelf is assured and no longer questioned, not only because it is precious to Alison – in a way that the technically efficient and typographically superior *Mr Fairweather and his Family* (written by Margaret Kornitzer for the express purpose of explaining adoption to pre-school children) has never been but because it taught me an invaluable lesson. The artistically worthless book – hack-written and poorly illustrated – may, if its emotional content is sound, hold a message of supreme significance for a particular child. If it does, it will be more important to that child's development than all the Kate Greenaway Medal-winning books put together.

For a book by itself is nothing – a film shown in an empty cinema: one can only assess its value by the light it brings to a child's eye.

From *Books* volume 2, National Book League, Winter 1970

Chapter 14

The effect of light and noise on pupils with Asperger syndrome

Bernhard Menzinger and Robin Jackson

Bernhard Menzinger is the education co-ordinator at Camphill School Aberdeen and Robin Jackson is an honorary fellow of the Karl Koenig Institute, Aberdeen. In this chapter they report on a study carried out in the school to better understand the responses of children with Asperger syndrome to light and sound intensity. They make recommendations regarding four practical steps that can be taken by staff to minimise negative effects, but they also urge for caution when interpreting behaviour and attributing cause and effect.

Introduction

We too often judge behaviour without understanding the cause of it. For carers, teachers and teaching assistants it is important to further their understanding of the underlying causes of certain types of behaviour. Over the past few years an increasing number of children with Asperger syndrome have been referred to our school. As teachers we at times struggle to understand the causes for pupils' often sudden and strong behavioural responses. Clearly their behaviour interferes with their own and other pupils' learning. It is our professional responsibility to provide a stimulating and congenial learning environment in the classroom. However, there is a fine line between an environment experienced as stimulating and one that can be too challenging for the pupil. The focus of this study is the behavioural response of pupils with Asperger syndrome to light and sound and the development of ways to help them to cope with such stimuli. Children with Asperger syndrome often have a very complex and disturbed sensory relationship with the world and themselves, which will inevitably cause anxiety, frustration and fear; this can result in very strong behavioural responses.

Source: An edited version of Menzinger, B. and Jackson, R. (2009) 'The effect of light intensity and noise on the classroom behaviour of pupils with Asperger syndrome' *Support for Learning, 24* (4), 170–175. Reprinted with permission from Blackwell Publishing.

Research design

In a recent research study, individual pupils were observed within their classroom setting or educational activities. The observation period extended over three consecutive seven-week terms. The first term was used for a pilot study. The second term was spent examining pupils' reactions to changing colour/light intensity and the third examining pupils' reactions to increasing noise levels. There was one working/observation period for each pupil each week. The duration of each working/observation session lasted 45 minutes. The idea was to undertake the research as a practitioner with the intent of bringing about changes in the school. The case study approach seemed the most appropriate choice for this research.

Three pupils were involved in the study. One was 6, one 11 and the other 14 years old. A clinical/educational psychologist had diagnosed all with Asperger syndrome. Two of them were residential pupils and one was a day pupil. (The names given below are fictional.)

John

John showed frequent outbursts of aggression from the age of three onwards. There was also little eye contact. His language was delayed. Various reports described him as always needing to get his own way. He had great difficulties in turn taking and needed to be the first in everything. This extended to all areas of life. He had a major aggressive outburst because he could not be the first on a bus. When he was in a larger group he spoke louder than anybody else. In school his aggression was mainly directed to children of his own age. He got on slightly better with younger children and adults. It was obvious from early on that he could not read social situations. His ability to sequence events was also very poor.

In 1999 at the age of five he was admitted to an Assessment Centre. Due to his 'defiant and aggressive behaviour' formal assessment was not possible. In 2000 he was diagnosed with Asperger syndrome. The report highlighted that John had no sense of danger. He also had no idea how dangerous his behaviour could be to others. It was also observed that he tended to focus on the details and was unable to see the overall picture. All activities linked to his own interests could be very obsessive. In break time he preferred to play on his own. Transition from home to school or to a lesser extent from one activity to another was challenging for him. The report concluded by stating that it was difficult to envisage how John would cope with a busy playground or a large group. The report of the occupational therapist highlighted the fact that John's finer motor skills were very poorly developed. After having experienced expulsion from two schools, John came to our school.

Peter

Nursery staff reported difficulties at the age of three. Peter's behaviour was described as 'bizarre'. A report stated that he could be 'off the wall', made inappropriate facial movements and noises, swore and showed extreme aggression. He showed interest in other children as long as the interaction was on his terms. He had no sense of danger and was very sensitive to sound. When he was anxious, he would soil himself. This was a situation which greatly upset him and it resulted in prolonged and aggressive outbursts. As he was very sensitive to touch, he would not allow anybody to help him get changed. When his parents first heard about his behaviour, they attributed it to the incompetence of the nursery staff. Peter was diagnosed at the age of five with Asperger syndrome and Semantic Pragmatic Disorder. The report highlighted Peter's strong obsessional nature. At the time of the report he was fixated with guns, cigarettes and knives. He also showed destructive behaviour towards himself and others.

Paul

At the age of three Paul was diagnosed with Asperger syndrome and possibly Semantic Pragmatic Disorder. The latter condition was later confirmed. Paul had been known to the Speech and Language Therapy Department from the age of three. He had very well-developed verbal skills which were described as 'sophisticated for his age'. The report also stated that he took everything literally which often led to bouts of confusion, frustration, anxiety and aggression. He had the greatest difficulty in understanding the behaviour of others. Other reports described him as loud, challenging and insistent. He showed extreme aggression towards others but not himself. He tended to play on his own.

It is interesting to note that with all three boys, difficulties were first diagnosed at the age of three. All three: (a) had difficulties in reading social situations; (b) wanted to make friends but did not know how; (c) had difficulties in understanding the meaning of what was said to them; (d) felt generally confused by life around them; (e) needed to be in control of every situation; and (f) were described as being very loud or at times making very loud noises.

Methodology

The main aim of the first seven weeks of the project was to see if the three pupils reacted either positively or negatively to colour or light intensity. The following situations were closely studied and subsequently discussed by the professional group; (a) we looked at the school activities of the three pupils in order to see what could be observed without changing the lesson plans; and (b) having established our possibilities for observations we then tried to align them to the Sensory Assessment Scale to the best of our abilities.

The reaction of the pupils in different situations was examined:

- *Sitting by the window for certain tasks with the daylight shining on to the desk*
  (Is there any noticeable reaction to changing daylight, for example irritation; complaints of headache; wanting to switch on the light as soon as it is overcast?)
- *Strength of light during outdoor activities*
  (Does he look for a place in the shade; put his hood over his head; shield his eyes with his hands; express any feeling of discomfort?)
- *Lighter or darker places*
  (Does he look for lighter or darker places?)
- *Computer work*
  (Does he turn away; complain of headache or feeling sick; or is he fascinated by the light and therefore cannot do his work?)
- *The changing light*
  (Is there any sign of irritation; lack of concentration; feeling uncomfortable when curtains are closed; or if there are sudden changes from daylight to electric classroom light?)
- *New people entering the room*
  (Does he lose concentration; show anxiety; stop working?)
- *The possibility of scanning the environment*
  (Is he aware of what is going on around him; can he orientate himself in the room?)
- *New charts or pictures in the classroom*
  (Is he disturbed by any changes in charts or pictures or their colours?)
- *New and/or bright clothing of people working with him*
  (Does he show any reaction to bright colour; make any comments?)

Results

Reaction to changing colour/light intensity

None of the pupils reacted either positively or negatively to colour or light intensity. Studying the sheets of the Sensory Assessment Scale relating to the visual system drawn up during or after direct observations, it is evident that there was no strong reaction to most of the areas observed. There was no strong reaction to changing daylight; a darkened room during a slide presentation; or the ever-changing light of the computer screen. Out of doors the pupils did not seek places in the sun or the shade. These findings were supported by the class teachers but came as a surprise to some other professionals. This would be consistent with Attwood's suggestion that sensitivity to particular levels of illumination or colour is a rare characteristic associated with children with autism and Asperger syndrome (Attwood, 1998). Myles *et al.* (2000) found that almost half of the 42 children they studied responded to visual input in the same way as those who had no special needs. Less than 20% had definite visual–related problems including visual oversensitivities and an additional 19% possibly experienced difficulties in this sensory area. It is interesting to note that in a study undertaken by Dunn, Myles and Orr (2002) only 19% of the people with Asperger syndrome showed definite differences in their visual perception.

Reaction to various and increased levels of sound

There were very strong reactions to increased levels of sound, particularly unexpected and shrill noises. This would appear to support the findings of Myles *et al.* (2000) where it was found that 85% of the children had definite or probable auditory problems. Difficulties in this area have also been described by Sainsbury (2000), Hall (2001) and Gerland (2003). A brief description follows of the pupils' responses to different levels and types of sound.

Normal activity and sound and humming to shut out noise

As soon as the sound of normal classroom activity increased slightly both John and Paul became very tense in their posture, looked agitated and started to hum or sing. John showed his distress especially clearly. It was typical for John in such situations to grip his pen, pencil or paintbrush very hard and start to scribble rather than write, draw or paint. If the noise increased further then he started to shout and to remind everybody to be quiet. Paul's response to increasing noise was to sing and to rock on his chair; these were well-observed and clear signs for Paul to let us know that moments of great discomfort were approaching fast.

We observed Peter, who is not part of a class, in the break-time activities. He was always active on the periphery, never joining the main group of pupils directly. If the noise level of the main group increased, he would start to shout and then remove himself to another part of the school's grounds. If on any particular day he felt already burdened by something, he would not go near the group but would withdraw to his tree house in the school's grounds which is surrounded by high bushes. All three boys had established some form of defence mechanism in order to cope with this particular problem. This is an important achievement since not all people with Asperger syndrome manage to do this (Sainsbury, 2000).

Unexpected sounds and shrill and distant noises

We found that three factors were often observed together. The unexpected sounds were often the telephone or a high-pitched sound made by a pupil. This sound could be an expression of joy, anger or pain. It could be near to the pupil or at times far away (the other end of the corridor or the opposite side of the playground). No other factor observed caused so much distress. This would appear to support Attwood's (1998) conclusions which he drew from clinical observation and personal accounts of people with Asperger syndrome.

The reaction of all three pupils was violent: either physical or verbal aggression. In all but two incidents, it was both. On all but one occasion in the sessions observed, the violence was directed towards the originator or source (person or object) from which the unexpected or shrill sound emanated. On one occasion aggression (punching, hitting or kicking) was directed to the nearest person. It is important to note that on some occasions the unexpected sound came from quite far away. This did not seem to diminish the anxiety level in the slightest. On one such occasion Peter threw a sizeable stone at a group of pupils who were on the other side of the playground. Myles and Southwick (1999) describe this observed behaviour as 'defensive panic reaction'.

There is however a difficulty here, for it is not possible to establish if these strong reactions are due to auditory hyper-sensitivity or the unpredictability of these sounds and noises. The meeting of professionals came to a similar conclusion. It is interesting to note that initially some thought that the number of aggressive outbursts had been much higher than it actually was.

On rare occasions during the period of observation when sudden noise was anticipated, the pupils usually took themselves away from the potential source of noise. One occasion when this did not happen involved John. He was anxiously watching a girl who was capable of producing loud and high-pitched noises. Eventually he got up, rushed to her and kicked her hard. When asked why he had done this, he said it was because she was noisy; however, she had made no noise on this occasion to provoke such a response. He clearly could not live with the suspense and his rising anxiety. We found that anxiety, even fear, that something unexpected might happen was always present in all three pupils. The fear of the unexpected is well described by people with Asperger syndrome (Myles *et al.*, 2000; Myles and Southwick, 1999).

Mechanical noises

Although it is known that a fascination for mechanical noises is not unusual for people with Asperger syndrome (Baron-Cohen, 2000), these noises had little effect on John or Paul, as long as they were warned well in advance that there would be a noise. John and Paul showed no positive or negative reaction to the noises made by a vacuum cleaner, a food processor, a slide projector, a mechanical drill, a fan or electric kettle. However, they could not tolerate the telephone. We assume that this had more to do with its unpredictability rather than the sound of it ringing. After the initial shock neither of them minded when it continued ringing. To begin with the ringing was mostly accompanied by short but loud verbal aggression. Other children might feel startled if there is a sudden noise but most of them would not have the need to become verbally aggressive.

The picture was very different for Peter. He is attracted to mechanical noises and movements and is generally delighted to hear the noise of mechanical equipment. At the time the research project was undertaken there was plenty of mechanical noise since we had a building site on the school's grounds. Peter was especially interested in watching diggers and there was a stage when he would not do any school work as he wanted to spend his time watching the diggers.

The meeting of professionals came to a similar conclusion. The fact that Peter's strong reactions were not due to mechanical noises was a surprise to some people. The findings regarding Peter are confusing and need some explanation. His strong reactions were *not* due to mechanical noises but to the fact that he was unable to watch the diggers. Once time for watching the diggers was included in his timetable his reactions changed dramatically and positively.

Discussion

These findings prompt a number of questions. It is not clear if some reactions are the result of sensory problems or are due to the general state of the pupil's well-being. It is possible that delayed reactions to events that had occurred on previous days may have played a part. One needs to be cautious about interpreting some behaviour as resulting from sensory stimuli without acknowledging the possible impact of other factors that may have contributed to a strong behavioural reaction.

It is interesting to note that the expectations of members of the professional groups were quite different from our own observations. Members of these groups had unanimously expected strong reactions by the pupils to changing light. One member thought she had clear 'evidence' that showed that one of the pupils was hypersensitive to light. On the basis of that assumption she had structured some of her educational activities to take account of that 'fact'.

As has been mentioned, varying light intensities had little or no impact on the classroom behaviour of the three pupils involved in this research. The first hypothesis for this research, 'that any sensory overstimulation in the visual domain, especially light intensity, has an adverse effect on the classroom behaviour of pupils with Asperger syndrome', was not supported. The effects of various sounds (human: loud, high-pitched; mechanical: shrill, ringing of a bell, etc.) did impact significantly on the classroom behaviour of the pupils. If the sound/noise came unexpectedly, it could result in physical and/or verbal aggression.

Everybody involved in this research project now acknowledges that detailed and ongoing observation of pupils is essential (Bell, 1999; Edwards and Talbot, 1999; Robson, 2003). Conventional forms of day-to-day classroom observation are clearly not detailed enough. The importance of a questioning attitude cannot be overstated. It has become clear to us that in order to understand the behaviour of a pupil we have to look at the way we are meeting certain behaviours and behaviour patterns. If that is accepted then we have to find the trigger for the behaviours.

Once we had established the connection between sensory experiences and the behaviour of the pupils observed, we were able to look for ways of minimising the effect of these experiences (Myles and Southwick, 1999). In order to do so, it was important to get as full a picture as possible. It was not enough to observe a pupil in just one teaching and learning situation. We found that pupils often behave very differently in different situations, so the observations of other professionals were essential. These observations need to be shared in multidisciplinary meetings and on a very regular basis – in our case this means weekly meetings. Once appropriate actions have been agreed then their impact is assessed and reviewed in future meetings. It has become clear that where actions have been successfully implemented, it is due to collaborative working (Connor, 1999).

There are a number of practical ways of minimising the negative effects of various sensory stimuli. Firstly, it is necessary to establish 'a place of safety' for every pupil who needs it (Myles and Southwick, 1999; Myles and Hubbard, 2005). It is acknowledged that this might be complicated by the number of pupils who might need recourse to it. The most important consideration concerning 'a place of safety' is not that it is big or small but that it will never be used by anybody else without the explicit permission of the pupil. No one is excluded from this – whether the school cleaner or the mechanic who has come to repair a broken radiator. 'A place of safety' clearly needs to be a *safe* place since it will be used when a person is highly distressed.

Secondly, pupils need to have a clear understanding of the programme that has been designed for them. They need to know where and when the potential danger points are likely to happen (for example ringing of the school bell, the use of mechanical instruments, etc.). Pupils need to know who will be there to help them and offer support when potential danger threatens. Thirdly, our research has shown that it is as important to reflect on the day that has passed as on the preparation for the day to come. This gives staff the opportunity to get to grips with the vast information gathered during the school day; it also provides a chance to look at how certain situations could have been dealt with in a better way. This time for reflection is beneficial for the pupil and for the teacher and therapist. Such reflection can add to an understanding of how pupils experience certain situations.

Fourthly, while it is well established that people with Asperger syndrome tend to possess good verbal skills, their comprehension of the spoken word frequently does not match their verbal ability. This is especially so during moments of high stress or anxiety (Attwood, 1998; Myles and Southwick, 1999). In a number of different situations it was found that the use of pictorial communication acted as a 'lifeline' for these pupils. We also found that it was important for the pupil to be involved in developing the format for that communication which he or she could use and which would be known to everybody working with him or her. Clearly it cannot differ significantly from the communication system used for the majority of the pupils in the school. Fifthly, as important as a predictable timetable is a consistent and predictable approach to the pupil.

This research project has proved invaluable to all within the school, for it has succeeded in dispelling the notion that research and 'the real world' are in some way divorced from each other. It has also demonstrated that if effective supports for learning are to be put in place for children with special needs then research has to be seen as an integral part of a school's work.

References

Attwood, T. (1998) *Asperger's Syndrome*. London: Jessica Kingsley.

Baron-Cohen, S. (2000) *Is Asperger Syndrome/High-Functioning Autism Necessarily a Disability?* Online Asperger Syndrome Information and Support. [Online at http://www.udel.edu/bkirby/asperger]. Accessed 08/04/05.

Bell, J. (1999) *Doing your Research Project*. Buckingham: Open University Press.

Connor, M. (1999) *Autism and Asperger Syndrome*. National Autistic Society (Surrey Branch). [Online at http://www.mugsy.org/ connorl.htm]. Accessed 08/04/05.

Dunn, W., Myles, B. S. and Orr, S. (2002) Sensory processing issues associated with Asperger syndrome: a preliminary investigation. *American Journal of Occupational Therapy*, 56, 97–102.

Edwards, A. and Talbot, R. (1999) *The Hard-Pressed Researcher*. Harlow: Pearson Education.

Gerland, G. (2003) *A Real Person*. London: Souvenir Press Ltd.

Hall, K. (2001) *Asperger Syndrome, the Universe and Everything*. London: Jessica Kingsley.

Myles, B. S., Cook, K. T., Miller, N. E., Rinner, L. and Robbins, L. A. (2000) *Asperger Syndrome and Sensory Issues*. Kansas: Autism Asperger Publishing Co.

Myles, B. S. and Hubbard, A. (2005) *The Cycle of Tantrums, Rage and Meltdowns in Children and Youth with Asperger Syndrome, High-Functioning Autism and Related Disabilities*. CDROM ISEC 2005 Inclusive and Supportive Education Congress. [Online at www. inclusive.co.uk]. Accessed 10/09/05.

Myles, B. S. and Southwick, J. (1999) *Asperger Syndrome and Difficult Moments*. Kansas: Autism Asperger Publishing Co.

Robson, C. (2003) *Real World Research*. Oxford: Blackwell.

Sainsbury, C. (2000) *Martian in the Playground*. Bristol: Lucky Duck Publishing Ltd.

Chapter 15

School buildings: 'A safe haven, not a prison . . .'

Catherine Burke and Ian Grosvenor

In 1967 The Observer newspaper ran a competition entitled 'The School I'd Like'. Just over 30 years later, in 2001, The Guardian newspaper repeated that competition. In this chapter, Catherine Burke, a lecturer at University of Leeds, and Ian Grosvenor, the director of Learning and Teaching, University of Birmingham, report on one aspect of the second competition. They describe children's responses related to the design and the quality of school buildings and they urge educators, designers and architects to take note of what children have to say in order that stimulating 'spaces for learning' might be better constructed.

The School We'd Like is:
A beautiful school
A comfortable school
A safe school
A listening school
A flexible school
A relevant school
A respectful school
A school without walls
A school for everybody.

The school building, the landscape of the school, the spaces and places within, the décor, furnishing and features have been called 'the third teacher' (Edwards, Gandini and Forman 1998). A beautiful, comfortable, safe and inclusive environment has, throughout the history of school architecture, generally been compromised by more pressing concerns, usually associated with cost and discipline. The material history of

Source: Burke, C. and Grosvenor, I. (2003) 'School buildings: "A safe haven, not a prison . . ." ', in *The School I'd Like*. Reprinted by permission of Taylor & Francis Ltd.

schooling, as conveyed in school buildings, is evident still in the villages, towns and cities of any nation. In the UK, one need not look far to locate, still functioning as schools, stone-built 'voluntary' schools of the mid-nineteenth century. The 'Board' schools of the late nineteenth century still stand, as red brick emblems of the cities in which they were built in an era which placed enormous faith in 'direct works' and 'municipalisation'. The schools built in the 1920s and 1930s reflected changes in educational policy indicating the beginning of a recognition of the diverse needs of children and consideration of health and hygiene. These decades saw the building of looser groupings of units, classrooms with larger windows and with removable walls being capable of being thrown almost entirely open. Architects worked to precise standards of lighting and ventilation as set out by the Ministry of Education. The post-war building plans saw the erection of buildings utilising modern prefabricated materials. Schools were built in large numbers, quickly and cheaply with the view that they would provide a stop gap until greater resources were available. 'Finger plan' schools, featuring one-storey classrooms set in parallel rows with a wide corridor to one side were popular. Thus started, for children, the long journey to toilets, hall and dining room as the buildings sprawled over large plots.

Already in the late 1960s, it was estimated that nearly 750,000 primary school children in England were being educated in schools of which the main buildings were built before 1875 (Department of Education and Science 1967:389). Standards were poor in general but there were particular problems, such as the 65 per cent of schools whose toilets were located in school playgrounds.

The new buildings erected in the 1960s and 1970s were needed to accommodate the swelling numbers on the school roll, the adoption of comprehensive secondary education and the extension of the school leaving age after 1973. Architects often used prefabricated assembly systems to help reduce costs and most new schools tended to resemble factories in their construction and style. Design aesthetics and comfort were usually given less importance than economy. However, many of the ideas about the flexible use of school buildings, first voiced by Henry Morris in the inter-war years, were revisited during this period. It was argued:

> Society is no longer prepared to make available a set of valuable buildings and resources for the exclusive use of a small, arbitrarily defined sector of the community, to be used seven hours a day for two-thirds of the year. School buildings have to be regarded therefore as a resource for the total community available to many different

groups, used for many different purposes and open if necessary twenty four hours a day.

(Michael Hacker of the Architects and Buildings Branch, Ministry of Education, cited in Saint 1987:196)

Open-plan arrangements reflecting child-centred pedagogy were criticised during the late 1970s and early 1980s. Educational policy under successive Conservative governments emphasised the importance of traditional methods of instruction and whole-class teaching rather than group collaboration and teacher facilitation. A recently concluded research study of classroom arrangements in the UK suggests, however, that for the majority, tradition overcame fashion (Comber and Wall 2001:100).

After decades of having to meet the enormous costs of refurbishment and repairs, the UK government in 1992 adopted the policy of financing public services including the building and refurbishment of schools via the public–private finance initiative (PFI). The first privately financed state primary school was opened in Hull in January 1999. At the time of writing, 20 public–private finance initiative contracts are already operational, a total of 30 new, rebuilt, or extensively refurbished schools are now open and another 500 are planned (*Guardian,* 30 September 2002). However, there is some disquiet among the teaching profession about the standards and quality of buildings that have recently emerged and concern that the design of schools today will rapidly become outdated as the organisation of learning changes in the future. The UK government's own watchdog on architectural matters, the Commission for Architecture and the Built Environment (CABE) has recently voiced concern over design standards of new schools built under the initiative. Their chief executive, Jon Rouse has stated, of the 30 PFI schools already built, many are like 'sheds without windows', and fail to comply with best-practice standards of natural light (Rouse 2002).

CABE has warned that there is insufficient effort being made to consult the users of school buildings. 'Schools need to get involved in that process and be specific about what they need. The whole process has got to be led by the curriculum' (CABE 2002). However, CABE does not advise that children and young people should be involved in the design process.

It is remarkable, in view of the fact that architectural education is very rarely provided within compulsory schooling, that there was such a wealth of ideas from children (in both the 1967 and 2001 competitions) about the shape and design of schools. However, some have argued that children are 'natural builders' or 'have a natural talent as planners and designers'

(Hart 1987; Gallagher 1998) and that the school curriculum might be better organised to recognise this. Writing in the USA, architecture and design educator Claire Gallagher has noted, 'The typical means of instruction in our educational culture is either linguistic and/or mathematical. Rarely is any attention paid to visual or spatial thinking or problem-solving' (1998:109). Her work with 'at risk' elementary school children in designing and planning their own neighbourhoods has illuminated how children have a distinctive knowledge and understanding of spatial environments that policy-makers rarely tap.

The 'School I'd Like' competition spontaneously produced dozens of models, hundreds of plans and thousands of implied designs of ideal sites for learning. In addition there was produced a remarkable collection of drawings and paintings through which children have expressed their ideas on curriculum, use of time, role of teachers and form of school. These design ideas address more than the shape of building and the ordering of spaces; they tell of a vision of education that reaches beyond the strict mechanics of building science.

The 1967 competition had also produced entries which were architectural in approach. Indeed, one of the winners at that time was a detailed plan produced by a 17-year-old pupil, said to want to become an architect. Like many of the plans and models contributed in 2001, this plan featured domes and pyramidal structures, circular spaces and a lot of glass.

Blishen was compelled to comment on the number of circular designs suggested by the 1967 competition entries. He noted that the young designers,

> having none of the problems of an actual architect . . . let themselves go and there can't for a very long time have been such a lavish decreeing of pleasure domes.
>
> (Blishen, 1969:43)

He suggested that such a quantity of circular schemes were, in fact

> reactions against a quality in school buildings that many inveigh against: their squareness. . . . Most were tired of squareness: where an actual shape was suggested, nine times out of ten it was a round one.
>
> (ibid.)

The 1967 cohort wanted schools not to resemble schools at all, but to resemble the adult world where individual privacy, comfort and relaxation were permitted. And it was not only the classrooms and building shell which were subject to the circuitous but also the organisation of bodies in spaces more generally:

> There would have to be a school with rooms, but furnished with soft chairs in a circle.
>
> (Richard, 15)

Within a circular school with circular classrooms and spiral staircases, what becomes challenged is the institutional: the regulation and ordering of bodies in precise spaces; the processing of children as in a factory; the rehabilitation of individuals as in a prison. An alternative regularity found in nature is envisaged in schools as colonies of life and development. The outer membrane, as in a cell, is penetrable, filled with light, transparent and attracts public view.

Jerome Bruner has proposed that the curriculum should be conceived of as a spiral to suggest how learning is achieved through a series of ever deeper encounters 'in the processes of meaning making and our constructions of reality'. The object of instruction should not be 'coverage' but rather 'depth', and the teacher is a collaborative learner and guide to understanding which begins with an intuitive impulse, 'circling back to represent the domain more powerfully or formally as needed' (Bruner 1996: xii). When describing the spaces for learning as 'caves' and the corridors as 'spirals', the children here could be seen to be expressing their instinctive cultural understanding of how learning occurs.

We could argue that the preference for dome-like features in the recently collected archive can be explained simply through acknowledgement of the fact that domes are features of leisure environments that children and young people frequent. These features are representative of enjoyment, freedom, play and excitement. Perhaps it could be argued, however, that we have here in this collection of material, responding to the same question over time, evidence of constancy in childhood. Traditionally the school room is square, has corners and contains rows of bodies in disciplined rank. The comments of children about the significance of this in contrast to their preferred spherical arrangements betray an understanding that a shift occurs in the organisation of authority and control in moving from the rectangular to the circular.

A recurring theme of likening school to a prison is found in competition entries, both past and present, suggesting that, from the point of view of those compelled to attend, little has altered in the basic character of school in spite of the vast extent of policy intervention over the intervening period. Blishen said of the contributions to the 1967 competition,

'When I was reading these essays, the image of the prison returned to me again and again' (1969:14): '. . . we're like caged animals!' is a remark which speaks for many in the more recent collection.

Comfort, privacy, space for social activity and rest, and colourful, softly textured, inviting interiors are called for by countless numbers of participants in the 2001 Archive. Once again there is continuity with the demands from the past. 'They cry out for colour, and are very conscious of the drab uniformity of many of the walls within which they sit' (Blishen 1969:43).

Toilets continue to be an appalling problem in many schools, over 30 years after the Plowden committee recognised the severity of the problem, and there were very few ideal schools, whether in essay, design, photographic or video format, that did not feature strongly a major criticism of the school toilets. Many suggest practical ways they can be improved but most wanted them to be less institutional, more comfortable and accessible. For many children, not being able to lock the toilet door safely causes distress.

Many children are still compelled to attend school buildings designed and built half a century ago. Distressed about the poor state of the fabric of their schools, most want more space and recognise the limitations of school design in relation to inclusive school policies. Young people in special schools who have difficulty just getting around the inadequately designed school spaces, take the opportunity to recommend change. Some argue convincingly that if the overall appearance of the school were improved then children would be more likely to want to attend and not to truant.

What emerges from the material is evidence that children have the capacity to examine critically the normal and everyday spaces in which they learn and can articulate their future in previously unimagined ways. They want to feel proud of the school to which they belong but many feel embarrassed by their surroundings. Children seem to regard the built environment as 'the third teacher'. To listen to these voices past and present is instructive to all educators, architects, designers and policy-makers who have responsibility for conceiving and constructing the spaces for learning which children inhabit. Seeming to understand the perspective voiced here, Paulo Freire once argued:

> One of our challenges as educators is to discover what historically is possible in the sense of contributing toward the transformation of the world, giving rise to a world that is rounder, less angular, more humane.
>
> (Freire, in Macedo 1996:397)

References

Blishen, E. (1969) *The School That I'd Like*. London: Penguin.

Bruner, J. (1996) *The Culture of Education*. Cambridge, MA: Harvard University Press.

CABE (2002) *Client Guide: Achieving Well Designed Schools Through PFI*. September. London: CABE.

Comber, C. and Wall, D. (2001) 'The classroom environment: a framework for learning', in: C.F. Paechter, R. Edwards, R. Harrison and P. Twining (eds.), *Learning, Space and Identity (Learning Matters)*. London: Paul Chapman Publishers.

Department of Education and Science (1967) *Children and their Primary Schools. A Report of the Central Advisory Council for Education (England). Vol. 1: The Report. (Plowden Report)*. London: HMSO.

Edwards, C., Gandini, L. and Forman, G. (eds.) (1998) *The Hundred Languages of Children*, 2nd edn. Greenwich, CT: Ablex.

Gallagher, C. (1998) 'The "Our Town" Project: a case for reform in urban design and classroom practice', in: *Emergent Paradigms in Design Education: Sustainability, Collaboration & Community*, Sydney, NSW: University of New South Wales.

Hart, R.A. (1987) 'Children's participation in planning and design. Theory, research and practice', in: C.S. Weinstein and T.G. David (eds.), *Spaces for Children. The Built Environment and Child Development*. New York: Plenum Press.

Macedo, D. (1996) 'A dialogue: culture, language, and race'. *The Harvard Educational Review*, 42, 383–98.

Rouse, J. (Chief Executive of CABE) (2002) Interview for the BBC Newsnight programme, 16.10.2002.

Saint, A. (1987) *Towards a Social Architecture. The Role of School-Building in Post-War England*. London: Yale University Press.

Chapter 16

Joining Gabriel's play

Kayte Brimacombe with Roger Hancock

> Kayte Brimacombe lives in North London and is the mother of three children. Kayte talked with Roger Hancock, a senior lecturer at The Open University, about her experience of helping her son Gabriel to play in order to stimulate his wish to communicate with others. Kayte's involvement in setting up play opportunities within the context of her home raises a number of considerations related to parental involvement in children's education, schools learning from parents, and particularly, what it is for adults to become truly involved in children's play.

My son Gabriel is nine and he has Down syndrome and autism. Children with Down syndrome have an extra, critical portion of the number 21 chromosome present in some or all of their cells. This can alter the rate of different aspects of their physical, cognitive, social and linguistic development, often resulting in learning difficulties. Children with autism typically experience difficulties with social interaction, social communication and imagination. They often resist changes in their routines. They also show repetitive behaviour patterns and can get stuck in such movements, usually called 'stimming'. For them, getting stuck might be important or pleasurable – flapping their hands is a common example. It could be said to be their way of playing. However, because it's repetitive it seems to be of limited value developmentally.

A place to play

We have set up in our home a play-based programme for Gabriel based on the Son-Rise Program® (see, ATCA 2004). This sees a child with autism

Source: Brimacombe, K. with Hancock, R. (2004) 'Joining Gabriel's play', commissioned by The Open University for *Primary Teaching Assistants: Curriculum in Context* (London: Routledge). Reprinted by permission of The Open University and Taylor & Francis Ltd.

as the teacher and suggests that parents and carers 'join' with them instead of taking an approach that goes against what they might wish to do.

There is a room in our house which is dedicated to play and fun. It's an ordinary sized bedroom with plain walls and the window is covered to minimise distractions. It's got a very soft floor covering because a lot of play takes place on the floor. The shelves are high so that Gabriel needs to communicate in order to choose something to play with. One of the main difficulties with autism is children can't select out stimuli – the radiator humming or the clock ticking can draw their attention as much as a face. When distractions are minimised adults become much more interesting and this increases the likelihood of communication. This is difficult for Gabriel in a normal family environment where there are many things happening.

Interestingly, limiting the number of distractions has a positive effect on adults too. When we go into the playroom no one else enters, so this allows us to really focus on Gabriel and keep our minds on play.

In the playroom we adults need to be very energetic and enthusiastic, have fun, and stretch ourselves in terms of building up our ability to play. Gabriel then becomes motivated to say 'more' or 'again' or 'up' or 'down'. These are very simple communications but he's stimulated to make those sounds and words because he's in on what is happening. In this way he is encouraged to share in the experiences of others.

Enlisting others

In addition to playing with members of his family, including his five-year-old sister, Gabriel also plays with trained volunteers. This gives him additional experience of communicating with other people and it also helps us if we can share what is a challenging family involvement. We recently went to the United States to receive further training from the programme's originators and this has given us more confidence when working with volunteers.

Currently, three volunteers are involved. They are given in-house training to help them build up their play skills, and taught how to be 'present' with Gabriel. The play room has an observation panel so sessions can be observed and feedback can be given on what is effective.

Gabriel's sister is the best person to play with him. She's quite happy to spin round and round in circles with him for ages and ages. Adults can't do this without feeling dizzy. She's also very good at linking with his body language so that there can be times when she truly connects with his experience.

Learning to play

The central message of the Son-Rise Program® is, therefore, that children with autism should be 'joined' in whatever they are doing. This is so even if they are engaged in something that might not normally be seen by adults as play. To some extent joining involves mirroring Gabriel's play. However, it's not just mimicking him but getting into his experience and understanding what he might be getting from what he's doing. For example, the way in which he's moving an object might provide interest for him because the light is bouncing off it in a certain way. So, an adult needs to discover what lies behind his involvement. It's a way of learning about his way of experiencing things and also being very understanding and accepting of him. This acceptance helps him to become interested in others. In this way, a bridge can be built which facilitates shared interests, communication and pleasure.

Time in the playroom has successfully built up Gabriel's communication skills. Sometimes, however, he's not in the mood and this has to be accepted. But mostly he realises that when he's in the play room he's in for a lot of fun. He can't really do anything wrong in there – anything goes, so it's known as the 'Yes' room.

A lot starts off through rough and tumble play, play that might also be appropriate with a toddler – swinging around, up and down games, for example. There's a big mirror that helps eye-contact with Gabriel. There's a great big ball and a rocker and a little trampoline. Physical games help build up his initial interest, get a smile from him and help him to want to play. He then might indicate that he wants more of something. On the shelf there are different things like big cars, skittles and huge bricks and he might indicate that he wants to go up and choose something to play with. It's therefore a positive cycle of him getting what he wants and then him wanting more of it.

At the moment the focus is on eye contact and this has improved dramatically in the last four months. Very simple vocalisations are developing – like 'up', 'down', 'more', 'ball', 'push', and 'jump'. Gabriel makes approximations for these words so they're not that clear. However, he is a nine-year old child who hasn't spoken since he was two so it's a very dramatic effect for the family.

The key to success with Gabriel is to genuinely have fun and not to fake this. The people who are best at playing with him are those who can really enjoy it themselves. Lots of different people have, over time, become involved and this includes teachers and teaching assistants at his school. Often, there is a nervousness about being with a child with autism. Inexperienced people tend to 'flatten out'. They seem to lose a lot of their energy and their enthusiasm. It seems as though they're picking up on the perceived lack of feeling coming from Gabriel. So they tend to get stuck as well and unintentionally they can reinforce his 'stuck' situation. The secret is to work at successfully joining him and then try to change whatever's happening ever so slightly.

Given Gabriel's progress at home, the staff at the school are now adapting how they work with him to incorporate the principles of joining. The approaches they have been using to date have not enabled him to make very much progress. Gabriel is a little more sociable than many children with autism so this has helped his progress with the Son-Rise approach. The school has created a play room for him where he can go for short sessions. They have observed Gabriel's home programme and seen a video of him at play with different volunteers. Although there's some carry over of the family's approach to school, Gabriel's main programme continues to take place at home during evenings and weekends.

Conclusion

The Son-Rise approach has proved to be effective for Gabriel. To a large extent its principles are basically common sense, however. It is about removing the distractions which children with autism can't screen out easily for themselves, joining them in whatever they are doing, and then using enthusiasm, engagement and fun to help them to be drawn into social interaction.

For many adults, the process of joining can be very hard at first because grown-ups tend to have many things on their minds. However, once the skill of being 'present' in play has been acquired, then new ideas, creativity and playfulness can seem like very natural things. A lot of the qualities that people would wish to develop in themselves are valuable when people play together – like being authentic with someone and being 'alongside' them.

Working with Gabriel has done much to increase family and school understanding about the nature of play and about the act of playing. Those closely involved feel they have not only learnt to join him when playing but that this skill has a wider significance for the way in which adults collaborate with children to support their play and their education more generally.

Reference

ATCA (Autism Treatment Center of America) (2004) See: http://www. autismtreatmentcenter.org/contents/other_sections/index.php

Chapter 17

Grandparents and children's learning

Charmian Kenner, Tahera Arju, Eve Gregory, John Jessel and Mahera Ruby

The role of grandparents in children's learning is a neglected area of research, but as the authors of this chapter, members of a research team at Goldsmith's College, University of London, discovered, their contribution is worth further consideration. Grandparents often have a close and special relationship with their grandchildren and the research team found many examples of them involved in a range of learning events in the home, where the grandparents sensitively joined with children in a process of discovery or shared their knowledge and experience. Schools may wish to consider how they could extend their notions of partnership to include grandparents and other family members.

Setting the scene

Sumayah, her cousin and her grandmother are showing our research team how they work together in the small garden of their terraced house in Tower Hamlets, London's East End. First there are leaves to be swept up. Five-year-old Sumayah is determined to do the job and begins pushing the broom. After letting Sumayah sweep for a while, her grandmother takes over and demonstrates the firm strokes needed, then leaves Sumayah to finish the task. Next there are trees and plants to be watered. In this tiny space, Sumayah's family grow apples, pears, lemons, pumpkins, tomatoes and herbs, using the agricultural knowledge brought by the grandparents from Bangladesh. This knowledge is now being passed on to Sumayah and her cousin; it is they who are left in charge of the garden when their grandparents are away on visits to Bangladesh.

Source: Kenner, C., Arju, T., Gregory, E., Jessel, J. and Ruby, M. (2004) 'The role of grandparents in children's learning' *Primary Practice, 38* (Autumn), National Primary Trust.

Learning from experience

What do the children learn from this experience? As they do the watering with three sets of hands grasping the watering-can handle – Sumayah's, her cousin's and her grandmother's – they find out how much water to give each tree or plant. They also know that not every plant is watered on every occasion; some need more water than others.

Sumayah points to the growing tip of a lemon tree seedling, commenting that the leaves are a different colour from the others because they are new. Her cousin shows three plants in a line of pots and explains while pointing to each one that two of them are his uncle's and one is Sumayah's. Sumayah is responsible for her own particular plant and she will thus find out in detail how to nurture it. For example, she knows whereabouts in the garden the plant has to be placed to receive the right amount of light. Her knowledge goes beyond the classic primary school experiment of growing cress under different conditions in order to discover that plants need light and water to thrive. As well as being aware that these elements are essential, Sumayah also knows what quantities are necessary for each plant.

The project

Our research project with grandparents and grandchildren in English-speaking and Bengali-speaking families in East London revealed a wealth of such learning events taking place between the older and younger generations. We had suspected that this little-investigated inter-generational relationship was of special importance to children's learning, but we were surprised by the wide range of activities going on.

An initial questionnaire, answered by eleven Bangladeshi British families and three Anglo (English-speaking) families, offered a list of 20 activities and asked grandparents whether they engaged in any of these with their three- to six-year-old grandchildren. Figure 17.1 shows the spread of activities.

Firstly, the questionnaire demonstrated that Bangladeshi British as well as Anglo families took children on outings to the park, played and read with them, involved them in cooking and gardening, told them stories and recited rhymes together. This finding challenges the assumption often made that ethnic minority families do not offer their children these kinds of learning experiences.

Secondly, the Bangladeshi British families placed a high priority on 'visiting others' and 'talking about members of the family and family

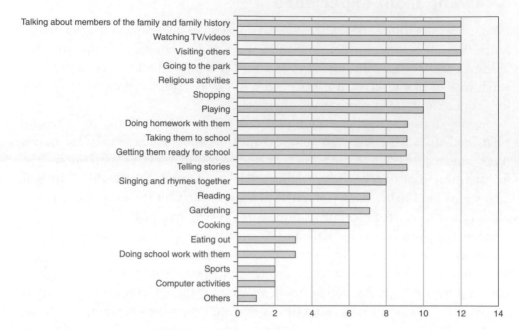

Figure 17.1 Activities carried out jointly by children and their grandparents, showing the number of grandparents reporting each activity.

history'. These were categories which the Anglo members of our research team had not originally thought of including, until two of the researchers – themselves from Bangladeshi backgrounds – made the suggestion. They explained that family visits are of considerable importance in Bangladeshi culture. When children go to see relatives, often accompanying their grandparents, they learn how to greet each person appropriately and how to behave within the social group. They gain knowledge of each relative's place in the complex kinship network and where they themselves fit in, giving them a sense of their own identity. Conversations with grandparents enhance their understanding of family history. These are important types of learning experience often overlooked by mainstream educators, and largely absent from the National Curriculum. We need a wider definition of the term 'learning' in order to encompass the rich variety of knowledge children gain from spending time in family settings.

The study

Having gained an initial idea of the kinds of learning experiences happening between grandparents and grandchildren, we approached 12 families who agreed to participate further in the project. Six were Sylheti/Bengali-speaking of Bangladeshi origin and six were monolingual English-speaking. Four families had children in the nursery class, four in Reception and four in Year 1. In interviews with grandparents and video recordings of learning events at home such as cooking, gardening, storytelling and computer activities, we examined the following questions:

- In what ways do grandparents and grandchildren take the lead in the learning interactions?
- In what ways are the learning interactions co-constructed by the participants?
- What kinds of knowledge are exchanged between the younger and older learners?
- What is the role of the computer in the cultural, linguistic and technical aspects of learning?

A special relationship

Children's relationship with their grandparents involved a sense of mutual vulnerability. Grandparents were recognised as needing care due to age and a certain amount of frailty. Sitting at the computer with his grandmother Hazel and observing her hand as she held the mouse in front of him, three-year-old Sam suddenly raised his own hands and declared: 'I'm not getting old . . . I've not got old skin.' Hazel agreed with amusement, noting that she indeed had wrinkles while Sam did not.

The grandparents in the project were keen to take care of their young grandchildren, and expressed this through a supportive use of touch. The close physical relationship between the generations was noticeable in the events we video recorded: Sahil's grandmother Razia linking her arm through her grandson's as they talked about the books they read together, Hazel patting Sam's tummy while talking about the computer game they were playing. The children's response showed a reciprocal use of touch: Sahil's younger siblings climbed on their grandmother's lap as she and Sahil read a poetry book, while Sam rested his head against his grandmother's shoulder as he listened to her comments on the computer game.

Guidance through touch

Touch was an important means of communication between young children and grandparents. As well as building children's sense of security and self-confidence, it was used by grandparents to guide kinaesthetic learning. The example was given above of Sumayah's grandmother helping her grandchildren to water plants in the garden. Through her touch, she indicated at what angle to hold the watering-can and how much water to give. We also observed Sahil's grandmother guiding his hand as he wrote in Bengali, enabling him to experience the flow of the pen on the page to inscribe the pattern of each letter. Once again, guidance through touch could be reciprocal. Moments later, Sahil placed his hand over his grandmother's to show her how to operate the mouse on the computer.

Learning exchanges around language

Grandparents often considered themselves responsible for particular areas of their grandchildren's learning. In the case of the Bengali-speaking families, one of these areas was language. For example, Sahil's grandmother Razia was seen by the family as responsible for maintaining the children's knowledge of Bengali. Sahil's mother, having grown up in Britain, tended to speak English as well as Bengali to her children, but wanted them to develop their family language in order to retain a link with their heritage and culture. Razia entered into her task with considerable energy. She used books brought by the children's mother from Bangladesh, including stories such as 'Snow White' in Bengali which she knew the children would enjoy.

Sahil was able to identify different categories of Bengali book – alphabet primers, 'chora' (poetry) books, and the 'Snow White' storybook – realising that each had a different purpose. When reading the 'chora' book with his grandmother, he closely followed her lead. The oral recitation of poetry was enjoyed by Sahil and also by his younger sisters, who ran into the room to join in when they heard the rhythm of their grandmother's voice. As well as developing their vocabulary and expression in Bengali, the children were receiving an introduction to rhyme – a skill considered very important by early years educators.

Meanwhile, Razia was learning English from her grandchildren, in an inter-generational language exchange. Along with other grandparents in the study, Razia mentioned that contact with her grandson added to her knowledge of English. When Sahil was asked by the researchers whether his grandmother knew English, Razia (understanding the question perfectly) told her grandson in Bengali 'say Granny doesn't speak English'. She was maintaining her role as the resource person for Bengali within the family, but throughout the video recorded event her knowledge of English was evident. When Sahil was asked what he most enjoyed doing with his grandmother, he thought for a few moments and then replied in English 'I enjoy she telling me what the word means in Bangla' ('Bangla' is the term often used for Bengali). Contented, Razia smiled and kissed him, once again showing her understanding.

Several of the Bengali-speaking grandparents were also introducing their grandchildren to Arabic for the purposes of reading the Qur'an. Sumayah and her grandmother spread out a prayer mat on the carpet and sat together on the mat, with Sumayah reciting verses of the Qur'an after her grandmother. This early introduction to the sounds and intonation of classical Arabic was a prelude to a gradual understanding of the content of the verses, just as children participating in hymn-singing or prayers in an Anglican church would be inducted into the richness of language which they would later comprehend more fully.

Learning exchanges around computers

It can be seen from the questionnaire results that few grandparents engaged in computer activities with their grandchildren. For the Bangladeshi grandparents particularly, computers were unfamiliar and there were language constraints – computers operate in English script unless special software is obtained.

The potential for learning from computer activities was emphasised by our video observation of Hazel with her grand-daughter Lizzie. Hazel and Lizzie frequently used the Internet at Hazel's house to search for information to enhance the other learning activities they did together. For example, they often looked at wildlife in the garden and once discovered an unusual moth which they could not then find in Hazel's reference book. Via the Internet, they identified its picture, with the name 'Quercus' and information about the male and female moths and egg-laying habits. They then printed out this page and glued it into Lizzie's scrapbook.

Hazel's support for Lizzie's learning was sensitively given, allowing Lizzie to take the lead when doing the typing or clicking the mouse on the appropriate spots. At some moments, Lizzie's responses preceded those of her grandmother. While Hazel was working out what step to take next on the search engine 'Google', Lizzie had already pulled out the keyboard ready to type the search word. Hazel stated that she was less confident about word processing than her grandchildren, 'but now that Lizzie is learning at school, hopefully she'll teach me'.

In this exchange of competencies, Hazel helped to structure the stages of the learning event for Lizzie and supplied alphabet letters to complete the word 'moths' when Lizzie was unsure. Lizzie's eager confidence in using the word processing commands suggested that she would indeed soon be instructing her grandmother in this area. Her desire to go beyond the limits of this particular investigation by printing out information about another moth on the same website (despite her grandmother's attempts to keep to the original task) would exploit the possibilities of hypertext and introduce new areas of learning for them both.

A different form of support

In comparison, the activities conducted by Bangladeshi grandparents (when the research team supplied a laptop computer for them to use with their grandchildren) at first seemed more basic. The children were unfamiliar with a laptop although they had used other types of computer at school, and for most of the grandparents it was their first chance to use the technology. The children mostly typed their names, working out how to use the different form of mouse incorporated in the laptop keyboard.

However, a closer examination of these events reveals that the grandparents, sitting quietly beside their grandchildren, were playing an important role similar to that of Lizzie's grandmother. Through their presence they helped to structure the event, for example by ensuring that the child was the main actor and an older cousin did not take over, or by suggesting the activity of typing the child's name and supporting the child's efforts through their own knowledge of English letters. By giving their attention through gaze or pointing, even though they did not touch the computer, they helped the child maintain concentration and accomplish the task.

Furthermore, the grandparents showed a growing interest in what was happening on the screen. Their curiosity indicated a potential to develop knowledge and expertise if they were to have access to software or websites, which operated in their own language, as Lizzie's grandmother did. One aim of the research project is to increase family involvement with computers at our partner school in the study, Hermitage Primary School in Tower Hamlets. If Bangladeshi grandparents can attend family workshops with tutoring and resources in Bengali, this could lead to positive outcomes for their own learning and that of their grandchildren.

Grandparents may need special encouragement to come into school and share their wisdom and experience. When invitations were issued to a 'Grandparents' Coffee Morning' at Hermitage School, a number of grandparents attended, some having dressed in their best clothes for the occasion. The grandparents were proud that the school had acknowledged their importance in their grandchildren's education – and the children were delighted to bring to school these key figures in their learning lives.

Conclusion

This research project has begun to open up a fascinating world of learning between grandchildren and grandparents, hitherto little-known to schools, particularly with regard to ethnic minority families. Our findings suggest the potential benefits if teachers widen their links with 'parents and carers' to ensure that the significant role of grandparents is recognised and built upon in home–school interactions.

Chapter 18

Learning at home is not like learning in school

Alan Thomas and Jane Lowe

In this chapter, Alan Thomas, visiting fellow at the Institute of Education, London, and Jane Lowe, founder of the Home Education Advisory Service, take a broad view of home education approaches, including more formal and structured ones, and compare them with common school practice. Their intention is to show how home education, however it is practised, is very different from school education.

We are all products of our own education and it can be surprisingly difficult to envisage anything that is radically different from our own experience. Many years ago when one of us, Jane Lowe, was an English teacher at a secondary school she remembers using an extract from a course book which was about a boy who was educated at home. She discussed it with her Year 7 class and they talked about what home education would be like. But when they were asked to write about what they would do if they had the freedom to learn anything they wished at home, they typically came up with a daily routine of half-hour lessons in all their normal school subjects. In the same way, when parents embark on home education they often think of it as school at home, with mum (because often it is mum) teaching a child(ren) sitting around the kitchen table, setting exercises and marking them, the same as a teacher only with just one or two children. However, as parents adapt, they find that learning at home nearly always turns out to be very different from what they expected initially.

Home education differs fundamentally from the school model in a number of ways. Table 18.1 gives a summary of the most significant differences which certainly apply if and until children study for GCSEs.

Source: A revised version of Thomas, A. and Lowe, J. (2007) *Educating Your Child at Home* (London: Continuum) pp. 8–19.

Table 18.1 Comparing home and school as places for learning

Home	School
No formal qualifications are needed to teach	Teachers are qualified
The national curriculum does not apply at home	The national curriculum is obligatory
Detailed planning is not necessary; parents may change and adapt as they go along	Detailed long term planning is needed
Timetables are not necessary	Lessons are timetabled
Prior knowledge is not necessarily required; parents may learn alongside their children	Teachers must have a very good grasp of the content of each lesson beforehand
Lessons are rarely provided all day; most common may be an hour or two at most; in some cases no formal lessons or structured teaching	Children have formal lessons all day
Informal learning is very important	Little planned informal learning
Written evidence is far less important; parents generally know what stage their children have reached	Children constantly produce written work as evidence of learning and attainment
Marking is unnecessary at home because any mistakes or difficulties can be dealt with as they occur	Children's work is marked, compared and graded
Almost all teaching is individualized	Lengthy individualized teaching by teachers is quite rare
For many parents, talking with their children contributes more to learning than anything else.	Reduced opportunity for learning through conversation with teachers.
Training for teaching reading is unnecessary	Teachers are trained to teach reading
As much time for reading for pleasure as children want; many are avid readers	There is reduced time for reading for pleasure
There are restricted opportunities for group learning; these have to be created e.g. by linking with other families for such things as drama, and sport	There are many opportunities for group/shared learning activities; also drama and sport
Very little competition at home where personal best is more of a motivator	Competition, real or subtle, is integral to classroom learning
Social interaction needs to be arranged; some children may be isolated.	Plenty of opportunity for social interaction – at least with age mates

The comparison is restricted to teachers and home educating parents. We tried out a version including teaching assistants but their roles are simply too diverse to fit into a generalised comparison so we refer just to teachers and parents. The table is over-simplified, of course. Hopefully however, it will serve to stimulate thinking about the differences, before we go on to discuss the two learning contexts, home and school, in greater detail.

Qualifications

Parents who educate their children at home do not need to have teaching qualifications. In fact, home educators who are also teachers sometimes say that their professional training is not that relevant because the task of teaching large groups of pupils in school bears little resemblance to teaching one or two children at home. Parents are able to guide their children's learning on an individual basis at home without any specialist subject knowledge, at least up to preparation for GCSEs. At this stage some parents may prefer to seek some input from web sites, correspondence courses or from tutors, but others carry on by themselves by obtaining the specifications and some suitable books and materials.

The national curriculum

The national curriculum decides, even prescribes, the content of children's learning in nearly all maintained schools. It is not obligatory at home and there are no compulsory subjects. Parents are free to establish their own philosophy and goals for their children. Moreover, there is no evidence to support any theory of 'best practice' in home education and parents use a wide variety of methods and approaches. These range from formal, structured arrangements to informal approaches which are completely child-led. Once they have settled down to learning at home, most home educators seem to evolve their own approach which falls somewhere in the middle between these two extremes. Even when home education takes place in a formal and structured manner, it still tends to differ greatly from the way schools organise learning.

Planning

At school, detailed long-term planning is essential in order to ensure 'delivery' of the national curriculum to all children. If they wish to do so, parents who teach their children at home may dispense with planning altogether in order to adapt to the ever changing nature of learning. They sense when it's time to insist, when to desist and when to try a different teaching tack. There is time to listen to a child to see how a task is conceived or to get a fuller picture when they have difficulty in understanding. At home parents can adjust teaching to each child's, minute by minute, in a way that is difficult for teachers in the classroom. It soon becomes evident that detailed preparation is largely unnecessary at home where you don't have to prepare a lesson to teach a whole class of children.

At home, you can simply start from where you left off last time. If you want to, you can get a step ahead as you are settling down together.

Timetables

Timetables are the historic bedrock of school organisation. At home there is obviously much greater flexibility. Lessons can be as long or as short as needed. If a child is not concentrating for whatever reason, a lesson can be put off for another time; there is nothing to be gained from persevering if you can break off and come back to the task later. On the other hand, if a lesson is absorbing, it can go on as long as necessary. This can extend to learning in 'blocks', exploring a topic for days or longer. The flexibility which could allow for this kind of learning is completely impractical in nearly all schools.

Specialist knowledge

A good grasp of the knowledge necessary to teach the curriculum and subject content is absolutely essential for teachers in the classroom, but not at home. A teacher who wants to give a lesson on volcanoes, for example, has to find out about the subject well before the lesson. By contrast, a parent at home may be perfectly open about the fact that they know very little about volcanoes and they may share in the child's pleasure and excitement as they find out about the subject together.

Children also learn how to learn, the rhetorical aim of all education professionals. Many parents comment on the unexpected bonus that home education has brought to them personally as their own knowledge has been broadened and extended as a result of working with their child. What many parents do have to offer, through their personal experience, is a better understanding of how to learn, to act as a kind of guide.

Lesson time

It's normal for children in school to have lessons all day long and it might appear from this that school is an environment where learning takes place intensively. Surprisingly, education at home turns out to be more intensive than school as most families find that part of the day – usually mornings – spent on formal work is enough. We know that children spend generally less than two-thirds of their time on task (Good et al, 1983). Even then all that we know is that they are doing something; we don't know for certain that they are learning anything. In school a lot of time is spent on non-teaching activities including registration, assembly, organizing the classroom, and dealing with all the interruptions that crop up. Also, in secondary schools, children spend time moving around from one classroom to another.

Informal learning outside lessons

There is little time for planned informal learning in the classroom. At home informal learning is very important and many parents discover this for themselves as they settle in to home education. For children in school, there is also evidence that informal learning at home may contribute to academic progress. Most important may be informal learning through social conversation. A child might describe much of this kind of activity as just chatting with mum or dad. Obviously, at first glance it might seem to be just a pleasant addition to more structured or formal education. However, most parents begin to see that such activities do make a valuable contribution to learning. As time goes by they see that these 'casual activities' are not just a supplement to structured, more formal learning, but they are potentially of equal value, running alongside it. A few parents begin to think that what their children are learning informally, without realising it, could even replace a lot of what they learn during structured sessions. At home children may also learn a lot by following their own interests, playing with their friends, using the computer or helping with shopping, cooking and other household tasks.

Written work

In school, children constantly produce written work as evidence of learning and achievement. At home, written work is far less important, as parents know what stage their child has reached. They point out that it's simply not necessary to write things down in order to learn. Also, just as you are not going to learn much from reading something in which you have little or no interest, there may be no point in writing down anything unless you have something that you want to say. Of course it's necessary to be able to write effectively for various purposes; that's not in question. It's just that the quantity of writing necessary to become a proficient writer is much less.

Individualized teaching

Individualized teaching by a teacher is rarely possible in the classroom and then only with very little time to spend with each pupil. Working closely with a child individually means that you are always aware of the stage that the child has reached in their understanding of a subject. You can help them to advance from that level and you are also able to deal with any difficulties, misunderstandings or errors there and then. Feedback on any exercise is almost instantaneous. Home educated children tend to expect assistance as soon as they need it, and they may grumble if the help is not at hand as speedily as they would wish.

Another aspect of individualized teaching at home is that children have the opportunity to influence the course of learning in a way that would be very difficult at school. When we were in school the first thing most of us learned was to feign attention to what the teacher was saying, often becoming quite expert at it. At home this doesn't work. Because it is one-to-one, parents know immediately when their children stop listening. There's just no point in going on. There is nothing as pointless or unproductive as insisting on teaching someone who is not learning. Yet this inevitably happens in classrooms because children are unlikely to speak up every time they find they do not understand something or are even not interested in what is being taught.

Teaching reading

Perhaps the most significant and fundamental area of learning which differs markedly between school and home is the teaching of reading. In school, reading is taught by teachers who have been trained to teach it but at home it isn't necessary for parents to have had professional training. Parents often worry about teaching this crucial skill to their children but it may be that the amount of individual attention which the child receives is the critical factor for success (Thomas, 1998). Also, children in school generally learn to read with an emphasis on a single method – synthetic phonics currently being in vogue. At home children learn by a variety of methods, maybe including phonics, maybe not, maybe a combination of methods depending on the child. Children in the same family may learn to read in very different ways, according to what seems to work for them.

Both for children at home as well as in school, learning to read may well be facilitated through board and computer games, by children's interests and reading to them. Outside the home there are countless opportunities to practice and improve literacy through reading for a real purpose – bus destinations, street and shop names, shopping and so on. It's just that home educated children are likely to get more of these opportunities. An important aspect of learning to read at home is that parents generally allow children to learn at their own pace whereas at school children are expected to have reached a certain age-related standard by the end of Key Stage 1. At home the age at which children learn to read may differ widely from these norms (Thomas, 1998).

Children at school have very little time for sustained reading during the school day. During the secondary years the demands of homework and coursework also make inroads into the time which is available for personal reading in the evenings. The situation is very different in home education, where many are avid readers. They simply have the time.

Shared learning, group and social activities

Teachers routinely offer many opportunities for children to learn together as a whole class, not only for traditional academic subjects but also to discuss a topical subject of interest, arising from the news for example. There is learning of all kinds in pairs and small groups. There are group activities in drama, sport, music and school assemblies. Children at home do not have such readily available opportunities. They have to be sought out in after school activities, through sporting and drama clubs, or by joining a choir or musical ensemble. Of course not all children will have access to these.

Competition

Some people might argue that competition in school is a necessary preparation for life in the 'real' world. Although school constantly fosters a competitive spirit, the downside is that, by definition, only a few can succeed. When a child is educated at home and they have the opportunity to work at their own pace the question of competitiveness doesn't arise. Not surprisingly, competitiveness is something which virtually never featured in Thomas' study of 100 home educating families (Thomas, 1998). Nevertheless, parents and children are not untouched by living in a competitive society and children will want to succeed when they are older and many will wish to sit public examinations. But it is not necessary for them to compete for years against their peers and to be assessed by way of preparation.

Lastly, it is the social experience in school which contrasts most markedly with the social life of home educated children. There is a general belief that children need to mix with same age children. Most home educating parents would not disagree with this, only in the amount of social contact. While children at home usually have fewer social contacts, especially with children of the same age, they are likely to mix far more with children of all ages and adults they meet socially in home educating groups. There is certainly no evidence to suggest that home educated children, including those who have never experienced school, are in any way socially deprived when they enter formal education or the workforce. On the other hand, some children may feel isolated, especially if they live far away from other home educating families.

Concluding remarks

Clearly, some of the above is not directly applicable to the role of the teaching assistant. Although, looking back at the table, teaching assistants often seem to be positioned between teachers and parents i.e. between home and school. Teachers understandably see the first priority for teaching assistants is to help them teach the national curriculum to all children.

So what might teaching assistants glean from this comparison of home and school to influence both the way they see their roles and how they work on a day-to-day basis? We suggest that teaching assistants have a great deal in common with home educators, most obviously because they often teach individuals or small groups of children. But there is more to it than this. Notwithstanding higher level teaching assistants, most teaching assistants are not professionally qualified to manage the learning and social development of a class of children at the same time. However, they have much more time to develop alternative strategies, to take account of any factors affecting learning and to understand learning difficulties from a pupil's point of view. Also they are better placed to relate to them at a personal level, getting to know children's likes and dislikes, their interests outside school and so on. This is in keeping with the dictum that in order to teach you first have to know the pupil. A teaching assistant can take advantage of a relatively relaxed relationship with a child when it comes to advancing their learning, especially as most of the pupils they work with have encountered difficulties with learning in the classroom.

Another point to consider is that while most home educating parents are not qualified to teach they do have a great deal of life experience to bring to their task. This is something that very many teaching assistants also bring to their jobs.

Finally, in case you think that we have painted a rosy picture of home education, we ought to deal with some of its drawbacks. It is undoubtedly a huge commitment with a massive responsibility. If a child in school is failing and the school has fulfilled all its obligations then the school cannot be held to account. At home, on the other hand, the parent is much more likely to be blamed. The responsible parent, nearly always the mother, has to forgo the personal status and financial benefits associated with being in the paid workforce. Relatives and friends may even be disapproving. All costs of home educating have to be borne by parents. In order to ensure adequate social contact it may be necessary to do a considerable amount of costly car journeys to home education groups and/or to take part in after school activities.

The intention of this chapter has been identify a number of ways in which learning at home is not like learning at school. However, in doing this we feel we have also highlighted areas of similarity and overlap. If teaching assistants and teachers have insights into ways in which parents go about educating their children at home, it is our belief that they stand to increase their understandings about children's learning (see Thomas and Pattison, 2012) and also are very likely to improve their classroom practice.

Author note

To include teaching assistants, this is a revision of a chapter that appears in Educating Your Child at Home by Jane Lowe and Alan Thomas (2002) London, Continuum International Publishing Group.

References

Good, T. (1983). Classroom research: A decade of progress. *Educational Psychologist,* 18, 127–144.

Lowe, J. & Thomas, A. (2002) Educating Your Child at Home. London, Continuum International Publishing Group.

Thomas, A. (1998) Educating Children at Home, London. Continuum International Publishing Group.

Thomas, A. & Pattison, H. (2012) Informal home education: philosophical aspirations put into practice. Journal of Education and Philosophy (in press).

Section 3

Working together

This section explores some of the different ways in which teachers, teaching assistants, and parents work together to support children's learning. Teaching assistants draw on a wide range of skills and experience, knowledge, and understanding in carrying out a range of roles. In Chapter 19, Jackie Marsh, highlights the increasing popularity of virtual worlds with young children and considers the way in which these worlds have been marketed to families as safe places for children to spend their time.

Jenny Houssart worked in the role of a learning support assistant in a number of primary classrooms. In Chapter 20 she describes the knowledge, skills, and understandings that learning support assistants bring to the task of supporting children's mathematical thinking and reflects on the important contribution that their observations can make to children's learning. This insider account considers the interpersonal sensitivities that can exist between teachers and teaching assistants and the extent to which the latter felt free to comment on, or act upon, their classroom observations.

Some teaching assistants are bilingual and speak the languages of children and parents in their schools. They often draw on their knowledge and understanding of other languages and cultures in facilitating the learning of bilingual pupils and home–school relationships. In Chapter 21 Carrie Cable discusses the particular contribution these staff can make to children's learning. In Chapter 22 Lindsey Haynes (with Anna Craft) describes how she works in close collaboration with her class teacher to develop children's creativity through encouraging children to be active participants in their own learning and in the creation of their learning environment.

Home––school relations, and projects to enable productive collaboration between families and schools, feature in Chapter 23 by Anthony Feiler. The four initiatives described provide novel curriculum-related ideas that can, wholly or in part, be replicated by others. In Chapter 24, Rose Schofield writes about the theme of transition between home and schools and, specifically, the experiences of her son James. Although many young children look forward to starting school and the structured and organised world that school is, it is important to remember that some need time and support to become used to this.

The final chapter in this section looks at pupil involvement in their own learning. In Chapter 25, Ruth Dann argues that pupil self-assessment should be an essential component in formative assessment because it will provide valuable insights into children's thinking and understanding and tell us what children consider to be important about their own learning.

Chapter 19

Children's play in online virtual worlds

Jackie Marsh

Children are increasingly attracted to the fun and stimulation that virtual worlds offer them. In this chapter, Jackie Marsh, professor of education at the University of Sheffield, explores the relationship between play and technology and reports on a study that asked 175 children aged 5 to 11 years to complete an online questionnaire. This initial phase was followed up with interviews of 17 children who used virtual worlds.

Introduction

Young children's home lives are becoming increasingly shaped by their engagement with a wide range of new technologies (Marsh et al., 2005; Rideout et al., 2003). Much of this use of technology is playful in nature. Play in this context can be viewed as a phenomenon that, drawing from play theorists such as Broadhead (2004), Pellegrini (1991), Sutton-Smith (1997) and Wood and Attfield (2005) can be defined in numerous ways, but must be seen as an activity which is complex, multi-faceted and context-dependent. The study outlined in this article focused on young children's playful engagement with online virtual worlds. Online virtual worlds are immersive 2D or 3D simulations of persistent space in which users adopt an avatar in order to represent themselves and interact with others. They may or may not include game elements. The study is set within a context in which both the relationship between technology and play and the dynamic between the 'real' and the virtual have been subject to extensive critique.

There have been a number of anxieties expressed in relation to young children's playful engagement with technology for some years. For example, Levin and Rosenquest (2001) suggested that electronic toys posed a threat to children's ability to engage in open-ended, imaginative play. The Alliance for Childhood has promoted a similar negative view of the role of technology

Source: An edited version of Marsh, J. (2010) 'Young children's play in online virtual worlds' *Journal of Early Childhood Research, 8* (23), 23–39.

in early childhood (Cordes and Miller, 2000), arguing that technology does not promote a healthy childhood and is not developmentally appropriate. More recently, similar concerns have been raised in relation to notions of a 'toxic childhood' (Palmer, 2006). Plowman et al. (in press) outline the socio-cultural, cognitive and affective disadvantages that critics suggest are prevalent because of children's use of technology, such as obesity, language delay and social alienation. However, there is a lack of research evidence to suggest that technology leads to these deficits and that play and technology are, therefore, incompatible (Yelland, 1999). In studies of children's use of technology in the home, children's play with technological hardware and software has been identified as being active in nature rather than passive (Marsh et al., 2005; Plowman et al., in press) and children have been identified as gaining a range of benefits from the use of technology, such as technical and operational skills, knowledge and understanding of the world and subject-specific knowledge in areas such as literacy and mathematics (Marsh et al., 2005; Plowman et al., 2008).

A further area of concern in relation to play and technology is the issue of the commercialization of childhood. In much of the discourse surrounding children's use of technology, we can see, as Miller and Rose (1997) depict, the child constructed as the ' "subject of consumption", the individual who is imagined and acted upon by the imperative to consume' (Miller and Rose, 1997: 1). Young children are the targets of commercial advertising from a very young age and their technological playthings are linked to a web of commercialized products. However, the relationship between childhood and consumerism is co-constitutive, and, as Cook suggests, is established well before birth:

> . . . it is important for scholars to be cognizant of the often unexamined assumption that posits children as somehow outside the realm of economic life who are then brought into it either by caring adults, like parents or teachers, or dragged in by media and marketers. That line which divides 'in' from 'out' fades every day as structures of capital help structure the imagining of the worlds into which a child enters well before its post-partum existence.
>
> (Cook, 2008: 236)

Club Penguin™ and Barbie Girls™

Club Penguin™ was developed by the media company New Horizon Interactive in Canada and opened to public use in October 2005 with approximately 25,000 users. In 2007, there were more than 12 million registered accounts and the world was subsequently acquired by Disney Inc. for $350 million. *Club Penguin*™ is currently reported to have 22 million registered accounts.[1] *Barbie Girls*™ was developed by Mattel Inc. and launched in 2007. It currently has approximately 17 million registered accounts.[2] The worlds differ in terms of their affordances, but both *Club Penguin*™ and *Barbie Girls*™ enable children to create and dress-up an avatar, decorate their avatar's home, buy and look after pets and play games in order to earn money to purchase items for their avatars and homes.

The *Club Penguin*™ site is well designed, with strong use of primary colours and stylized features of the landscape (for example, snow, sea, mountains and forests) that are depicted across all areas of the world, thus offering a coherent and well-defined environment. The use of multicoloured penguins as avatars means that cultural representations of identity are not narrowed in the way that they are in other worlds that use human forms, such as *Barbie Girls*™. However artefacts, including clothing and furniture, throughout the world are generally 'Westernized' in nature and there is little to denote cultural heterogeneity.

Barbie Girls™ is a very restrictive world in comparison. Whilst *Club Penguin*™ appeals to both boys and girls, the home page for *Barbie Girls*™ makes it clear that this world is intended for girls only. Representations of femininity are very limited and stereotypical in nature. The range of skin colours that users can choose for their avatars is restricted, as is the range of hairstyles, most of which appear to be more appropriate for Caucasian ethnic groups. The predominant colour used throughout the world is pink and there is a high level of use of pastel shades, a pattern that is often seen in relation to young girls and technology and is a phenomenon I have referred to elsewhere as 'pink technologies' (Marsh, in press). Unlike the environment of *Club Penguin*™, which features shops and buildings within a natural environment, the landscape of *Barbie Girls*™ is that of a shopping mall, with a single park that enables avatars to mingle. The discourse here is similar to that surrounding numerous texts and artefacts aimed at young girls, as Carrington has outlined in her analysis of Bratz dolls (Carrington, 2003). 'Barbie bucks' are easy to earn in a range of games which include painting nails and giving Ken a make-over. Ken is described as 'totally crushworthy', which emphasizes that throughout this hetero-normative world, the 'heterosexual matrix' (Butler, 1990) is writ large.

Commodity purchasing is a key activity in both *Barbie Girls*™ and *Club Penguin*™. Users earn coins by playing games and then are able to spend the coins dressing their avatars and homes. Both virtual worlds offer free membership and an additional layer of paid membership which provides access to additional goods and in-world opportunities. It would appear that just as forms of capital (Bourdieu, 1990) operate in virtual worlds inhabited by adults, such as *Second Life*, the child-orientated worlds are also shaped by social, economic and cultural capital. In addition, the global flows of mediascapes and ideoscapes (Appadurai, 1996) can be seen to permeate the world of sites such as *Barbie Girls*™, which is located within a nexus of commercialized practices that operate across online and offline worlds (Grimes, 2008).

This overview of the virtual worlds offers a review of the key discourses that frame their use. Against this backdrop, I will now explore the nature of young children's play in these online worlds. There is a need to determine the extent to which children's online and offline worlds relate, as many assumptions are made about the relationship between both in critiques of play and technology. The research question addressed in this article is: 'What is the nature of young children's play in online virtual worlds?'

The study

The study was undertaken in a primary school in a large city in England. The school serves a primarily white, working-class community located on a housing estate. An online survey was set up, using 'Google Docs', which asked children a range of questions about their Internet use, including asking children to identify if they used virtual worlds outside of school and, if so, how often. Questions also focused on the nature of children's activities when using virtual worlds, that is, if they shopped, played games, read the in-world texts and chatted to friends. Many of the questions were multiple choice to enable ease of completion. Children were also asked 'What do you like about playing in virtual worlds?', which was an open question. Children were invited to complete the survey when they attended ICT lessons in the IT suite, which each class in the school did twice a week. The IT teacher in the school frequently used online surveys in 'Google Docs' and therefore the practice was not unfamiliar to the children.

A total of 175 children across all year groups (ages 5–11) completed the survey. Thirty-eight children aged between five and seven completed the survey. Some of the younger children were supported in their completion of the online survey in that questions were read out to them when necessary and their responses inputted by an adult, but the majority of children completed the survey independently.

Following the completion of the survey, 10 children aged six and seven and five children aged 10 and 11 took part in a series of group and individual semi-structured interviews. It was explained to the children in these age groups that I wished to ask questions about their use of virtual worlds. Four of the group of six- and seven-year-old children who were interviewed had not completed the online survey because they had been absent from the relevant IT sessions, but indicated at a later date that they used virtual worlds and so joined the interviews. The interviews took place in the school dining room and were digitally recorded, then transcribed. The interviews explored in depth children's activities when using virtual worlds outside of school. The interview data and responses to open questions in the survey were analysed inductively (Strauss, 1987) and emergent themes identified. Children's responses have been anonymized.

In total, 52 per cent of the 175 children aged 5–11 surveyed stated that they used virtual worlds on a regular basis. In this article, I focus on the data from the youngest children, aged five to seven, who stated that they used virtual worlds. The total number of children who reported using virtual worlds in the five to seven age group was 17 (13 of the 38 children in this age group who stated that they used virtual worlds in the online survey (34%), plus four children who had not completed the survey, but took part in the interviews with the group of six- and seven-year-olds). The article therefore reflects on the findings of the survey of 13 pupils and the interviews with all 10 children aged six to seven.

The use of virtual worlds

Twenty-seven of the 38 children aged five to seven who completed the survey were regular users of the Internet at home; 11 reported that they never went online at home (29%). Of the 27 in the survey who used the Internet, 13 reported that they used virtual worlds on a regular basis, six girls and seven boys. Four five-year-olds, three six-year-olds and six seven-year-olds stated that they used virtual worlds in the survey. Of this group of children, nine accessed virtual worlds once a week or more, three used them once or twice a month and one child used them less frequently than once a month.

The choice of worlds for this youngest group appeared to be gendered in nature. Five of the six girls who completed the survey stated that they used *Barbie Girls*™ and none of the boys stated that they used this world. The sixth girl could not remember the name of the world she used, but she said it was 'one with pets on it'. This could include sites such as *Neopets*™ or

Webkinz™, both of which are popular with girls. Five of the boys who completed the survey played on *Club Penguin*™ and two played on *Nicktropolis*. None of the younger girls who completed the survey played on *Club Penguin*™ although one of the girls interviewed, but who had not completed the survey, used the site. Whilst research relating to older users of virtual worlds suggests that people often adopt avatars of a different gender than themselves (Hussain and Griffiths, 2008), this was not the case with these young players, all of whom apart from one stated that their avatars were the same gender as themselves. In their responses to this question, issues relating to border-policing of gendered identities (Thome, 1993) could be discerned, as children expressed the reasons for not wanting differently gendered avatars to be one of aversion. For example, in an interview, Lisa suggested that her avatar was a girl because, '. . . boys are dirty and smelly' (Lisa, aged seven). Unusually, one boy's avatar was a girl and this was because, he explained, his older sister had made him adopt a girl avatar.

Children were asked why they used the virtual worlds. Playing games featured strongly in the responses across both the survey and interviews:

> It's [Club Penguin™] got some ski game. It's really good so I can ride on sleds and it goes really, really fast.
>
> (Leo, aged seven)

> It's all games. I like the games.
>
> (Ewan, aged five)

Games appear to be a major draw for young children in their use of the Internet (Marsh et al., 2005). Indeed, online gaming is not a phenomenon limited to childhood; it is a strong feature of older children and adults' use of the Internet (Livingstone and Bober, 2005). Some researchers have identified a range of learning opportunities related to the use of computer games (Gee, 2003) and there is further research to be undertaken regarding the educational benefits of using games in these online virtual worlds.

Play in virtual worlds

The types of play that children reported engaging in within *Club Penguin*™ included fantasy play, socio-dramatic play, ritualized play, games with rules, and what might be called 'rough and tumble' play, albeit that I am suggesting here a virtual version of offline physical play. I will consider each of these categories in turn.

Fantasy play involves children creating imaginative narratives involving characters and roles that are not necessarily based on 'real-life' examples. *Club Penguin*™ promotes fantasy play through the provision of costumes that enable children to adopt a range of imaginary personas, such as pirates and mermaids. The producers also develop narratives that run across specific time-scales and which invite children into narrative-related play. Each narrative theme involves children collecting special 'pins' that are placed in the virtual world for as long as that narrative runs. This encourages children to keep returning to the site and mirrors the collection-driven play offered by other commercial products such as *Pokémon* and *Beanie Babies*. Children reported collecting pins and dressing in fantasy costumes in order to engage in these narratives, but more frequently referred to socio-dramatic play. Sociodramatic play involves children undertaking play activities based on domestic, everyday practices and involves social interaction. Smilansky's (1968) set of defining characteristics of socio-dramatic play is still influential in the field and consists of the following elements:

- Imitative role play
- Make-believe with objects
- Make-believe with actions and situations
- Interaction
- Verbal communication
- Persistence

Each of these elements existed within children's reports of socio-dramatic play in *Club Penguin*™, although verbal communication was replaced by communication through text-messaging. As in children's sociodramatic play in the offline world, children reported adopting a range of adult roles in the virtual worlds and sometimes drew on adult-focused cultural scripts in this play, as reported in the interviews:

> Me and my friends and my cousins and strangers who come to my party, we all went to the disco room and then when we were all drunk we went back to my house and had a little lay down.
>
> (Brendan, aged seven)

As in the offline world, this kind of play was not always co-operative. For example, Lisa described in her interview how she sometimes behaved when she went to the parties of other penguins:

I like dance around and check if they've been looking after their puffles and if they've got security cameras, I throw snowballs at them and block them.

(Lisa, aged seven)

There was certainly some indication in this study that the relative anonymity offered by the virtual worlds meant that children engaged in behaviour that did not reflect their offline social activities, and this is a matter that needs further exploration. The behaviour reported by Lisa is playful rather than menacing in nature, but other types of anti-social behaviour were reported by older children (such as 'scamming' and stealing passwords). However, the discourse surrounding cyber-bullying is such that there is a need to tread carefully to ensure both that assumptions about patterns of behaviour are not made and that peer-to-peer bullying is recognized and dealt with appropriately (Shariff, 2008).

Children reported engaging in various forms of ritualized play whilst in *Club Penguin*™. For example, Billy stated in his interview that he had learned to demonstrate affection for other penguins by using the heart emoticon:

I like reading messages and falling in love with girl penguins. I have got about five girlfriends. You have to win a loveheart and then you can send them to them.

(Billy, aged seven)

The development of in-world rituals in *Club Penguin*™ is typical of similar online environments aimed at adults. In a study of Massive Multiplayer Online Games (MMOGs), such as *World of Warcraft*, Steinkuehler (2005:12) noted that 'In-game social groups devise rituals and performances . . . and generate in-game antics and adventures' which develop social communities of practice. A range of such rituals and antics can be identified in *Club Penguin*™, some of which are captured for posterity and posted as machinima[3] on YouTube for post-ritual celebration and reiteration of the bonds. For example, a machinima[4] which outlines a 'war' featuring various gangs garnered comments such as the following, which mark membership of a community of practice.

i was in that vid im naruto6168 awsome = D. (narutofreak616)
me was there. (homeofravensrh4755)
awesome! I was there!:) Thats my home server its usualy quiet, then one day it's full, amazing lol. (supposedcp)

cool 1 was there fighting with rpf. (pokemon12d)
same here, i rember dat. i think i was on the gold. (cplpg123)

In this context, ritualistic play serves the function of providing 'social glue' and enables users of virtual worlds to signal online allegiances in the way that such play is often used in offline spaces to cement friendships. Whilst the young children in this study were not recording their ritualistic play and posting this on YouTube, three children who were interviewed did report searching YouTube for *Club Penguin*™ machinima, thus acting as consumers of the recorded play of older children and young people.

For the children in this study, it was clear that the relationship between online and offline play was close and that there were many similarities between them. Primarily, play was a social practice that was constructed through interactions with others; this is the case both in the virtual world and the physical world. Many categories of play remain the same across these spaces. However, there are a number of differences between online and offline play. One key difference is that one does not always know who one is playing with online, although children in this study reported that they arranged to meet friends and relatives online. This correlates with other research, which suggests that older children and young people often interact online with people they know in the offline world (Davies, 2009; Thomas, 2007). A further difference relates to the materiality of the play and the way in which embodiment is related to play online and offline. Whilst children are not physically involved in the play in the virtual world other than the movement of arm, hand and fingers to control the mouse, they are embodied in the play through their avatars and as Karoff and Johansen (2009: 3) suggest is the case with play using Nintendo DS games, 'Simulating actual physical actions, it [play on screen] can be said to cross or at least challenge the borders' between offline and online worlds.

Conclusion

The young children involved in this study demonstrated engagement in a range of play activities that replicated offline practices but that also sometimes enabled interaction distinct to online spaces. The limitations of sample size mean that it is not possible to generalize more broadly from the findings, but patterns identified here were replicated in the larger sample of 175 five- to 11-year-olds. However, my intention was to focus particularly on the data relating to the children in the early years of schooling, for it is this age group that is frequently overlooked in analyses of online social networking. In virtual worlds, children have opportunities to construct, re-construct and perform identities and learn how to engage with others in online forums. Given the extent to which online social networking appears to be a popular activity with older children and young people (Dowdall, 2009), young children's engagement in online virtual worlds might offer useful opportunities to develop skills that will enable them to navigate online environments more safely and appropriately. Nevertheless, the restrictions in relation to gender, 'race' and identity and the commercial aspects of the worlds raise concerns and deserve further consideration by educators so that children's critical stances towards these aspects can be enhanced further. These virtual worlds are fast becoming a part of the online landscape of play for young children and rather than dismiss them as irrelevant, or deride them as potentially harmful environments, academics and educators need to examine their affordances more closely in order to identify what children gain from their playful engagement in these worlds and how their experiences can be built upon in early years settings and schools.

Notes

1   KZero research, reported in February 2009 at: [http://www.kzero.co.uk/blog/?p = 2700].
2   KZero research, reported in February 2009 at: [http://www.kzero.co.uk/blog/?p = 2700].
3   Machinima are films that are made within 2D and 3D worlds, such as computer games and virtual worlds.
4   'Club Penguin™ War' by Fever, posted at: [http://www.youtube.com/watch?v = NLUkm9ZdGSg].

References

Broadhead, P. (2004) *Early Years Play and Learning: Developing Social Skills and Co-operation*. London: Routledge/Falmer.

Butler, J. (1990) *Gender Trouble*. London: Routledge.

Cook, D. (2008) 'The missing child in consumption theory.' *Journal of Consumer Culture* 8: 219–43.

Cordes, C. and Miller, E. (eds) (2000) *Fool's Gold: A Critical Look at Computers in Childhood*. College Park, MD: Alliance for Childhood.

Dowdall, C. (2009) 'The texts of me and the texts of us: improvisation and polished performance in social networking sites', in R. Willett, M. Robinson and J. Marsh (eds) *Play, Creativity and Digital Cultures*. New York: Routledge.

Gee, J.P. (2003) *What Video Games Have to Teach Us about Learning and Literacy*. New York: Palgrave/Macmillan.

Karoff, H. and Johansen, S.L. (2009) 'Materiality, body and practice'. Paper presented at the IDC, 8th International Conference on Interaction Design and Children, Como, Italy, 3–5 June.

Levin, D. and Rosenquest, B. (2001) 'The increasing role of electronic toys in the lives of infants and toddlers: should we be concerned?' *Contemporary Issues in Early Childhood* 2(2): 242–7.

Marsh, J. (in press) 'New literacies, old identities: young girls' experiences of digital literacy at home and school', in C. Jackson, C. Paechter and E. Renolds (eds) *Girls and Education 3–13*. Buckingham: Open University Press.

Marsh, J., Brooks, G., Hughes, J., Ritchie, L. and Roberts, S. (2005) *Digital Beginnings: Young Children's Use of Popular Culture, Media and New Technologies*, Sheffield: University of Sheffield. Available online at: [http://www.digitalbeginings.shef.ac.uk/], accessed 11 June 2006.

Miller, P. and Rose, N. (1997) 'Mobilising the consumer: assembling the subject of consumption'. *Theory, Culture and Society* 14(1): 1–36.

Palmer, S. (2006) *Toxic Childhood*. London: Orion Press.

Pellegrini, A.D. (1991) *Applied Child Study: A Developmental Approach*. Hillsdale, NJ: Erlbaum.

Plowman, L., McPake, J. and Stephen, C. (2008) 'Just picking it up? Young children learning with technology at home'. *Cambridge Journal of Education* 38(3). 303–19.

Plowman, L., McPake, J. and Stephen, C. (in press) 'The technologisation of childhood? Young children and technology in the home'. *Children & Society*.

Shariff, S. (2008) *Cyber-Bullying; Issues and Solutions for the School, the Classroom and the Home*. London: Routledge.

Steinkuehler, C.A. (2005) 'Cognition and literacy in massively multiplayer online games', in D. Leu, J. Coiro, C. Lankshear and K. Knobel (eds) *Handbook of Research on New Literacies*. Mahwah, NJ: Erlbaum. Available online at: [http://labweb. education.wisc. edu/curric606/readings/Steinkuehler2005.pdf], accessed 4 April 2008.

Sutton-Smith, B. (1997) *The Ambiguity of Play*. Cambridge, MA: Harvard University Press.

Thorne, B. (1993) *Gender Play: Girls and Boys in School*. New Brunswick, NJ: Rutgers University Press.

Wood, E. and Attfield, J. (2005) *Play, Learning and the Early Childhood Curriculum*, 2nd edn. London: Paul Chapman.

Yelland, N. (1999) 'Technology as play'. *Early Childhood Education Journal* 26(4): 217–20.

Chapter 20

Supporting and enhancing primary mathematics

Jenny Houssart

To gather material for this chapter, Jenny Houssart, a senior lecturer at the London Institute of Education, worked in the role of teaching assistant in a number of primary classrooms. Her observations show teaching assistants bringing considerable knowledge and expertise to bear as they work with children developing their mathematical thinking. She concludes that the most successful partnerships are those where the teacher values and makes use of the observations teaching assistants make.

Over the past 35 years, I have worked in or visited primary classrooms in a variety of roles: student, teacher, parent, teaching assistant, tutor, researcher and advisory teacher. Each role has its own delights and challenges, but of them all, that of teaching assistant appeared to me to offer the most potential for close observation of individual children and how they respond to activities. The roles I have listed have different statuses too, and although I was made to feel welcome when working as a teaching assistant or unpaid helper, my views were less likely to be sought than when I visited in 'higher status' roles. It is sometimes tempting to take the pessimistic view that assistants hear and see more but are listened to less than other groups, but fortunately this is not always the case. There are classrooms where teaching assistants are able to feed back their observations to teachers and even act on them independently. The case study at the heart of this chapter is an example of such a classroom.

The study is set in the context of mathematics lessons for a small group of children considered to be 'low attainers' in mathematics. Recent research

Source: A revised version of Houssart, J. (2004) 'Supporting and enhancing primary mathematics', commissioned by The Open University for *Primary Teaching Assistants: Curriculum in Context* (London: Routledge). Reprinted by permission of The Open University and Taylor & Francis Ltd.

confirms that it is common for teaching assistants in primary schools to work alongside those children who have the greatest difficulty in mathematics and English (Blatchford et al. 2009). The same research points to the many positive benefits of involving assistants, but questions whether their presence has any positive effects on children's measured attainment, a finding not dissimilar to earlier research focusing on numeracy (Muijs and Reynolds, 2003).

In recent years, there has been an increase in the advice available to teaching assistants to enable them to work effectively in mathematics lessons, focusing on developing both their own mathematical knowledge and understanding and their awareness of appropriate pedagogic strategies (eg Compton et al. 2007). Such skills are important, but still leave assistants with sometimes delicate decisions to make about how they use their knowledge and, in particular, if and when they are allowed to speak up. This is acknowledged by Fox (2003) who suggests that teachers and assistants should establish ground rules for working together and that assistants need to know what authority they have when working in the classroom. The question of the assistant's authority is considered below in more detail where I address the question: 'What interventions are possible and appropriate as a result of what teaching assistants see or hear in a mathematics lesson?' The next section explores some possible scenarios.

What would you do?

The following scenarios are suggested to prompt questions about what an assistant might do in particular situations. Suppose you were working in a primary mathematics lesson, as a teaching assistant, or perhaps as a volunteer assistant and you felt that one of the following was happening:

- A child is struggling with the work being explained by the teacher.
- A particular activity is not working well for several children.
- The work is too easy for one or several of the children.
- The teacher is saying something confusing, or even incorrect.
- The amount of time allowed for a task is inappropriate for some children.

How might you respond to these scenarios? The answer is likely to depend partly on what you would choose to do and partly on what you felt would be accepted by the teacher. Some possibilities for each are:

- Do and say nothing.
- Raise the issue with the teacher tactfully, after the lesson.
- Raise the issue openly when it occurs and in the hearing of the children.
- Take action to deal with the issue without consulting the teacher.

The scenarios suggested may provoke different reactions. These may range from feeling these things only happen in 'bad' classrooms, through an acknowledgement that they can sometimes happen to most people, to the view that they represent the complexities of teaching and learning and are ever present. Another key issue is that all the scenarios hinge on the teaching assistant's opinion of what is happening. How seriously this is taken will depend on how the assistant's view is valued, especially if it potentially contradicts the teacher's view. One approach is that teachers are highly trained experts, so their view is paramount. Certainly the training and knowledge of the assistant is a closely related issue and this varies widely.

However there are other points to consider. First, assistants are in an excellent position to observe individual children, partly because they do not normally have to maintain a teacher's awareness of the whole room, presenting the lesson and considering what changes to make. Second, some assistants work closely with individual children, sometimes across several years. They develop pictures of strengths and difficulties that a teacher might not have.

My experience of working alongside teachers and teaching assistants in mathematics groups containing high proportions of children with special needs, is that very different approaches can be taken to the scenarios listed above. In one classroom, for example, assistants often took no action, though they occasionally shared their observations quietly with each other. The view was that other adults like them were not expected to speak when the teacher was teaching the class. There was also a feeling that making suggestions or pointing out problems, even tactfully and outside the children's hearing, was an unacceptable threat to the teacher's authority. In another classroom, however, assistants commonly raised issues with the teacher as they occurred. They also sometimes discussed issues afterwards, or occasionally took action themselves. In the following section, this classroom is taken as a case study of effective practice.

Case study

The following incidents occurred in a small lower attaining mathematics set in a large primary school. The children were mixed Year 3 and Year 4. All were considered to have special needs in mathematics and some had statements. The teacher was supported by two assistants, Mrs. Taylor and Mrs. Carrington. The latter was assigned to work mainly with one child, James.

I was present at lessons once a week as part of my research into mathematical tasks. I adopted a role similar to that of the assistants, working alongside children as directed by the teacher. When possible, I made notes about children's responses to the tasks. The following incidents from my notes all show that an assistant noticed something about the child's response.

Open discussion

In these incidents the assistants raised issues as they arose and in the teacher's hearing.

Coins in a jar

The children were sitting on the mat, working on counting activities. One activity involved 2p coins being dropped in a glass jar. The children had to close their eyes and count in twos in their heads, using the sound of the coins dropping in the jar. When 12p was dropped in the jar, Neil said it was 22p and Claire said 10p. Most others seemed to get the correct answer.

The next example was 20p. Only three hands went up at the end, two of them offering the correct answer. The next example was 14p. Several incorrect answers were offered, for example 12p, 16p, 22p, 31p. The next example was 18p and this again led to several incorrect answers.

At this point the teacher and Mrs. Taylor started to discuss the activity. They seemed surprised at the difficulty the children had with this compared to similar activities. They talked about the fact that the children did better with numbers up to 10 and concluded that they needed to concentrate on counting in 2s between 10 and 20 in future activities.

The end of the adults' discussion suggests that they were trying to work out on the spot what was proving difficult for the children. Similar short discussions occurred on other occasions, often amounting to a comparison of two activities. One example of this was counting alone rather than as a group. Another was counting in fives starting from a number higher than zero or five. The discussion above also suggests that an idea arose about possible future activities. Incidents where the adults talked about possible next steps occurred in other lessons; sometimes immediate changes were made as a result.

In all the examples above, the adult discussion was about the responses of the group in general to an activity. The example given below concerns an individual child's response.

Spider

The children were on the mat and the teacher was leading an activity using a large hundred square and a plastic spider which she moved around the square. The children started by being asked the number 10 more than the one the spider was on. Later questions included 20 and 30, more and less.

At one point the spider was on 64. The teacher said that his dinner was on '20 more' and the children had to say which number this was. Douglas was asked but said he was not sure and didn't give a number. Other children then answered correctly.

The activity continued with different examples and Mrs. Carrington helped Douglas, who was sitting near her. A little later she told the teacher that she thought Douglas was 'struggling' and asked if he could move nearer to the hundred square so he could touch it. The teacher initially agreed, but then had the idea of giving Douglas a smaller hundred square to work with. She handed the hundred square to Mrs. Carrington, who worked with Douglas on the next examples using it. Neil, who was sitting nearby, also made some use of it.

The next example was 20 less than 55. Douglas continued to have problems. He seemed to moving in ones rather than tens and said to Mrs. Carrington, 'I'm looking at the next door neighbour numbers.' After further examples, Douglas was getting correct answers and was encouraged by Mrs. Carrington to put his hand up and answer.

Looking back at this incident, I wonder whether Mrs. Carrington started watching Douglas when he didn't give an answer to the teacher's earlier question. Because her intervention was immediate, Douglas was given something to help him with subsequent examples. Raising the matter afterwards would not have had this effect. However, provision of the hundred square did not enable Douglas to answer the questions straight away. What it did was to give the adults more information about his difficulty, enabling him to be helped further. After more help and encouragement from Mrs. Carrington, Douglas answered the questions correctly. Provision of the hundred square was also helpful to Neil.

This suggests a particularly significant point of more general use: that what appears to be a difficulty confined to one child may in fact be more widespread in the group. In other words, an 'individual difficulty' reveals a more widespread one.

This incident also suggests shared values between the teacher and Mrs. Carrington in wanting to help the children understand the mathematics, rather than just giving correct answers. A potential problem with this example however is that it involves an individual child's difficulty being discussed very openly. Perhaps for this reason, individuals were sometimes discussed before or after the lesson when the children weren't there – something considered in the next section.

Discussion outside lessons

Before-lesson discussions sometimes arose when the teacher told other adults what was planned for the lesson and speculation followed about possible outcomes and possible changes. Individual rather than apparently 'whole group' problems were more commonly raised in this way. After-lesson discussions occurred when adults informed each other about children they had worked with individually or in small groups, as shown below.

Smartie graphs

The lesson had just finished. The main activity had been to draw a graph of colours from a tube of Smarties. The children had gone to play, taking their Smarties with them. The adults were putting the graphs in the children's folders.

Mrs. Taylor, who had worked on the same table as James, talked about how well he had done today. She said he needed less help than expected with the graph and she thought he really understood what he was doing.

This led to a discussion of James and how much he can do by himself. Mrs. Carrington, who usually works with James, talked about some other incidents. She said that although she was there to work with him, she wanted to encourage his independence rather than sit with him every minute.

The after-lesson discussions lacked the immediate impact of 'on the spot' discussions, but they nevertheless had advantages. One was that there was more time for discussion. Confidentiality was another.

The discussion about James and the Smartie graphs moved on from reporting back on his work to discussing a key issue, that of how assistants assigned to individual children maintain the balance between helping them and encouraging their independence. Major issues were also sometimes discussed as a result of reflecting on how a particular task went, or talking about what would be done next. One such discussion was about how much time should be spent on consolidation and whether children should still be moved forward if they seemed to have difficulties with current work.

Also discussed was the difficulty children had when activities were varied, for example from counting in twos to counting in fives or from adding to subtracting. The teacher and the teaching assistants talked about whether it was legitimate to keep the activity the same in the hope that children might keep getting correct answers. They contrasted this with the hope that children should be able to respond to variations in the task rather than just repeating the same thing. None of these discussions were apparently planned, they arose naturally from a situation where the adults talked openly to each other about the children's responses to the work.

Other issues

In the examples above, assistants suggested changes to the teacher and hence I was aware of their suggestions. It is obviously harder to know whether they made any changes to tasks without saying anything. On the occasions when I worked close to another adult, I sensed that it was considered acceptable to make minor changes according to how the activity was going. Often these were mentioned in casual discussion afterwards.

There were also occasions when assistants suggested that children got pieces of equipment to help them, without asking the teacher. It seemed to be accepted practice for assistants to provide support or extension for tasks, albeit in small ways, without necessarily asking or telling the teacher. Sometimes the issue of time needed for a task arose. There was some flexibility here, with teaching assistants occasionally judging that a child needed more time to complete a task as the others returned to the mat, and this was usually agreed with the teacher.

It will be clear from the incidents above that there was a good working relationship between the adults in the classroom. There was also a certain amount of shared humour, helping to diffuse potentially embarrassing situations. If a mistake was made or an answer forgotten by the adults, one of the others was usually able to step in under the shared joke that we were having a bad day or had forgotten where we were up to.

Discussion

Impact on mathematics

The incidents above suggest that the way this classroom team worked together had some impact on the mathematics. Sometimes the impact was fairly direct and obvious, as in the 'spider' example, where adult intervention enabled Douglas' difficulties to be considered more closely. As a result Douglas succeeded with a task which he had originally not seemed able to do.

Sometimes the effect of intervention was more subtle. In the 'coins in the jar' incident, the combined views of the adults were used to inform decisions about what might be done next. The combined views of the adults were also sometimes used to consider the strengths and difficulties of individuals, usually in discussions outside the lesson. The success of this team in considering and acting on pupil difficulties is notable given that reports have highlighted this as something teachers find it difficult (e.g. OfSTED, 2001) and, more recently, as something likely to be tackled successfully when mathematics teaching is good or outstanding (OfSTED, 2009). The latter report also identifies the provision of appropriate support throughout the lesson from well informed teaching assistants as an aspect of effective practice.

Finally, the climate of open discussion and sharing of views often led the team of adults to reflect on and consider important and complex questions. Issues such as how much help assistants should give children they are assigned to and how much children with learning difficulties should be encouraged to move forward, seemed to flow naturally from discussions about incidents during lessons.

Factors influencing approaches

It is worth speculating a little on the factors that enabled this team to work in the way described. Certainly the teaching assistants had the mathematical knowledge and understanding to make useful contributions. Perhaps more importantly the teacher was aware of this knowledge and understanding and valued it. This may be because she took time to talk to the assistants and got to know their strengths. It is also worth noting that the assistants were involved in numeracy training within the school, meaning that all the teachers had some awareness of the knowledge of the assistants and also meaning that assistants and teachers were likely to share some understanding of issues and approaches.

Matters were helped by the teacher's openness to ideas and by the fact that the adults appeared to get on well socially and to value each other's views and experiences.

Conclusions

The case study outlined above supports the view that children's learning is enhanced if use is made of the observations of teaching assistants. In this case study classroom, an atmosphere had been established where assistants felt free to comment on or act upon their observations. As a result, the adults worked effectively as a team, doing their best to diagnose and act on children's difficulties. Their teamwork was also evident in their discussion of complex issues related to teaching, supporting and assessing pupils with learning difficulties. Assistants' views were not just rhetorically 'valued' by the teacher in an abstract sense, they were welcomed and turned to positive effect to assist learning. This was especially valuable where 'individual' problems were shown to affect many more children, and teaching was consequently improved for the whole class.

My more recent research concerning the views of teaching assistants (Houssart, 2011) confirms that they have a strong sense of the ground rules they operate under. Although many assistants talk of variation between individual teachers, there is also a sense of schools having an overall policy about what is expected. A positive example of this comes from the interview extract below from Jan:

> '. . . as a group of TAs in my school, we're definitely well supported, in the sense that we know what to do, when to do it and we can kind of take it upon ourselves. Like I said, if the kids can't access the work, I'll change it. I'll give them the harder sheet, or I'll take it down a level and they're not expected to necessarily complete the sheets all the time. And the teachers are very understanding, if I go in and say, "You know what, they really struggled with that?" You know? And she's happy for me to revise that the next day rather than move them on. We are quite supported in that sense.'

Jan's quote suggests that this way of working is positive from her point of view and that of her teaching assistant colleagues and she presents it as a form of 'support' for assistants. I would go further and suggest that such an approach is ultimately positive and supportive as far as the children are concerned.

References

Blatchford, P., Bassett, P., Brown, P., Koutsoubou, M., Martin, C., Russell, A. and Webster, R. with Rubie-Davies, C. (2009) *Deployment and Impact of Support Staff in Schools*. Research Report No DCSF-RR148, DCSF Publications.

Compton, A., Fielding, H. and Scott, M. (2007) *Supporting Numeracy: A guide for school support staff*. London: Paul Chapman Publishing.

Fox, G. (2003) *A Handbook for Learning Support Assistants: Teachers and Assistants Working Together (revised edition)*. London: David Fulton.

Houssart, J. (2011) ' "I can be quite intuitive": Teaching Assistants talk about how they support primary mathematics', paper presented to BSRLM conference, 12th March 2011.

Muijs, D. and Reynolds, D. (2003) 'The effectiveness of the use of learning support assistants in improving the mathematics achievement of low achieving pupils in primary school', *Educational Research*, 45(3), 219–230.

OfSTED (2001) *The National Numeracy Strategy: The second year, An evaluation by HMI*. London: Office for Standard in Education.

OfSTED (2009) *Mathematics: understanding the score, improving practice in mathematics teaching at primary level*. London: Ofice for Standards in Education.

Chapter 21

Reflections on bilingual practice

Carrie Cable

The job descriptions for teaching assistants do not always reflect the complexity of their roles. In interviews with Carrie Cable, a senior lecturer at The Open University, three bilingual teaching assistants/instructors reflected on the similarities and differences between their roles and those of monolingual staff. These staff were working in different education authorities in England but shared many similar views on the special contribution they make to children's learning, teachers' understandings and effective home–school relationships. These insights can also help to inform the thinking and work of other staff working with bilingual children.

Supporting bilingual children's language development and learning

Many children begin to learn English when they start school or are in the process of developing their English language skills and ability throughout their primary schooling. They may speak another language at home and be developing literacy in that language supported by their parents or through attendance at complementary schools. Research suggests that it can take between 5 and 8 years for children to learn the English needed to fully engage with subject knowledge learning and the complexities of English language use for different purposes (see Cummins, 2001). Guidance produced by the National Strategies in England (DCSF 2007, DfES 2006) clearly highlights the importance of home languages and the desirability of bilingual support:

Source: A revised version of Cable, C. (2004) 'Reflections on practice: three bilingual teaching assistants/instructors reflect on their roles', commissioned by The Open University for *Primary Teaching Assistants: Curriculum in Context* (London: Routledge). Reprinted by permission of The Open University and Taylor & Francis Ltd.

Bilingualism is an asset, and the first language has a continuing and significant role in identity, learning and the acquisition of additional languages.

(DCSF, 2007:4)

Secure and trusting relationships with a key person are vital to a child's development in all areas. Bilingual support is a highly desirable resource but it has to be accepted that appropriate first language support may not be available for all children in all settings all the time.

(DCSF, 2007:6)

Given the caveat in the last quotation it is important that monolingual practitioners in primary schools learn to draw on the expertise of their bilingual colleagues and children's parents as well as the children themselves to inform their thinking and practice. Learning to listen to and engage with the knowledge and insights of colleagues is an important aspect of continuing professional development. Reflecting on how this can inform planning and deciding how to integrate and utilize this knowledge in practice will enhance practitioner's ability to meet the social, emotional and learning needs of bilingual children. The following reflections are offered as a contribution to this process.

The bilingual teaching assistants/instructors

Surinder works as a bilingual instructor, and as a member of a centralised team of bilingual staff, for a large, mainly rural county where her work involves her in supporting isolated learners in different primary schools on a peripatetic basis. She speaks Punjabi and some Urdu and Gujerati. Margaret worked as a bilingual instructor for a centralised team but was deployed full-time to one primary school with a large number of children learning English as an additional language. She speaks Twi, Ga and some Arabic and was educated and qualified as a teacher in Ghana. Amina is employed full-time as a bilingual assistant by an inner-city primary school. She works across a number of classes spending half a day in each class, mainly supporting literacy and numeracy activities, but also other areas of the curriculum. She speaks Bengali and Sylheti. In semi-structured interviews they reflected on how they utilised their knowledge and understanding of other languages and cultures to support bilingual pupils in their schools.

Utilising their cultural knowledge and understanding

All three bilingual staff felt that knowledge and understanding of the cultural backgrounds of the children and their families was one of the important contributions that they made to the education and care of the children they worked with. They were able to communicate these understandings to teachers and help them gain valuable insights into children's skills and behaviour, especially when they first started school or nursery.

Surinder outlined some of the cultural differences that she felt it was important for teachers to understand, including sleeping, eating and routines.

Surinder: It's quite a norm to wait till the parents go to bed and then turn in. There are few parents who will actually be very firm about it . . . It's much easier, rather than having to coax them, so it's a way children don't cry, you don't want them to cry, so they normally sleep with the parents in their bed. There is a cot but the child is quite good at manipulating, jumping out of the cot – they work that one out at a very young age and milk it to the full . . . They eat later – they eat their meals later – so it's a totally different pattern to life compared to what we traditionally do in the UK, and then people brought up that way, I think, have those life-long habits which they don't see there's anything wrong with because why? It's not wrong, that's the way it has always worked and their children fit into that pattern as well.

Although they acknowledged that practices in different communities varied, they all felt that it was the knowledge that there could be differences which was important, and that their explanations helped monolingual and monocultural staff to better understand parents and children's needs. As well as helping teachers to understand important elements of children's home backgrounds, they also, when necessary, helped parents to become familiar with the customs and practices in UK nurseries and schools. They saw their role as supporting children's social integration, well-being and self-esteem, and fostering their independence so that they would be able to thrive in the nursery or school.

Mediating communication between home and school

All the bilingual staff were involved in working closely with parents, including those parents who did not share one of their other languages. Although many teaching assistants are involved in informal contact with parents at the school gate before and after school; few of them have formal contact or are asked to specifically make contact with parents.

Margaret: When the children come in, I do a home visit, talk to them about their backgrounds – so at first I develop that relationship, that special relationship with the parents from the home. That, you know, brings them to the school and when they come to the school, I take them round the school to familiarise them with the school surroundings and I tell them how the school functions, about the timetable and the things that the children require. Sometimes when the school is on a visit, outing, I make sure, you know, I get one of the parents to come along so they will know more about the school.

As well as having a role in helping parents to understand the educational system, the curriculum and the demands of the school, they were involved in providing workshop sessions about the curriculum for parents. They also talked about the importance of involving parents in the life of the school and inviting them in to share stories or prepare and cook food with the children. Sometimes contact involved 'trouble-shooting' or 'problem-solving'.

Surinder: I had one child who transferred from another school and he had an appalling attendance record. I worked out that one of the days he wouldn't be in school was the day that we went swimming. So I stopped and called the mum one day and said: 'He's missing a lot of school, which means he's missing a lot of lessons, can you find ways of working with me on this one? Is there a problem?' I said to the boy: 'Are you afraid of going under water? How come I wear my swimming costume?' He smiled at me. You say to the child: 'It's fun, don't miss out on swimming.' So he'll go home and say: 'I'd like to swim, can I have my towel?' And then say to his mum that swimming is really good. Maybe mum was thinking he would be wet and he wouldn't dry himself and catch a cold so the day of swimming he didn't go to school. Anyway this mum was absolutely brilliant, she was one hundred per cent supportive. He was really struggling in Year 1 and not getting very far in Year 2, now he's in the top end of the class results. It's the little things you know.

On occasions they were also approached, sometimes confidentially, by parents who wanted to share a concern or obtain information.

Margaret: If there was a problem they would always come to me first, always come to me first – because of my background I understand them better.

They felt more comfortable if they complained to me, that I won't go back and tell the teacher and she won't be angry with the children. And maybe I'll be able to explain it to them in their language better, better to them because I understand them better. In a language they will understand, you know the vocabulary I use, the vocabulary they will understand.

Both Margaret and Amina described how they would attend interviews at the parents' request with staff and parents even though they did not share the parents' first language and the parents spoke some English. They both said that staff also felt that this 'interpreting' role was valuable in communicating with parents. Margaret thought that parents were happy to approach her because, even when they did not share the same first language, there were elements of their backgrounds and experiences that were similar and she was not white and monolingual. Parents, they felt, saw them as people they could trust and as people who would represent their views.

Amina and Surinder, and to a lesser extent, Margaret, were involved in interpreting for parents through the medium of their first language and Amina was also involved in translating some information to be sent home to parents. This was not a major part of her role however, and she felt that drawing parents' attention to and discussing the information that was sent home in English was more helpful for parents and ensured that they understood what was intended. These discussions usually took place informally before and after school. However, they all felt that having bilingual staff wasn't enough on its own for effective communication to take place.

Amina: To be able to do that, you need a couple of things: one of the things you need is support from the school which needs to be quite proactive about it, not to sit on the back burner; two, you need to feel perhaps a certain amount of standing or power to be able to do that, you need to have a certain amount of confidence to say: 'Let's do that.'

They felt that they could communicate with parents – whether or not they spoke the same first language – and represent parents' views. They empathised with parents and wanted the schools to understand and take account of their concerns and perspectives. At the same time they saw themselves firmly as members of the school staff and used the 'language' of school. At times they moved backwards and forward between the two 'languages', but did not find this difficult.

Margaret: Perhaps it's because I understand that English is not the master language; there are other languages through which we can communicate.

Contributing to assessment

All the staff were usually involved in making some kind of assessment of children new to the school. They felt that schools did not automatically seek out this information as part of their procedures and relied on them to do this through informal contacts with parents or with siblings.

Surinder: It means you have to stop at the gate and say can you provide me with information on your child . . . for example, asking siblings about literacy levels, etc.

They were not involved in carrying out assessments in the mother tongue except on an ad hoc basis. Only in instances where the child was perceived to have a difficulty in learning did the possibility of a mother tongue assessment arise and only then in some cases. Cline (1998) has identified clear omissions in guidance relating to the assessment of bilingual children who may have learning difficulties and recommends the involvement of bilingual staff at every stage.

They felt that teachers had a better understanding of the distinction between the needs of children learning English as an additional language and those with a learning difficulty than in the past. However, Surinder said that there were still schools in her area who 'put children on the special needs register'. She spoke of the long-term effects this could have on children's learning and self-esteem when it also meant they were assigned to groups labelled as 'low ability' and provided with inappropriate support.

Surinder: And once you are in there, it's very hard to break away – very, very hard. You have to really fight to bring a child out of SEN [Special Education Needs] and by that point they've usually a few friendships.

Supporting and mediating children's learning

Margaret and Amina spent most of their time supporting children in classroom activities. They usually worked with mixed groups of bilingual and monolingual learners. The nature of Surinder's role meant that she was more inclined to work for short, intensive periods with an individual child once or twice a week. Amina and Margaret were more fully involved in planning and attended after-school planning sessions. Margaret also usually planned her own activities to do with the groups she worked with. Amina worked with groups especially during the designated group times in literacy and mathematics lessons, but she was also involved in working alongside the class teacher – sometimes role switching and sometimes using Bengali with the whole class. They were all involved in feeding back their observations of children's achievements and areas for further development to teachers and for monitoring the progress of the bilingual children they worked with. Supporting children's learning prior to Key Stage 1 and 2 assessments was something they had all been involved in and their help in preparing children for these tests was sought by the schools.

Margaret commented on the importance of the groups that children were in and her role in selecting monolingual children to join her groups who would provide good language role models for children.

Margaret: I always selected a few monolingual children, so as we did the activity they'd pick up the language from their peers . . . children learn more from their peers – it's always better to have a mixed group, especially [for] very confident ones to be with them, and usually they pick up the language from them. It's also easier when they work with their friends, because, you know, they pick up language from their friends.

Socio-cultural perspectives on learning emphasise the social and cultural contexts for learning and the role of adults in supporting learning. The assistants emphasised the importance of drawing on children's knowledge and experience and enabling them to make links with their prior experiences and learning.

Amina described how she would utilise a variety of measuring instruments to introduce children new to UK schooling to measuring activities and ensure that they developed a clear understanding of the concept before using rulers or measuring tapes. She would use Bengali or Sylheti to support children's learning in these situations.

Amina: In other countries, when we are doing measuring, we would use different measuring devices, like the feet, because some of them, you know, might not have seen a ruler or a measuring tape before, you know, they use the palm or the arm and they are familiar more with these devices – so starting from what they know and what they are already aware of makes the lesson more interesting to them.

Margaret described a lesson when she was working with a child who had recently joined the school:

Margaret: There was this lesson on water and I took him and two other friends and I started off on how you use water and I started telling them about my childhood and how we used to go and have our bath in the river, wash our clothes and hang them by the river and these boys started saying: 'Yes.' 'Yes.' 'Yes, back home my mother used to do that, we used to do that.' So after the lesson I told him to make a picture of himself at the riverside and the activities that go on there back home in India. He produced a nice picture, and when I took that picture to the teacher she was really surprised and said: 'Oh this boy has all this in him and he never speaks to me in the class.' She put it on the board. It made that child very proud, and after two terms this boy was among the best three children in the class because of the support he received from the beginning, that got out the confidence in him.

She felt that there were experiences common to people from both an African and Asian background and the fact that she could use examples in her teaching that children would be able to relate to gave them starting points into developing both their linguistic and curriculum knowledge. In the above example she was also acting as an advocate for the child, ensuring that his understanding was communicated to and acknowledged by the teacher.

They were also involved in giving advice with respect to the curriculum. Amina was involved in selecting bilingual resources and in preparing some of these herself. She was in charge of the 'multicultural resources', which included toys, games and musical instruments, and for ensuring that they were available in different classrooms to support role-play, themes and practical activities.

They also all talked about the additional and non-verbal ways of communicating meaning, including drawing, signs, symbolic representations, drama, and role play, as well as gestures, actions and facial expressions. They felt that, because they were used to communicating with other people who did not share their languages, they utilised these devices both consciously and unconsciously in working with children.

A key element of their role was supporting children's learning and language development. However, although they were all committed to children maintaining and developing their skills and competence in their first languages, they did not see this as primarily their role in school.

The importance of bilingual staff

Surinder: My perception of this is they relate to you, you are possibly somebody who is one of them, especially if you are an only child coming into school. It [school] is very much monolingual, very much white – culturally, linguistically, in every way. I think they probably feel a sense of belonging – that's OK. Like saying to this child – I'm going to bring my sense of identity to this; it's normalised something for them. I think that's important.

They felt that constructing a 'normal' experience for children, one in which they could see and have access to people who they could perceive, not necessarily as speaking the same language or coming from the same cultural background as themselves, but who they could perceive as not white and not monolingual, was very important.

Margaret: So long as they know that there is someone else whose language is not only English, you know, but who has a different language or who understands them. Because, usually, if I don't understand the language at all, it is possible they come from a country where we have similarities in doing things – so the fact that there is another person whose first language is not English brings confidence to them, they talk to you.

Concluding thoughts

My aim in talking to these three bilingual teaching assistants/instructors was to find out more about their perceptions of their role and contribution to children's learning. They all felt that they made significant contributions to children's learning that could not be provided by monolingual staff. These were related to fostering the social conditions necessary for learning as well as to supporting language development in the classroom.

The knowledge and understanding of children's cultural backgrounds and home experiences, other languages and parents' concerns enabled these teaching assistants/instructors to facilitate and enhance communication between home and school in ways that would otherwise not have happened, or at least not to the same extent. They acted as 'Funds of Knowledge' (Moll *et al.* 1992) by providing information for staff, mediating communication, and facilitating children's understanding of and engagement with the school curriculum. They also helped to give children a sense of identity through their sense of their own identities as bicultural and bilingual people living and working in the UK.

It is noticeable that it does not always have to be the ability to speak a child or parent's home language that helps to facilitate learning and communication. Developing intercultural understanding and a willingness to engage with other ways of seeing, doing and behaving are also important. As the National Strategies guidance (DCSF 2007) suggests, this approach also connects with views of the child as unique, with building positive relationships and with providing enabling environments. For a further discussion of the benefits of bilingualism and other practical suggestions for supporting bilingual learners first languages and their learning of English see:

Northcote, A. (2010) 'Responding to Linguistic Diversity' in J. Arthur and T. Cremin 2nd edition *Learning to Teach in the Primary School*, London, Routledge

The NALDIC website (naldic.org.uk) also provides a wealth of information and suggestions.

References

Cline, T. (1998) 'The assessment of special educational needs for bilingual children'. *British Journal of Special Education*, 25 (4), 159–63.

Cummins, J. (2001) 2nd edition *Negotiating Identities: Education for Empowerment in a Diverse Society* Los Angeles, Californian Association for Bilingual Education Department for Children, Schools and Families (2007) *Supporting children learning English as an additional language*, London, DCSF also available online at http://education.gov.uk/publications/standard/publicationDetail/Page1/DCSF-00683-2007 (accessed 18 March 2011)

Department for Education and Skills (2006) *Primary National Strategy: Excellence and Enjoyment; Learning and Teaching for Bilingual Children in the Primary Years: Professional Development Materials*, London, DfES also available online from http://education.gov.uk/publications/standard/publicationDetail/Page1/DFES 0013 2006 (accessed 18 March 2011)

Moll, L.C., Amanti, C., Neff, D. and Gonzalez, N. (1992) 'Funds of knowledge for teaching: Using a qualitative approach to connect homes and classrooms'. *Theory into Practice*, 31 (2), 132–41.

Chapter 22

Enabling children's creativity

Lindsey Haynes with Anna Craft

Lindsey Haynes, a teaching assistant, and Anna Craft, a professor of education at The Open University, collaborated in the writing of this chapter. Anna was a researcher with Lindsey and Jean Keene, the class teacher, exploring how they worked together to develop children's creativity and their own creative practice.

I am a full-time teaching assistant in a Reception class at Cunningham Hill Infant School in Hertfordshire, England. There is a close working relationship between all staff and the teaching assistants are encouraged to take a proactive role within the school. All teaching assistants are included in the weekly staff meetings and have the opportunity to contribute ideas. Teachers and teaching assistants also have regular opportunities to plan together: in my case the teacher asks for my suggestions at a very early stage and we develop ideas together.

Each year group has parallel classes and all of them have a full-time teaching assistant. I have my own clearly defined areas of responsibility: helping with administrative functions, ensuring materials are adequately stocked, dealing with injuries, but most importantly I support the teacher and the children in the classroom. I work with the children in all aspects of the curriculum, either with individual children, small groups or on occasion the whole class. I also have regular contact with the parents.

Setting the context for developing our children's creativity

The school does not have its own nursery so the children enter Reception with a wide range of pre-school experience. During the first few weeks the

Source: An edited version of Haynes, L. with Craft, A. (2004) 'Enabling children's creativity', commissioned by The Open University for *Primary Teaching Assistants: Curriculum in Context* (London: Routledge). Reprinted by permission of The Open University and Taylor & Francis Ltd.

class teacher and I introduce the children to each other, the classroom and the school. We go as slowly as necessary at this stage to ensure the children feel safe and begin to gel together as a unit. We set clear and consistent boundaries and have high expectations of the children. We share information and observations throughout the day and in that way are able to adapt quickly to the children's needs and interests. The ability to work in this way has developed during the five years we have worked together. It is from this foundation that we develop the children's creativity, and we do this as a partnership.

From the very beginning the teacher made it clear to the children and their parents that we would both be important to their children's education. At first this seemed somewhat daunting, as I had little experience, but knowing I was trusted was a source of encouragement and as my skills and knowledge of the class routines developed I began to offer suggestions and take on more responsibility for working independently. Working together in this way means that the teacher is able to delegate tasks while retaining overall responsibility, and I am very positive about my role. I feel that this relationship has been made because I work with the same teacher on a full-time basis. Over time, she has learned about how best to use the skills that I have. These include art and craft, listening skills, and the capacity to stimulate and record children's own ideas, both individual and collective. She expects us to share our perceptions of the children's creative learning on a regular basis and offers me opportunities to suggest activities that might extend the children's ideas. I feel highly valued and a vital part of the team in this class and in the school.

The building blocks of creativity in the Reception class

While in Reception the children are taught basic skills and techniques: we see it as essential to make firm foundations. We endeavour to make these sessions as interesting as possible. The children may use flashcards within the classroom or we may go to the library and use the labelling on the shelves. The children count the numbers for lunch each day and find the corresponding figure on a numberline and then we might practice further by playing hopscotch outside. These types of activity are available for the children to choose during child-initiated sessions and the children often report finding a particular number or letter in a new setting.

From only a few weeks into being in the class, we then encourage all children to develop their skills and knowledge creatively, often through a whole class project. Any project of this sort is planned by the teacher with my input. All projects will include cross–curricular elements, with a clear set of learning objectives, which include developing children's creativity. We aim to develop the children's ability to:

- ask questions
- make connections
- envisage what might be
- explore options
- reflect critically.

These are the five areas of the creativity framework originally developed by the Qualifications and Curriculum Authority (QCA 2005a, 2005b). On the basis of the way that we work on creativity, we were chosen by QCA to be one of five focus classrooms for a training video made for other practitioners, produced in 2005.

Each of these creative processes are developed across the physical space – indoors and outdoors – as well as right across the curriculum. The children's own ideas inform the ways that we develop and engage with our learning environment. The display boards are often used for large interactive displays deeply influenced by the children, and very much 'owned' by them, whilst the role-play area has, again at the children's suggestion, been converted into many things including a café, a castle and a ferry. The outdoor classroom has housed a garage and a film studio. The children suggest ways that we might develop a particular part of the classroom, and together we make the transformation. The children have ownership and control over how they develop play in these areas, and we encourage diversity in both what they do and how they reflect on it later, encouraging children to give each other feedback.

This type of work may take days to complete and will be used for several weeks so it is important that alterations can be made to extend the children's learning.

So how exactly do we get the children to share their ideas, and how do we facilitate the expression of these in our classroom? Many of our class projects are focused through the collaborative construction of interactive displays, which involve many ideas proposed and developed by the children. These displays then become a learning resource for them to use and play with at many points in each day. The displays form such an important part of the way we work that when our new intake joins us in September we always retain some displays made by the previous year group, for the new children to play with, learn from and, hopefully, be inspired by. We feel that making and using interactive displays stimulates children's curiosity and creativity and this is what I will focus on in the rest of this chapter.

Developing creativity through the use of display

Asking questions, making connections

We try to engage in creative practice throughout any project, as well as nurturing the children's creativity. We encourage the children to generate both questions and connections, right at the start.

Each new project is introduced by the teacher to the whole class, and a theme is suggested for the display which will symbolise the project.

Everybody is encouraged to offer ideas for both the project and the display, which may include what they know already, and also suggestions for what we could find out next, and what we might proceed together with for the project. All of the ideas are valued and recorded.

I take part in this introductory session by supporting children who have specific needs. We feel that it is important to be seen to value all the ideas as this encourages the children to think creatively rather than being restricted to ideas they think will be accepted. So, by arrangement with the class teacher, I often sit close to children who might otherwise be shy of suggesting their ideas in the whole class group, and I can either voice ideas that the children may share with me, or encourage such children to talk to the whole class themselves about their idea.

Figure 22.1 Listening carefully to children and giving them time to think is an important part of creative practice.

Once the class has had a go at generating some initial ideas, I will then work with small, mixed-ability groups to discuss ideas for the project in more detail. I encourage them to think about how their knowledge and skills can be used, I help them plan achievable targets and I ensure that the equipment they require is available.

A recent project and display were based upon a discussion of 'the seasons'. The teacher had encouraged the children to consider how our display might include the changes that occur in the natural environment during the autumn and to watch how this changed over time. Straight after the whole-class discussion, we took the class outside to look at the changes as they were occurring. The children collected leaves, seeds and berries. They studied the hedge very closely and when we returned to the classroom the children themselves began, excitedly, to explore the possibility of this forming the basis of the display. They generated ideas about the background to their autumn scene, ways that they could represent the hedge itself, as well as objects that they could show in, under, next to and above it.

Listening carefully to the children's enthusiasm for their hedge idea, the children chose which aspect of the display to work on. Having decided as a whole class that paint was their chosen medium, I supported the children in making the display. I encouraged each group to focus on the colours and shapes of the objects they wanted to represent.

Some of the groups chose to paint large sections of the hedge, while others painted individual fruits and seeds. At one stage there was a long discussion about the difference in colour between a blackberry and an elderberry. We had purple available to use but one child asked if we could make a new colour, as the berries were 'not the same sort of purple'. All of the group then studied the fruit more closely and decided the elderberries were a much darker colour. I was then able to use this opportunity to show the children how to mix colours, encouraging them to explore the possibilities. We are very aware that although we are encouraging the children to have and express ideas, we need to build their knowledge and skill all the time, and this will mean that some sessions will be adult-led – in this case mixing colours – but the children are always given the opportunity to return to an activity and explore further themselves. The work that is produced during these independent sessions is used to inform future planning. In this case I reminded subsequent groups of the need to look very closely before they started their pictures, they responded by including the red colour on the elderberry stems and different shades on the leaves.

Envisaging what might be, exploring options and reflecting critically

Imagining possibilities, taking ideas further and reflecting on these are all integral to our class practice in developing creativity through our projects.

In this case, the children, who were in their first term in Reception, drew on their previous knowledge and skills, to develop the display further over the weeks that followed. They often brought objects from home.

The first change was the addition of leaves, nuts and berries they found. One child brought a sweet chestnut in its case. She thought that it looked like a hedgehog and asked me if she could stick on some berries to make eyes. 'Henry', as our hedgehog become known, stimulated a great deal of class discussion: What did he eat? Where did he live? What other animals might live in the hedge? Such questions arose in all kinds of interactions, including when the class were sitting together on the carpet. During different lessons and using resources such as our class and school library, and the Internet, children were encouraged to research their questions.

Eventually a house for Henry was added along with mice, birds, badgers, insects and their homes. The house was made by covering a box with natural materials, grass, leaves, etc. The insects were drawn using a computer package; the mice and owls were made using collage.

Through the representation of an autumn scene, the children were learning about animals, their habitats, the changes that occur and some of the reasons for these. They were also developing early research skills and improving their mouse control skills. Individuals and groups then shared their learning with the whole class, giving us the opportunity to celebrate their achievements.

My role in supporting and enabling the interactive displays

We feel strongly that creativity should be at the heart of teaching and learning in our classroom. This means motivating the children to feel what they are doing has both relevance to them and can be shaped by them. Therefore it is important to us that the ideas for any project should come from the children.

My role is to listen and by asking questions encourage them to explore these ideas within the broad framework, which is suggested by the class teacher, rather than offer my own. I try to ask questions that allow the children to move forward themselves. During the hedgerow discussion the animal theme became extremely popular and ideas ranged from owls to zebras. I then asked the children to think about where these animals lived and together we refined their choice to the animals that may actually be found in that environment. I want the children to learn to share their own ideas and by opening a discussion allow them the space to reflect on these to refine their ideas.

The time spent with the children at this stage is extremely important as it is their opportunity to envisage what might be and with my support work out which materials and techniques they will need to bring their ideas to fruition. We feel that resources are vital. We have a cupboard full of collected and found objects as well as standard art and craft materials, which support our work on interactive displays. Although I always provide a range of materials to start a project as soon as the ideas have crystallised, I allow time to enable the children and myself to collect any additional material that we may need.

The displays are a tool for the children to use independently and as such I need to ensure that they are accessible, robust and wherever possible interactive. The children are shown how to use the display; for example, the animals in the autumn project were all free standing. The children were able to move them within the display and then to other areas in the classroom making links and extending their learning through play. In this display, the children were able to weave long 'leaves' in and out of the static and three-dimensional leaves of the hedge. The children returned to this display for many weeks during their free choice time. The interest in Henry continued for the whole year, and he became part of several subsequent displays, having a holiday home in a display based on the nursery rhyme, 'One, two, three, four, five, Once I caught a fish alive'.

As the children begin to work with an interactive display they often come up with new ideas to extend it. Part of my role is to be available and listen to these while the ideas are fresh in their minds and plan a time for the children to make the necessary changes. The ability to be flexible and to develop a project in line with the children's interests is something that is encouraged throughout the school. However it is made possible by the teaching of basic skills and by developing the children's ability to work independently. As the children's confidence grows they are more willing to offer ideas and are able to support them. When the autumn project took place the children were new to the class and the school and were only just beginning to make sense of this new environment. The framework for this type of work is still decided by the teacher but with each subsequent project their involvement grows. In a display later in the year the children were asked to think how we might record our memories of the school year. Most of the children wanted to offer suggestions and the most popular was a memory quilt. They wanted it to be made of material like a patchwork quilt. I worked with this and found material and fabric pens, which the children used to record the things they had enjoyed the most during the year. I joined the pieces together and then the children helped to display it. The children want to be involved in all aspects of a display and enjoy sharing their knowledge with others in the class and visitors, parents, etc.

As the children move through Reception their ability to think creatively and to make links across the curriculum, coupled with a grasp of new techniques, allows quite complex displays to be undertaken. The children have increasing ownership over this complexity, being encouraged to consider how the display might be used, its aesthetic dimensions, as well as its robustness. I will be told where to put particular items in a display, be asked to move things if they are insufficiently accessible and recently was asked not to cut out as this was something that they could do for themselves!

Valuing creativity in the classroom and school

I really enjoy working in reception and being allowed to take such an active part in the class is very satisfying. I am fortunate to work in a school where class teachers and their assistants work as a team, where the role of the teaching assistant is valued and where thinking and working creatively is promoted.

Creativity in our class is developed through all parts of the curriculum, but in this chapter I have focused on demonstrating how the creative process is modelled and supported through concrete, often art-and-craft-based activity, while acknowledging that creativity is much broader than art. My role in the creative process is to act as facilitator, to help the children use the basic skills that they are taught to make connections and envisage what might be.

I have the time, which is not always available to the teacher, to listen when it is convenient to the child. I talk to the children, ask questions and encourage them in their thinking, making choices and connections. The skills I need and use during the making of a display are equally valuable throughout all activities.

Chapter 23

Successful home-school projects

Anthony Feiler

Anthony Feiler is reader in education (special educational needs) at the University of Bristol. In this chapter, taken from his book on parental engagement, he examines four home-school projects that are deemed successful. These are: 'The Letterbox club' for looked after children and foster parents in the Leicester area; 'Drop in for coffee' for parents in the North Perth area of Scotland; the 'INSPIRE' project involving Birmingham parents in reading and mathematics; and 'The home-school knowledge exchange' project for families in the Bristol area. All of these initiatives have antecedent projects dating back to the 1970s but the chapter helps show how such projects can be revisited in order to make them more appropriate for current parental needs.

Introduction

The approaches presented here have been selected for a number of reasons. The design and focus of these approaches make them particularly relevant for schools working with harder to reach parents. This may be due to the fact that the projects were developed in areas characterized by poverty, where there exist various constraints on families that make it more difficult for parents to liaise closely with teachers. These approaches include examples where non–deficit approaches to involving parents were deliberately adopted and where schools recognized that families had much to offer their children. They also included forms of adaptation on the part of staff, where schools recognized the needs of families and made adjustments to accommodate such needs. The initiatives each contain features that can be readily taken on by staff, or adapted and developed so that they fit a range of different contexts and different situations. The projects used inventive, imaginative approaches to parental involvement where ingenuity and sensitivity mattered more than large amounts of funding.

Source: An edited version of Feiler, A. (2010) 'Successful projects in the United Kingdom', in A. Feiler *Engaging 'Hard to Reach' Parents* (Chichester: Wiley-Blackwell) pp. 81–99.

The Letterbox Club

The government report *Care Matters* (Department for Education and Skills, 2006) presents a worrying account of the poor progress made by many children in care at school: stark differences in achievement exist at all ages, and at the age of 15–16 years the proportion of looked-after children attaining good GCSEs in 2005 was five times less than other children. The long-term outcomes are equally worrisome: children who have been in care are less likely than other young people to be in training after the age of 16, and are more likely to become teenage parents, unemployed, drug users and imprisoned.

Approximately two-thirds of looked-after children live with foster parents, and the remainder mostly live in children's homes or with their parents whilst being the subject of a care order. Foster parents can play an immensely important role in supporting the education of children in care. The *Letterbox Club* presents a practical approach for improving educational outcomes for children aged 7–11 who are looked after by foster families. This scheme was instigated by Rose Griffiths at the University of Leicester's School of Education and is managed by Booktrust (www.booktrust.org.uk).

During the early stages of this initiative, a pilot project was developed for children in foster care attending four schools. One of the pioneering approaches used in this creative scheme was to supply resources direct to children. This decision was taken because it emerged from interviews with a sample group of foster carers, before the start of the project, that although some of the foster carers welcomed the option of helping their foster children at home with reading or mathematics, others were less enthusiastic. Some foster parents expressed a lack of confidence about their role in supporting children's learning or anticipated that the children would not be motivated to participate. So it was agreed that books and other materials would be sent straight to the children by post in personally addressed packages, and the children were free to decide whether to use them and whether or not to share them with others in the foster home. There was no expectation that foster parents had to be involved. The goal of the project was to improve the children's attitude and attainment in literacy and numeracy; in addition, the scheme aimed to increase the children's foster parents' confidence in helping learn at home.

Before the *Letterbox Club* project started, one foster parent expressed reservations about children receiving posted materials as this might result in one of her foster children receiving letters from members of his family who were prohibited from making contact. So the materials were sent in red envelopes with 'Letterbox Club' stickers on them. During the initial stages of the project, each parcel contained one or two books (fiction, poetry or non-fiction), a mathematics activity and any necessary stationery items for tackling these activities such as scissors or glue. The packages were sent once a month for 6 months. In each packet, there was also a letter personally addressed to the child. The children's attainment in reading and mathematics was assessed at the start of the project, and the books and mathematics activities that were subsequently sent were chosen according to the children's age and level of achievement. One of the parcels contained an audio to accompany a storybook, and this proved to be very popular. Mathematics games were also well liked, as were the sheets of personalized name labels with the message, 'This book belongs to . . .', and the child's name inserted.

In terms of outcomes, 20 children aged 7–11 and their foster parents and teachers participated in a pilot evaluation of this scheme. For the nine children who were still at primary school at the end of the pilot phase, five of the children made better progress with reading than they had previously (three of the children made gains in their reading ages of 14, 16 and 18 months). Six of the nine children showed improvements in mathematics. Several children referred to the significance of opening a personally addressed *Letterbox Club* package, commenting that it was the first time they had ever received a letter or parcel.

A number of minor difficulties were noted by the author of this project. None of the children joined the local library, even though library membership forms and leaflets were included in three of the six parcels. Griffiths suggests that for future work it may be worthwhile sending children a library ticket (not just a library form) and information about specific library events. It also proved difficult to find suitable books and other materials that matched the children's interest and attainment levels.

'Drop in for Coffee'

The notion of schools offering a broader range of services to families evolved in the United States during the early 1980s and was initiated in response to educational underachievement in disadvantaged areas (The Scottish Office, 1998). This development recognizes that services need to adopt more holistic approaches in providing support for children and young people's educational, social, emotional and physical needs, and that schools cannot solve the problems associated with social exclusion and deprivation on their own (Wilkin et al., 2003). Karayiannis (2006) points out that the concept of school as a community resource is becoming increasingly acceptable internationally: like 'Full Service Schools' in the United States, Sweden has 'Open' schools, and Canada has 'School Plus'. The UK government is currently encouraging schools to become more extended in order to build stronger relationships with parents and the wider community (Department for Education and Skills, 2004, 2007). Dyson and Robson (1999) propose that schools that offer more extended services to families and the community should function as a resource for the community rather than viewing the community as a resource to the school. They also propose that in responding to the needs of the community, staff need to see this role as the core purpose of the school, not 'as a distraction'.

One such example is an inspiring project – the *Drop in for Coffee* scheme – described by Illsley and Redford (2005). One of the key aims of Integrated Community Schools in Scotland is to enhance engagement with families and the wider community. The *Drop in for Coffee* scheme was developed in a group of Scotland's Integrated Community Schools and centres in North Perth, and the key aspects are listed below:

- Parents were invited to 'drop in' for coffee in pre-school, primary and secondary schools.
- The initial approaches and invitations to parents (e.g. by teachers or community learning workers) were deliberately informal and were made in playgrounds, when parents dropped off their children at schools/nurseries, or during parents' evenings. Illsley and Redford (2005) report that when one of the mothers was approached about joining this project she commented, 'I don't do groups, but I'll come for a quick coffee.' This mother remained with the project for 3 years and has since addressed conferences about the impact the coffee groups made on her life.
- The numbers in the *Drop in for Coffee* groups (usually mothers) varied from 6 to 12, with creche provision for four to six young children or babies.
- The groups decided on their own programme of activities and these included art and crafts, healthy cooking and inviting head teachers to discuss issues such as secondary transfer.
- Subsequent groups (*Coffee Too* and *Coffee Extra*) supported further personal development amongst the parents including computer skills, literacy and numeracy, and creative writing. Various accredited certificate courses were offered – the majority of parents who originally

'dropped in' subsequently progressed to adult education, volunteering or family learning opportunities.

• All the groups were held in schools, nurseries or children's service centres (typically where education, social work and health services are brought together on one site). The authors note: 'The informality of the groups has contributed to the development of the shared space. School staff often took the opportunity to come into a *Drop in for Coffee* group to say hello to parents, taste any food made, admire crafts produced or simply have a coffee or a piece of fruit' (Illsley and Redford, 2005, p. 164).

In an (unpublished) evaluation of this project, a head teacher observed that parents were more willing to speak with her because she participated in the *Drop in for Coffee* group, whereas previously they had hardly lifted their heads when they saw her approaching (Humphris, 2004, cited in Illsley and Redford, 2005). It is likely that the informality of the *Drop in for Coffee* groups contributed to parental engagement, helping to put families at ease and to overcome feelings of apprehension. The authors emphasize that many parents had negative experiences when they themselves attended school, had not achieved academic success and had no formal qualifications.

The project demonstrates a thoughtful approach to involving parents, offering support to families in a highly sensitive manner that was deliberately designed to avoid embarrassment or discomfort. It offered parents the opportunity to extend their range of knowledge and skills and brought together professionals from a range of agencies. Tett (2005) notes that Integrated Community Schools in Scotland have concentrated particularly on socially excluded families, who experience a range of difficulties including poverty, poor housing and health and low educational attainment. Such difficulties can present severe challenges not only to the families but also to teachers and other professionals who offer support. An important aspect of the work of Integrated Community Schools is that school staff are not expected to undertake this work in isolation. Tett (2005) emphasizes that one of the strengths of working in this way is that no single agency is left to respond to the complex range of difficulties such families face.

Involving parents in reading and mathematics

Beryl Bateson (2000) presents an engaging overview of the INSPIRE initiative (involving school parents in reading and mathematics). The scale of this project marks it out from many other parental involvement initiatives: INSPIRE was developed across the 370 primary and nursery schools in Birmingham, and was aimed at involving all parents, rather than being targeted at specific groups judged to be in need of help.

Strong support for INSPIRE was provided by Birmingham Local Authority. This backing had its roots in an earlier Local Authority focus on adult learning. It was recognized within the authority that those with low levels of basic skills in literacy and numeracy were more likely to experience social exclusion and to be unemployed or employed in low-paid unskilled jobs, and were more likely to be homeless or to offend. In order to improve levels of literacy and numeracy in Birmingham, the Core Skills Development Partnership (www.coreskills.co.uk) was formed in 1996. It consisted of various city council departments and voluntary services as well as the national Basic Skills Agency. The aim of this initiative was to improve literacy and numeracy skills across all communities and age groups in Birmingham. A key goal was to engage parents and families in literacy and numeracy learning. This gave an important boost to the development of the INSPIRE programme with its focus on families with children attending primary schools.

Staff working on the INSPIRE scheme recognized that negative judgements and assumptions can prevail about what parents can offer. The INSPIRE project aimed to change the beliefs and attitudes of teachers and other professionals working with parents, as well as parents themselves, in order to raise expectations:

Research quotation

'Many acknowledged that parents often do not have the confidence to be involved in school or to help in their children's education; that they may have had bad experiences in education themselves; that they may not have had access to knowledge on how to be involved or that they needed their information to be updated; and that not all teachers or all schools make it easy for them to be involved. These barriers run alongside practical difficulties such as no available accommodation in school, little non-contact time for teachers, no child-care facilities for younger siblings and, with some families, no common language with which to communicate. And so we had to INSPIRE school staff that involving parents really could make a difference and it really is worth making this a priority . . . Teachers in turn had to INSPIRE parents and families about the value of what is done or can be done at home that supports the child's learning.'

(Bateson, 2000, p. 56)

The challenge for INSPIRE workers was to convince staff working in schools that parents from a range of social and cultural backgrounds could be productively involved in education and that this would have a significant impact on children's learning. Similarly, those who devised this scheme set out to convince and inspire parents that they could be constructively involved with their child's learning, see Bateson (2000).

It is worth noting that schools are not given prescribed lessons or materials to deliver, and the focus of workshops is not seen as training for parents:

Research quotation

'INSPIRE is offered purely as an opportunity for parents/carers to work with their child alongside the teachers and be involved in activities that support their child. This is what we believe parents really do want.'

(Bateson, 2000, p. 56)

Birmingham has many deprived areas with relatively large numbers of black and minority ethnic groups whose first language is not English. INSPIRE included not only those parents who were from more affluent areas of the city but also those from disadvantaged areas whose involvement with the school had not been extensive – parents who had not traditionally been strongly involved in education. Evaluation data indicate strong support from staff and parents, and the scheme was successful in attracting very high numbers of families across the city of Birmingham. INSPIRE developed links with a wide range of organizations providing services to families in hostels and refuges:

Research quotation

'These developments [INSPIRE] have recently been extended to include support for families in hostels and refuges. In the first six months a total of 156 parents and 204 children in 12 hostels have worked through a mix of workshops, short courses and book sharing sessions . . . The activities are supported by book loans within the hostels and encouragement for families to use the local libraries.'

(www.coreskills.co.uk)

The INSPIRE framework is applicable to schools in a wide range of contexts, and as the approach is strongly rooted in the National

Curriculum, it does not undermine teachers' main priority – their pupils' learning. The uncomplicated structure of this practical model renders its approach both flexible and robust. It should be noted that despite INSPIRE's straightforwardness it is a model underpinned by carefully considered and well thought-through principles such as giving children an empowering role in choosing who to invite to school and using activity-based learning to give parents and others access to the curriculum.

The Home-School Knowledge Exchange project

The Home-School Knowledge Exchange (HSKE) project was carried out between 2001 and 2005 by staff based mainly at the Graduate School of Education, University of Bristol. It was funded by the Economic and Social Research Council, and directed by Professor Martin Hughes. The author was a member of the research team that conducted this work; part of the work has been described in *Improving Primary Literacy: Linking Home and School* (Feiler et al., 2007). The account that follows has been taken from Feiler et al. (2006, 2008).

The HSKE project was based on the following supposition: parents and teachers have knowledge that is relevant to enhancing children's learning and this knowledge is often poorly communicated and under-utilized. Interventions involving parents may fail to recognize the skills and the approaches that they adopt and can result in school values and practices being imposed on less advantaged families (Hughes and Pollard, 2006). A key principle that influenced the design and implementation of the HSKE project was the desire to recognize and build on existing home practices, helping schools to become more sensitive to families' social capital and fostering links through the development of bridging mechanisms between families and teachers. The work of Luis Moll and other researchers (Moll et al., 1992) suggests that all families possess extensive 'funds of knowledge', including those who live in deprived or disadvantaged circumstances. The HKSE project aimed to develop knowledge exchange activities that would enable parents to make a valued and significant contribution to their children's learning, based on their funds of knowledge. This might include knowledge of how their children approach learning, what motivates them, what children know and what they would like to find out about. The corollary to the recognition that families have 'funds of knowledge' is that teachers too have a wealth of knowledge about the range of subjects that comprise the curriculum and about children's learning at school. Although teachers know a great deal about pedagogy and the content of the curriculum, they may know little about children's out-of-school worlds. Similarly, although parents know much about children's home interests, their skills and what they find exciting, they may know little about the content and teaching of curriculum subjects such as literacy and mathematics. The core goal of the HSKE project was to enable teachers and parents to pool their funds of knowledge in order to enhance children's learning.

There were three 'strands' of the HSKE project:

- Developing literacy at Key Stage 1 (children aged 5–7 years).
- Developing numeracy at Key Stage 2 (children aged 7–11 years).
- Facilitating transfer between primary and secondary schools (children aged 11–12 years).

Within each of the three 'strands', researchers on the HSKE project worked in four primary schools – two in Bristol and two in Cardiff – developing, implementing and evaluating a range of knowledge exchange activities. The discussion below has been taken from Feiler et al., (2006).

Using video to communicate with parents

There is a tendency for teachers to communicate with families in writing. However, using print to communicate can prove problematic for some parents, as one mother in the HSKE project indicated: 'I didn't [learn to read] until I was 11, I have to say . . . we used to do the Peter and Jane books and I used to take them home and my sister used to read them to me and I used to memorize them, so that's how they never picked up that I couldn't read . . . but there you go, I can now.'

Even where parents are able to read English, they may be disinclined to access information through this medium. One parent who participated in the HSKE project, who acquired English reading skills late, explained how she used the social network of parents waiting in the playground to determine the content of letters: 'when I go up to school there's usually a few of us and we all talk, "Okay, did anybody read that letter? Can somebody translate, so I don't have to read it?" . . . and then they put the input, "Well I think it's about" and I go, "Okay then", and off I go.'

In order to avoid an over-reliance on the written word, alternative strategies were developed for communicating with parents. A prime example was the use of video. At the start of the HSKE project, parents had expressed a desire to know more about the ways their children were taught in school. Videos were made of literacy lessons in all four of the schools, and of mathematics teaching approaches in two of the schools. Copies of the video were made for each family in case parents were unable to attend the school-based screenings that were arranged. The individual copies were accompanied by a booklet which included aspects the teacher wanted to highlight and ideas for helping children at home.

The highest turnouts for the video screenings (with around three-quarters of parents attending) were at the schools with lower proportions of children eligible for free school meals. One of these schools provided the only evening viewing. It was very well attended and included several fathers. The teacher at this school was surprised by the high turnout and also by which parents came (i.e. parents of a number of lower achieving children). At one school, in addition to sending out written invitations, the class teacher personally invited parents to the screenings during the course of parents' evenings. At the two schools where literacy activities were developed and where there were higher proportions of children eligible for free school meals, slightly less than one-half of parents attended one school-based screening, whilst less than one-third of parents came to the other. These numbers point up the importance of making the video available for viewing at home.

Whilst the literacy videos were edited versions of complete lessons, a different format was used for the numeracy videos. There was a focus on procedures for carrying out calculations and this was a response to the sense of deskilling that parents expressed, which resulted from the use of teaching methods that differed from those used in their own education either in the United Kingdom or in other countries. Two of the mothers commented: 'What confuses me is that they do their calculations slightly different to how we were taught to do them . . . I try and show her my way and she says, "Oh, you don't know what you're doing." And I give her answer with my own way, and then . . . we does it like a big way, difficult way, and she'll say, "Oh mum, like this way is easier" . . . I wish I went to school here, but I didn't.'

Building on home knowledge – using disposable cameras

There are varied reasons why participation in activities located at school may be difficult for some parents. In addition to language differences, parents may have family responsibilities such as caring for younger children or elderly family members, working hours that coincide with the school day, illness or transport difficulties. Sending video material home may help to overcome some of these barriers. However, it has been argued that focusing on school learning alone can be marginalizing since it excludes children's out-of-school experiences (Caddell et al., 2000).

The HSKE researchers sought to promote the exchange of knowledge between home and school as a two-way process, that is, knowledge flowing from home to school as well as from school to home. They were keen to explore strategies for bringing children's out-of-school worlds into the classroom. Photographs were used as a medium for tackling this, and children were given disposable cameras to use at home over a holiday period. They were asked to take photographs relating to class topics on making a model vehicle, living things, plants and growth and the local environment. Most parents helped their children at home with the photography.

In two of the schools (both with higher proportions of children eligible for free school meals), parents were invited to the school to help the children make a book from captioned photographs. Older siblings were also invited to join these sessions. In both schools, about half the children were supported in class by parents. Since they knew the provenance of the photos and the circumstances in which they were taken, parents developed specialist knowledge and were able to help the children express the meaning of the pictures as well as helping out with the practicalities.

Displaying children's work away from the school location

Some parents can experience feelings of insecurity and discomfort just because of being in a school; such feelings can result from negative experiences they had during their own school days (Whalley, 2001). In one of the HSKE project schools (with higher proportions of children eligible for free school meals), an exhibition of children's work was deliberately displayed away from the school site in a nearby supermarket used by many of the parents. The exhibition included photographs of previous project activities, for example photos of parents and siblings helping to make books from photographs taken at home, and explanations of the activities and other information were provided for parents. The class video of the literacy lesson was also played continuously.

The exhibition was open from 8 a.m. to about 6 p.m. on two consecutive days. Colourful invitations to the exhibition were sent out, which included a voucher for a tree cup of tea or coffee at the supermarket's café. It was difficult to keep tabs on the number of class parents who visited, as the place was sometimes very busy with parents from other classes and other members of the community also dropping by, but at least two-thirds of parents attended this event (this was more than double the number of parents attending the original video screening of the literacy lesson at this school).

The response to this activity was very positive, and the pattern of visiting was particularly interesting, with parents making more than a single visit and in different social groupings. For example, one mother of Indian heritage, who had not previously participated in any school-based events, visited with her children twice, and she also visited on her own; the children's paternal grandfather, aunt and cousins also visited. The visiting parents seemed to be at ease in this familiar territory, where expectations regarding school ways of doing things were less evident, and where members of the extended family and next-door neighbours could also take an interest in a child's education.

Conclusions

The four initiatives discussed in this chapter exemplify a number of factors that appear to underpin effective practice when schools reach out to engage with parents who might be described as hard to reach. Griffiths' work with *The Letterbox Club* represents a highly inventive response to the needs of children in care, aiming to improve their literacy and numeracy. There was a very clear focus on providing children with learning materials, and these were conveyed to the children in an imaginative, engaging manner. The perspectives of foster parents were respected and played a part in how this project was conducted. A feature of the *Drop in for Coffee* scheme that stands out is the successful strategy used for recruiting parents. The carefully thought-through informality of the approach adopted in this project appeared to avoid a typical danger of such initiatives – stigmatizing parents who participate. The simplicity of the INSPIRE framework for involving parents means that it is adaptable and can probably be used in a range of differing contexts, meeting the needs of a variety of parent and family groups. Finally, the core message from the HSKE project is that variety is important when designing strategies for engaging so-called hard to reach parents – diverse approaches may need to be considered in order to meet the needs of different groups.

References

Bateson, B. (2000) INSPIRE, in S. Wolfendale and J. Bastiani (eds) *The Contribution of Parents to School Effectiveness*, London: David Fulton, pp. 52–68.

Caddell, D., Crowther, L., O'Hara, P. and Tett, I. (2000) *Investigating the roles of parents and schools in children's early years education*. Paper presented at the European Conference on Educational Research, Edinbugh.

Department for Education and Skills (2004) *Every Child Matters, Change for Children in Schools*, Nottingham: DES Publications.

Department for Education and Skills (2006) *Care Matters: Time for Change* (White Paper), Nottingham: DES Publications.

Department for Education and Skills (2007) *Extended Schools: Building on Experience*, Nottingham: DES Publications.

Dyson, A. and Robson, A. (1999) *School, Family, Community: Mapping School Inclusion in the UK*, Leicester: Youth Work Press.

Feiler, A., Andrews, J., Greenhough, P., Hughes, M., Johnson, D., Scanlan, M. and Ching Yee, W. (2007) *Improving Primary Literacy: Linking Home and School*, Abingdon: RoutledgeFalmer.

Feiler, A., Andrews, J., Greenhough, P., Hughes, M., Johnson, D., Scanlan, M. and Ching Yee, W. (2008) 'The home-school knowledge exchange project: linking home and school to improve children's literacy', *Support for Learning*, 23 (1), 12–18.

Feiler, A., Greenhough, P., Winter, L., Salway, L. and Scanlan, M. (2006) 'Getting engaged: possibilities and problems for home school knowledge exchange', *Educational Review*, 58(4), 451–469.

Hughes, M. and Pollard, A. (2006) 'Home-school knowledge exchange in context', *Educational Review*, 58 (4), 385–396.

Humphries, K. (2004) *It's more than just a cup of coffee: a collaborative enquiry* – Project Report (unpublished). Dundee: University of Dundee. http://services.bgfl.org/services (accessed 9 September 2008).

Illsley, P. and Redford, M. (2005) ' "Drop in for coffee": working with parents in North Perth New Community Schools', *Support for Learning*, 20 (4), 162–166.

Karayiannis, C. (2006) 'Integrating and partnering services in schools – an emerging model in Northern Ireland', *Support for Learning*, 21 (2), 64–69.

Moll, L., Amanti, C., Neff, D. and Gonzales, N. (1992) 'Funds of knowledge for teaching: using a qualitative approach to connect homes and classrooms', *Theory Into Practice*, 31 (2), 132–141.

Tett, L. (2005) 'Inter-agency partnerships and integrated community schools: a Scottish perspective', *Support for Learning*, 20 (4), 156–161.

The Scottish Office (1998) *New Community Schools Prospectus*, www.scotland.gov.uk (accessed 5 March 2009).

Whalley, M. (2001) *Involving Parents in their Children's Learning*, London: Sage.

Wilkin, A., Kinder, K., White, R., Atkinson, M. and Doherty, P. (2003) *Towards the Development of Extended Schools*, London: Department for Education and Skills.

Chapter 24

It's hard being expected to work all the time

Rose Schofield

We can experience many transitions in our lives – birth, leaving home, changing jobs, getting married, moving house, finding a new partner, emigrating to another country, moving into a care home. Transitions can be exciting but also challenging, especially for children given that they may not have very much experience of being in transition. Starting school is a transition that most children encounter and to which they need to adjust. In this chapter, Rose Schofield, a mother and senior manager at The Open University, tells of the experiences of her son, James, as he encounters the formal curriculum of school whilst placing this against the background of what he enjoys doing at home and in the community.

When James first started school he was very anxious about going there and being left without me. Whilst he had been to a nursery from the age of 7 months he didn't know any of the children that he was going to school with and this made him apprehensive. In the Foundation Stage parents were asked to bring the children into the classroom and to settle them into an activity before leaving when the whistle blew. There was a 10 minute slot to do this. My experience was that this was actually very stressful, particularly on the first day when some children had both parents, plus grandparents, bringing them in for their first day at 'big' school. From my perspective this meant that the classroom was very crowded and absolutely over-flowing with grown ups. James said to me 'don't leave me mummy, I am frightened'. I could see his point as I felt a bit intimidated too. I feel quite strongly that the classroom should be the children's space and they should be made to feel happy and comfortable there, and that really the parents could be seen as intruders to the children's space.

This method of children starting school carried on for the first two terms. Whilst trying to settle James in for his day at school I also had to

Source: Commissioned by The Open University for this volume.

keep my eye on his 2-year-old sister, with quite strict instructions that younger siblings were not allowed to mess up any of the activities previously set up for the day ahead. It was literally mission impossible.

For the first 3 weeks or so James cried every time I dropped him off but then began to settle into the routine. We managed this by firstly making sure he was handed over to the teacher or teaching assistant. He would still cry but was happier that he was being comforted. Eventually, he was happy to be left on his own after having a kiss and cuddle with me. The routine since the final term of Foundation Stage and moving into Year 1 has been that James goes into the classroom on his own (apart from reading mornings) and sometimes he asks for a kiss and a cuddle and sometimes he doesn't want it. I let him make the choice.

When I asked him to think about what he did in Foundation Stage he said he couldn't remember because it was a long time ago. He did say that he can remember learning phonics and having lots of time to play. He enjoyed learning phonics and made good progress. During the phonics classes James learnt the sounds with the corresponding actions. We were also given a booklet to practise at home and the teachers also provided a phonics workshop for the parents. James's teacher advised me that he was progressing well with phonics at a parents evening. James also told me himself that he had been moved to a different group that he saw as a step up. I don't know whether this was the case or not, but he would come home and say 'so and so doesn't know this yet and so and so doesn't know that and they haven't been learning phonics at home'. He didn't ever really mention any of the other things he learnt and the usual response to 'what did you do today' was 'I can't remember'.

I was anxious for James moving to Year 1 as I thought, after the long summer break, he would be upset going into school. However, he surprised me by settling straight back into it. His Foundation Stage class was split into three classes of twenty each for Year 1 which suits James's shy nature much better. I also think he finds his current Year 1 teacher less intimidating (I know I do). On the flip side though, the class is made up of 14 girls and 6 boys. I often find that the girls seem to be steaming ahead while some of the boys are not (James, for instance) and that maybe this is demoralising for him, although this is purely speculation on my part.

James complains a lot about going to school as he says that in Year 1 he does not get any time to play. He told me that he has to work hard all the time and it is hard. I think by 'hard' he means that it is hard being expected to work all the time, rather than a particular activity being hard. Actually, I know he would like to play more. I asked him how often he gets to play at school and he said 'hardly ever' but normally once a week and he thought it was for half an hours 'golden time', but he wasn't too sure. James asks every day whether he has to go to school and how long it is until the weekend. He repeatedly tells me he does not want to go and that he doesn't like school. However, his teacher tells me he seems fine when he is there.

The teacher has identified that James might be dyslexic. Apparently, he has a higher rate than the norm for getting his letters back to front. However, by her own acknowledgment, all children of this age make those mistakes and it is too early to test him. I am sceptical of the implication of this, however, as I believe his difficulties are not significant but related to his age and will resolve over time. I am pleased that she has identified a potential problem and she is being very proactive to help him form his letters correctly.

I also raised with the teacher that James is uninterested in reading. For instance he enjoys listening to stories at home and we have recently started reading the Roald Dahl books to him. In comparison, I think the books he reads himself seem like dull stories where nothing really happens. James's teacher agreed that if he reads at home with me without making a fuss he will get extra effort marks (the schools reward system). This has worked to an extent but I would say James is still not overly interested in reading books for himself. I think we should be looking for ways to make reading interesting for him, rather than offering an alternative incentive to 'make' him read. My belief is that this will come in time as his reading ability strengthens and his motivation to read increases, and there is a larger range of interesting things for him to read.

Last week, James and I became so fed up with the books he has been reading (blue level on the Oxford Reading Tree) that we selected a red level book (the next level up) to try. James read this perfectly apart from two words, so I discussed this with his teacher and she agreed it was fine for James to read these books. One of the problems I have with the Oxford Reading Tree used at James's school is that children are placed on a level; they might then read all the books on that level several times before they are moved up to the next level. I also have no idea how it is communicated to parents that their children have been moved up a level as James has only been moved up when I have pushed for it. If I hadn't pushed I am left wondering whether he would have ever progressed. James was so pleased to move onto the red books and it has incentivised him to read as he feels like he is making progress and also has new stories to read. He must have been bored to tears with the blue books and I know I was bored to tears of hearing the same old stories.

James is happy at home. He likes to play with us, with his sister Lola, and sometimes on his own. He likes to play games like chess, dominoes, Operation, and the Hungry Caterpillar. He also likes to play with Lego, Ben 10 toys – both of which involve lots of role play. He likes watching cartoons on TV. He really enjoys riding his bike and scooter. He also likes going to football training on a Saturday morning and Beavers after school on Wednesdays. Like at school, James doesn't really tell me much about Beavers, and I don't like to hassle him too much for details. However, he has told me that they play lots of games, ones that he hasn't played before. I did see him engaging in a game of Chinese whispers and he seemed to be really enjoying it. He was also thrilled to bits last week when his six won the competition to make a musical instrument and then perform with the others in his six. He also really enjoyed growing cress out of the top of an egg shell (which he drew a face on) to make it look like the egg's hair. I know about these activities simply because they were brought home. He also has swimming lessons, which he is a bit more reluctant to go to, because he says he is tired and also his friend Charlie has been moved into the next group. However, once he gets there he enjoys it and I think swimming is a good skill to have.

James gets homework in different formats. Firstly, the children are expected to read at home three to four times a week, which will then gain them an effort mark – the reward system that the school uses. They can be issued for literally any effort the child makes whilst at school. I originally thought the effort marks were kept on a sheet in children's personal drawers but have since realised that they are also displayed on a wall chart next to each other so they (and the parents) can see how they are doing in comparison to their friends. This feels quite exposing of children to me.

James is supposed to be learning frequently used words (including spelling, writing, and reading them). I find it confusing as sometimes it feels like we are given lots of different print outs with words on and I am not sure what we are supposed to be focussing on. James doesn't really understand what he is expected to do and relies on me to guide him through. At the moment we have four different sheets of A4 with words to learn. I think it could be made easier if these were given weekly or even fortnightly, if you knew they were coming, and if there were just say half a dozen to focus on each time. The amount of work that comes home feels overwhelming to me so I can't imagine what it must feel like to James. On top of that he is given official homework that comes back to us in a homework book every Wednesday to be submitted every Monday morning. This could range from naming five facts about dinosaurs, making a dinosaur poster, learning double digit numbers, and learning rhyming words. I do find the homework burdensome and think it puts a strain on family time that could be spent doing other interesting and fun things. I also find it hard trying to balance the homework James gets with the needs of my daughter and the demands of running a home and working part-time. I think it is unnecessary for a 5-year-old to be given homework and that the learning they need to achieve should be managed within school hours as other activities outside of school are also educational. Issuing homework actually encroaches on family time.

I also think homework is unnecessary. However, I have been told that some parents have actively requested homework for their children as they feel this helps them prepare for later school life, particularly secondary school. It would be interesting to conduct an experiment to see whether setting homework so early in children's school lives actually makes any difference in their academic achievements later in life.

I was surprised at how little free play there is in Year 1 and think the transition from Foundation Stage to Year 1 is quite steep. I think the children should have more free time to play in the school day. For instance, they could have activities set up (painting, drawing, water, sand) as well as toys made available. The children could then 'choose' what they would like to do. Alternatively, they could perhaps have a longer afternoon break. However, these suggestions are based on what James describes the day to be, I haven't actually observed the day at school myself and haven't done because I don't have any free time given I work part-time and when I'm not working I am looking after my 3-year-old daughter.

I am also not sure about the various reward systems that schools use, particularly at such a young age. I noticed that James had considerably lower effort marks than his peers and raised this with his teacher. She told me she would work on this with James and that sometimes the quieter ones did not get as many as the louder more confident children. I think this is unfair as the same task could actually take a lot more effort for some children than others and how do you measure that? Whilst reward systems motivate the achievers they can actually have the opposite effect on others. I think any reward system at this young age should be personalised and not competitive.

Overall, despite my concerns, I am quite pleased with the progress James has made at school over the last year and a half. I think it is a shame that he feels pressured by school work at such a young age. This, combined with the homework that he is also required to complete each week, tips the balance in the wrong direction to my mind. Our family approach, however, will be to support him as much as possible and to liaise with his teachers when necessary. This should enable him to learn through his school work and to progress well throughout his primary school.

Chapter 25

Developing pupils' self-assessment skills

Ruth Dann

If assessment is to be meaningful for pupils they need to be involved in the process. If teachers and teaching assistants want to plan to support children's learning they need to know what pupils think about their own learning. Ruth Dann, a senior lecturer at Manchester Metropolitan University, argues that pupil self-assessment should be an essential component in formative assessment and one that will provide valuable insights into children's thinking and understanding and what they consider to be important about their learning.

- Pupil self-assessment is an essential component of formative assessment or 'assessment for learning'.
- The assessment process involves critical thinking so as to make judgments based on evidence about achievements.
- Pupil self-assessment will relate to pupils' understanding of the tasks they are completing, perceived expectations, and the importance they give to individual effort and enjoyment.

Self-assessment requires pupils to engage in a process, which requires a range of skills. Some of these skills may complement those required in other areas of the curriculum, whereas others may be additional ones.

Pupil self-assessment as a dimension of formative assessment

Our model of the National Curriculum and assessment requires teachers and teaching assistants to assess pupils' learning in relation to descriptors, which are progressively structured by levels. For some parts of the core

Source: A revised version of Dann, R. (1996) 'Developing pupils' skills in self-assessment in the primary classroom' *Primary Practice: The Journal of the National Primary Trust*, 5 (June).

curriculum, assessment of pupil achievement will be carried out by standard tasks/tests; the remainder will require teachers' own assessments.

Progression through the levels of the National Curriculum is envisaged to be at an average rate of one level every 2 years. Accordingly, the amount of detail offered through these assessment levels will be suitable for highlighting pupils' learning needs in relation to fairly large learning steps, but not in relation to more specific learning targets. If teaching is to be appropriately matched to pupil needs then teachers must be more informed about pupils' achievements at a more specific level. Assessing Pupil Progress (APP) has certainly helped with this by introducing sub-levels (DfE). However, engaging pupils more specifically in the process of assessment, so that the ultimate aim of closing the learning gap is possible, needs more considered attention.

In accordance with Torrance (1993), development of formative assessment practice must be built on research which seeks to examine the complexities of teacher–pupil interactions at a classroom level. This is further developed through research by Black et al. (2003) in considering developments in Assessment for Learning. Furthermore, as Gipps (1994) maintains, a key aspect of formative assessment is that 'the student comes to hold a notion of the standard or desired quality similar to that of the teacher, is able to monitor the quality of what is being produced at the time of the production, and is able to regulate their work appropriately' (p. 126).

In order to gain insight into pupils' learning, teachers must continually seek to understand pupils' achievements. Clearly, this will involve considering some of the following: marking finished work, observing classroom process, questioning (oral and written), understanding learning context, and establishing pupils' priorities and goals for their learning. Learning is a complex process that embraces more than cognitive learning and must be identified and examined within a context. If learning is to be realistically explored, and the achievements identified, a range of evidence will need to be reflected upon by the teacher. Involving pupils more directly in the assessment process offers a potential source of evidence, which is beginning to receive the attention it deserves in contemporary assessment developments. It is an area in which teachers and teaching assistants may have valuable insights and a wealth of experiences from which formative assessment can be further built and developed.

Self-assessment gives children the opportunity to judge their achievements for themselves. This allows (adults) to gain a greater understanding of children's own thinking about their learning. Additionally, and from the child's perspective, the self-assessment process communicates an important message – that teachers value pupils' opinion about their learning. The potential that pupil self-assessment may offer is highlighted by Holt (1974). He states that 'perhaps the greatest of all the wrongs we do children is to deprive them of the chance to judge the worth of their own work and thus destroy in them the power to make such judgements, or even the belief that they can' (p. 504).

The process of pupil self-assessment

The way in which pupils may be engaged in the assessment process will vary in relation to the age and experience of the children, as well as in relation to the focus of assessment. It may be that pupils' judgments about their work are sought by teachers through questions as part of the marking process. Alternatively, pupils may be invited to complete a self-assessment sheet requiring their judgment to be recorded in a general or specific form.

Task:
Creative Writing

Aims:
To develop skills in story structure – beginnings.
To develop imagination.

Objectives:
Pupils will develop the beginning of the story by: setting the scene describing location and atmosphere; describing characters.

Pupils will demonstrate their imagination by building into their story four stated objects, so that these objects form important parts of the story. The objects are:

- a fox
- a precious vase
- a knitted hat
- a tree house.

Pupil self-assessment can be encouraged by dialogue with the teacher, as in the example below.

> *Teacher:* Tell me – what do you think is the best part of this work you have done?
>
> *Child:* I think it was the bit I wrote about the vase. It was hard to put it into the story, but then I got an idea.
>
> *Teacher:* Yes, that was a good idea; I thought it was going to get smashed at first, but it didn't – I was glad. Was that the hardest part of the writing?
>
> *Child:* Well . . . sort of. It took me a long time to think of my story – trying to fit the four things in.

Example. Pupil self-assessment through teacher–pupil discussion.

This, however, is time consuming. For it to be adequately adopted in the classroom, only a small number of children can participate on each occasion. Giving every pupil an opportunity will require careful planning over a half-term or termly period.

Opportunities in which all pupils can play a part demand a written prompt for pupils to think about and record their achievements. These prompts may use a specifically task-focused proforma or could be in a more general outline form.

The type of self-assessment used must be matched to pupils' skills as well as to the task being considered. The purpose that pupils perceive for the process will greatly influence the way in which it is carried out.

Self-assessment may be aimed at encouraging pupils to make judgments about their work in relation to specific criteria. Alternatively, its aim may be to ascertain pupils' own priorities for and interpretations of their own work, which can offer useful information to the teacher when making assessments. Both are useful; each, however, demands different skills.

Pupil self-assessment using criteria

Criterion-referenced assessment may well be the focus for teacher assessment. It may also form the focus for pupil self-assessment. For consideration, however, is the way in which criteria are both shared and communicated. The National Curriculum offers statements grouped into level descriptions that form the focus for assessment, but these are not designed as criteria for assessing individual lessons. The focus for such criteria needs to be far more specifically related to individual tasks, if they are to give appropriate indication of pupil progress, which can immediately inform teaching and planning. These learning objectives may take the form of 'WALT' (what am I learning today) and the success criteria may take the form of 'WILF' (what I am looking for). These child–friendly forms for sharing learning intentions offer a first step in helping children be more fully engaged in understanding their own learning and subsequently judgments made about it.

To return to the example previously given in English (creative story writing), the objectives of the lesson are for children to incorporate four objects into a story; to structure the beginning of the story so that location and characters are described and the atmosphere portrayed. To move from these lesson objectives to achievement criteria demands another level of specification. For example, how will the children demonstrate their level of skill in relation to each of these objectives?

In order to account for varying pupil needs, it may be that for some pupils the objectives set will be different: perhaps only two objects are to be incorporated into the story. Accordingly, the criteria for success will reflect such differences.

But additional and crucial factors need to be probed in this example – what is meant by 'imaginatively' or (in relation to the other stated objectives) how do you successfully describe location, atmosphere, and characters? These areas should form part of the initial discussion with the children about the task. Illustration, example, and comparison are important tools for communicating to pupils what they should be aiming for. For example:

Teacher: Listen very carefully to this example:

It was Wednesday. Mum was late for work. She picked up her key and ran along the road to catch the bus. Mrs. Thomas was taking me to school. She had a red jumper with a rose on it. Wednesday mornings we always have hymn practice which is not much fun when you have a sore throat . . .

Tell me what you think about the way I have used the two objects key and rose?

Child: I don't think you have used them very well.

Teacher: Why is that, why do you think they are not used very imaginatively?

Child: Well, you have only just said the word in the sentence and not said anything else about what it was like.

Teacher: Good, thank you. What do other people think?

Child 2: I don't think it is imaginative because you have not said what will happen to them – it's just boring.

Teacher: Good. Who agrees that it is not imaginative? What would we have to do to make it a bit more imaginative?

Child 3: You could say that the key fell out of Mum's pocket as she ran for the bus and someone found it.

At the end of the initial task discussion, specific highlighted points, which have been elicited, can usefully be written up and left in a prominent place during the activity. For example:

Using the four objects imaginatively

*   Make sure something happens in the story and the four objects play a part in this.
*   Include something surprising or unexpected for each object.

Beginnings

*   Where is your story set?
*   How does this place make you feel?
*   What are the people in your story like?
*   Use adjectives (describing words) for each of these parts of your beginning.
*   Make the beginning interesting so you will want to find out what happens next.

If children are to be given an opportunity to consider their work in relation to the criteria for the task, then an appropriate framework must be constructed. This prepares the way for pupil self-assessment. The assessment process required pupils to judge their work. In the context of criterion-referenced pupil self-assessment a variety of skills are needed. Fundamentally, pupils are required to think critically about their work and to relate it to the stated criteria. This assessment process demands the complex skills of comparing, examining evidence, interpreting, reasoning and decision-making. These skills are important dimensions of learning and may be supported through other curriculum areas. They are skills which need to be developed throughout a child's education. Their use within pupil self-assessment is therefore a means of developing learning as well as judging it. A notion which can be called assessment as learning (Dann 2001).

What becomes crucial in the self-assessment process is the support and guidance given at appropriate stages. Children need to understand the conventions of assessment judgments that relate to different aspects of their work. For example, it may be appropriate to say, 'That is a good picture because I like it', but not 'the answer is three because I like its shape'. Some decisions will require recognition of precise rules, whereas others will require judgments that draw on creative process. Guidance is needed to direct the children towards the framework most appropriate for the given task.

With adequate support, children in Key Stage 2 show remarkable skill in relating their work to criteria. However, the extent to which their assessments are exclusively criterion-referenced must be further probed.

The influence of personal and social development

Children's learning cannot be developed or assessed in a vacuum that excludes personal and social influences. Although attempts may be made to minimise these influences, they cannot be eliminated. Children have a keen sense of 'fairness' in the assessment process. In a research study carried out to examine the role of criteria in pupil self assessment (Dann, 2001) pupils stated that they used the criteria given but also added their own priorities. Without this additional dimension pupils felt that their views were not fairly represented in the assessment process. For example, they considered their work in relation to what they had previously achieved, in relation to how much effort they put into it, as well as how much enjoyment they gained from it.

In self-assessment schemes, in which pupils were invited to assess their work only in relation to stated criteria, the pupils said that they included these additional issues themselves before reaching their final judgment. Thus they were not willing to dwell exclusively on curriculum-related criteria for their assessments. They would draw on other influences whether these were made explicit or not. Hence any attempt to develop pupil self-assessment must recognise the important role that pupils give to the social context of their learning and their personal priorities and expectations.

It is only through communication of this nature that teachers and teaching assistants can recognise the range of issues that influence learning and that enable further teaching to be effectively planned and taught.

The future

Effective teaching demands an understanding of pupil learning. A range of evidence is required for this to represent the variety of experiences and opportunities encountered and the way in which they are interpreted both by teacher and by pupils. Actively engaging pupils in the assessment process is an aspect of formative assessment which can yield valuable information for teachers as they seek to develop and understand pupils' learning. For pupils, it can provide a useful vehicle for developing critical thinking skills, for expressing concerns and priorities about learning, and for fostering a sense of trust and communication with the teacher. Pupils must be at the centre of teaching, learning, and assessment in the primary classroom.

References

Black, P. Harrison, C., Lee, C., Marshall, B., and Wiliam, D. (2003) *Assessment for Learning.* Berkshire: Open University Press, McGraw Hill Education.

Dann, R. (2001) *Promoting Assessment as Learning.* London: Falmer (DfE Assessing Pupil Progress National Strategies website).

Gipps, C. (1994) *Beyond Testing.* Lewes: Falmer Press.

Holt, J. (1974) The tyranny of testing, in G. Davis and T. Warren (eds), *Psychology of Education.* Lexington, MA: DC Heath & Co.

Torrance, H. (1993) Formative assessment: Some theoretical problems and empirical questions. *Cambridge Journal of Education, 23*(3), 333–343.

Section 4

Perspectives and voices

The chapters in this final section cover a range of perspectives, and a wide range of voices including those of children, teaching assistants, teachers, advisors, and a writer. We felt they all had something important to say about how children learn, what and how they should learn, and how they can best be supported in their learning. The chapters encourage us to stand back from our practice and to reflect on different views and approaches – an essential element in continuing professional development.

In Chapter 26 Ian Eyres and his colleagues describe the findings of a research project in which children were invited to describe the role of their teaching assistants. Although the official roles of teaching assistants and teachers are quite distinct, at classroom level there appear be more similarities than differences, at least in the opinions of the children interviewed. Enabling all children to express their feelings and views is the focus of Chapter 27 written by Ann Lewis and colleagues. Their chapter describes a technique that uses eight card pictures to elicit children's ideas.

In Chapter 28, Jonty Rix writes candidly about the professional advice given to him with regard to his son Robbie. The chapter reminds that all educational professionals need to be in touch with the reality of family life when they provide suggestions and guidance to parents. In his study of Bangladeshi families, Adrian Blackledge (Chapter 29) found that parents' willingness to engage in their children's literacy development was frustrated by the gap between home and school concepts of literacy and the lack of understanding of home literacy practices.

We would all wish that we could prevent every child from being abused. In Chapter 30, Ruth Pooley writes unequivocally about what she feels are our responsibilities to report worrying symptoms. She argues that teaching assistants are uniquely placed to 'break the taboo' by speaking out where they feel this to be necessary.

In Chapter 31, Philip Pullman reminds us that learning should be fun and that we learn more about language when we are in situations where we can play around with it and realise its power and potential through story, poems, and songs. In Chapter 32 Marsha Bell argues that the complexity of the English sound and spelling systems gives rise to the literacy problems that children have long encountered when they first approach reading and writing. The English spelling system she states is 'at the extreme end of alphabetic imperfection' using 185 spellings for 43.5 sounds.

Peter Woolston, co-ordinates a primary school breakfast club. In Chapter 33 he writes about the social and educational benefits of the club and also the roles that adults take on to enable children to enjoy and learn from a busy morning event. In Chapter 34 Dympna Meikleham establishes associations between Northern Ireland's enriched curriculum and the current foundation stage curriculum; and, against this policy background she reviews her role as an outreach support worker. Again, as in Chapter 24, we are reminded of how some children need personal support if they are to make successful transitions.

Chapter 26

'Whoops, I forgot David'

Ian Eyres, Carrie Cable, Roger Hancock and Janet Turner

Despite their unique perspective and the profound importance of many local and national initiatives to their everyday lives, the views of children need to be given much more consideration in educational research. This chapter, written by researchers from The Open University, features the voices of children in several English primary schools articulating their idea of the role of teaching assistants. It would appear that the clear distinction between the roles of teachers and teaching assistants conceptualised at the levels of management and policy breaks down somewhat in the context of real classrooms.

Over the past 20 years, teaching assistants have made up an increasing proportion of the primary school workforce. Children are the group most significantly affected by such educational innovations, but they rarely have the opportunity to comment on them (Norris, 1998). This study, therefore, set out to explore children's perceptions and experiences of teaching assistants. Seventy-three children between the ages of five and eleven years were interviewed in six primary schools. For younger children the interview began with a task in which they were invited to draw the adults in their classroom, and this proved a useful starter for discussion. The main findings of the study are set out below.

Children are happy to work with many different adults in the classroom

The 73 children reported working with a total of 66 teachers, 71 assistants and 2 adult volunteers: a total of 129 adults, of whom fewer than half were

Source: An edited version of Eyres, I., Cable, C., Hancock, R. and Turner, J. (2004) 'Whoops, I forgot David': Children's perceptions of the adults who work in their classroom. *Early Years*, 24 (2). London: Taylor & Francis Ltd.

qualified teachers and fewer than a third were their class teacher. The 'Teachers and headteachers' category were senior staff who occasionally work in classrooms, supply teachers who work regularly or occasionally with classes, and teachers who have specific responsibilities for supporting children learning English as an additional language or particular children with a learning difficulty or impairment. Assistants outnumber teachers by a factor of nearly three in most of the schools, and while many are employed part-time, the number of children with whom they have contact is increased by their working in more than one classroom in a week; some have other roles, for example midday supervisors.

As she drew them, Samantha, a five-year-old, named adults in the following roles (Figure 26.1, left to right): teaching assistant, deputy head, teaching assistant, teaching assistant, teaching assistant. David, the class teacher, is included only after the sudden realization: 'Whoops, I forgot David!'. She also includes a computer in the background—evidence of a perceived 'virtual teaching assistant'?

In his classroom, Alan similarly gave an impression that a number of adults were involved:

> There's Miss Ball, my teacher, Miss Audley, Miss Monroe and
> Miss Wells and sometimes Miss Morgan.
>
> (Alan, Year 3)

The number of adults mentioned by children tended to be greater towards the end of Key Stage 1 (Year 2) and at the beginning of Key Stage 2 (Years 3 and 4). In some instances adults were working with specific children.

Figure 26.1 'Adults in my classroom' (Samantha, Year 1)

More frequently the adults mentioned were working with groups, either inside or outside the classroom, on literacy 'catch-up' programmes such as Additional Literacy Support (ALS) (DfES, 1999). Children also mentioned 'going out of the classroom' or being taken in groups by teaching assistants for a range of activities, including reading, maths and science.

Some of the adults mentioned by children were qualified teachers, many engaged to support children with EAL or special educational needs. Some children encountered supply teachers on a regular basis and a few experienced a climate of constant change (one pair reporting that they had had 6 changes of supply teacher that year!). For some children the teaching assistant provided a sense of continuity they would not otherwise have experienced.

The overwhelming impression gained from this study is that children are comfortable with the number of adults they encounter and with their comings and goings, so long as there is some degree of stability and continuity. Many cited their class teacher as meeting this need, while a few others saw a particular teaching assistant as a more or less constant presence.

Children notice the different working patterns in the classroom and how they are managed

Apart from the class teacher, children appear largely to perceive the adults in their classrooms as being attached either to individual children:

> Rebecca only works with Kelly.
>
> (Billy and Sushi, Year 2)

Or to a particular group:

> I work with Miss Morris because I'm in the phoneme group.
>
> (Philippa, Year 3)

The link between teaching assistant and group appears to be strong in the minds of some children and a number of those interviewed identified the 'ideal' classroom as having one teaching assistant per group. With the arrival of the National Literacy Strategy (DfEE, 1998), much has been made of the new emphasis on whole-class teaching; at the same time, patterns of group-based working, with groups often adult-led rather than collaborative, have also become well-established and this organisational structure is certainly significant in the eyes of the children in this study.

As in the study carried out by Doddington *et al.* (2002), our data suggests that children are well aware of which group they and other children have been assigned to, and welcome and rely on the additional support they receive from teaching assistants in group work activities.

> We're in this little group and we usually just do what others do – but just easier because in our group we don't do . . . we can't do some of the hard stuff.
>
> > (Robin, Year 6)

> It isn't that easy to get help because if you're the bestest group, they think you can't have help.
>
> > (Naseem, Year 2)

Assignment to groups was largely perceived in terms of 'ability' and there was a sense in which 'higher' groups enjoyed higher status – Naseem's words, above, convey a sense of self-esteem.

It appeared that the children perceived differences in status between adults, especially between the class teacher ('our real teacher'):

> Mrs. Wilson is my teacher.
>
> > (Shamila, Reception)

> Miss McAngel is the actual teacher teacher teacher.
>
> > (Laila, Year 6)

and others who may be 'just' assistants:

> Barbara isn't a proper teacher: she helps us, she doesn't actually teach us.
> > (Mark, Year 6)

> He used to normally work in the lowest group because he just helps.
> > (Sadia, Year 4)

The second quotation suggests the intertwined low status of both adult and children.

Without the overall responsibility of the class teacher, qualified teachers in supporting roles did not appear to be perceived any differently from teaching assistants:

> He [Mr. Burke, EMTAG support teacher] works with us on Wednesdays . . .
>
> > (Ewan, Year 6)

Class teachers are not simply seen as 'more important' per se but also to have a management role, which sets them above the other adults in the class.

> [. . .] Helen and Chris [. . .] sort of sit and talk and Barbara sits and listens and then she, um you know, they would say, 'Oh, could you do this for us Barbara, could you do that? Or could you help these children please' and like, she would do that, you know.
>
> (Jane, Year 6)

These examples illustrate the way in which children see teaching assistants as assistants, lending support to the teacher's teaching role. The children didn't simply notice this relationship in respect of ad hoc support; the perception that teachers have higher status is reflected in the perception that they have overall responsibility for the management of classroom activity:

> She tells us what groups are doing and she tells us which group is doing group reading.
>
> (Joshua, Reception)

It would seem also that in at least some cases the class teacher's authority has some practical benefits:

> Melissa [class teacher] . . . sorts it [social problem] out quick . . . she would like really sort the problem out.
>
> (Jade, Year 3)

There are other instances of teachers being seen as the ultimate authority over behaviour, but there are examples where teaching assistants are seen as powerful disciplinary figures too.

Teachers and teaching assistants are different, but it's difficult to say how

This question was at the heart of much of our discussion with the children. On the face of it, teachers and assistants are very different. Teachers have usually followed at least four years of higher education before qualifying. Teaching assistants need no formal qualifications and provision of training opportunities is variable. The two groups have different conditions of employment, patterns of working inside and outside the classroom and very different salary structures. According to recent government guidance, teaching assistants should undertake a range of non-teaching tasks, thereby freeing teachers to teach (DfES 2002, 2003). Our interviews probed the extent to which children perceived teachers and assistants as carrying out different roles. Analysis of what children told us (Table 26.1), suggests an apparently clear distinction between the two groups' activities.

At the very least, this table does help to illustrate the variety of activities that adults were seen to be engaged in, both directly in working with children and, in the case of teaching assistants, in supporting the teacher's work. As the interviews focused on the role of teaching assistants it is not surprising that the right hand list is longer than the left. However, readers familiar with primary classrooms would doubtless identify many items which could appear in both columns and, of course, if a child says that teachers do a particular thing, that does not mean they think that teaching assistants don't do it and vice versa.

Table 26.1 Children's views of what teachers and teaching assistants do

A teacher:	An assistant:
• helps children write things	• does group reading
• tells stories	• helps with reading
• tells groups what they are doing	• hears people read
• tells which group is on the carpet	• helps children find reading books
• tells what assistants should do	• helps children write things
• tells us the work	• rubs things out and corrects writing
• tells us stuff	• watches children when they write
• tells us what to do	• watches what the teacher's doing
• reads a book on the (group) tables	• takes children's outside the classroom
• gives children work (D)	• helps on the computer
• makes us sit on the floor (D)	• does children's 'files'
• seems to mostly teach children	• helps with work
• teaches the class	• helps with sums
• teaches you different things	• helps with art work
• teaches all the stuff	• explains things
• teaches what we have to do	• translates things
• does much harder work	• works with children on the computer
• does more stuff	• tells children about the computer
• stays in the classroom	• tells you off if you're really being naughty
• has lots of jobs to do	• does literacy
	• does PE
	• helps the literature people
	• takes people out of the classroom to read with them
	• takes people out when they are less good
	• prepares things
	• talks to children
	• writes things on paper
	• shows children homework

Overall the lists give an impression of teachers who 'tell' and teaching assistants who 'help'. However, despite these apparent differences, many children seemed to have great difficulty in explaining how the activities of people whose standing in the classroom they obviously saw as different, differed in practice.

Interviewer: How is what *Jean* does different from what *Anna* does?

Heather: It isn't really. (*Heather,* Year 2)

> Well the helpers seem to help out and do what the teacher does and the teacher seems to mostly teach children. But sometimes the helpers teach children.
>
> (Sarah, Year 3)

Statements like these were often the result of much prompting and reached via a great deal of speculation on the child's part. One girl speculated about the different roles as though she were carefully unravelling the clues to a mystery:

> Well, there's something very, very, very, very strange about the teacher. The teacher does more maths than the other teachers and Miss Rose [teacher] is quite – is more active than all the other teachers . . . Er, let's see – Mr. Burke [EMAG support teacher] really does more stories than Miss Rose and about questions about stories about 'wish you were here' stuff. Let me think – there's something fishy . . . Mrs. Dell [helper] does more reading than Miss Rose. They all do more reading than Miss Rose.
>
> (Asma, Year 2)

It seems easier to identify the teaching assistant role when it involves more 'menial' tasks:

> Daniel like tells you what to do on your work. Daniel tells us the maths on the board. Tammi is like at the back of the class, like sharpening the pencils, and she sets out the things on the tables, the sheets we are going to write on.
>
> (Fraser and Jane, Year 1)

In the main we concluded that these children regarded teachers and assistants as doing very similar things. This echoes the findings of Moyles and Suschitzky (1997) that Key Stage 1 children were not very questioning about the two roles, although the children in this study were often willing to attempt to explain the differences. In fact they often saw the task as a stimulating riddle: they knew there was a difference but they just couldn't put their finger on what it was.

> Well Miss McAngel is the actual teacher, teacher, teacher. She actually teaches us everything because she's just a teacher and she teaches us everything. But, if you like, you've got another teacher, they teach us – pretty much they'd teach us everything but Miss McAngel would do different things with us – d'you know what I mean? – sort of, I can't put it into words really – but [looking towards Tim, her friend] can you help?
>
> (Lisette, Year 6)

Omar, a Year 2 boy, said he had to write more intensely when with his teacher, which perhaps is a token of the higher esteem in which the teacher is held, or perhaps of her superior motivational skills.

Overall our impression was of children racking their brains for evidence to support the view that people with different job titles must be doing different things, rather than articulating a difference they found obvious or even particularly visible within their everyday experience. Perhaps we should not be surprised at this. Hancock *et al.* (2002) found many assistants were taking on teaching-related activities with children, and the literacy and numeracy strategies have led to a considerable blurring of the teacher/teaching assistant boundary. Reports from Open University Specialist Teacher Assistant (STA) students suggest that even some OfSTED inspectors find it hard to distinguish between trained assistants and teachers.

The notion that teaching assistants 'help' may be less helpful than it appears

We have noted above the possible inference that 'teachers tell and teaching assistants help'. Certainly 'help' and 'helper' were words used often when explaining the teaching assistant role.

Raymond: I'm drawing Mrs. Monroe.

Interviewer: Is she your teacher?

Dushanti: No, she just helps.

(Raymond and Dushanti, Year 2)

In many of the schools, teaching assistants and other adults who were not teachers were referred to by other staff and by some of the children as 'helpers'.

[*Imogen*]'s our helper in our class.

(Rebecca, Year 1)

In fact the word 'help' occurred so frequently in the extracts we had selected for this paper that we felt the need to return to the full transcripts to see if some explanation could be found there. One thing we found was the frequent use of that word in the questions about teaching assistants. Questions of the type: 'How does Mrs. X help you?' abound. Three of the questions in the schedule which guided the interviews also emphasised the notion of 'helping':

- How does this [support for groups] help you with your work?
- Can you tell me more – (give an example) of how Mrs/Mr X has helped you?
- If you had a problem with your work, would you ask for help from anyone (any adult)?

This is not to suggest that the interviewer was leading the children's responses. However, given the interview schedule and the field of enquiry, 'help' was a word difficult to avoid. In the light of this we feel we should be very careful in drawing any conclusions from children's statements to the effect that they see teaching assistants as 'helping'.

As we have seen, some of the children articulated this relationship in terms of helping the teacher and others in terms of helping them or specific children in the class.

One boy emphasised the teacher–support role of an assistant and brought out the teacher's lead responsibility:

> Well I think it's different because the helpers, they come in and they help with things that the teacher needs help with and stuff like that . . . the teachers, they have to prepare most of the stuff and the helpers just help the children with their reading and writing when they need help.

(William, Year 4)

Some older children in the study appeared quite clear in their minds about the differences.

> Mary doesn't teach, she helps. She just helps us out with our work.

> Rachel [teacher] teaches what we have to do. And if we find difficulties, Rachel sometimes helps but Mary [assistant] is the main person to help.

> (Sasha, Year 6)

Perhaps, however, Sasha is not using the words 'teach' and 'help' in the way education professionals would. Is 'teaching us what we have to do' a matter of advancing knowledge and understanding or simply the setting of tasks? Certainly the examples of 'tell' more often relate to giving instructions than to fostering learning. On the other hand, when Mary 'helps', is it the same kind of help as in, say, 'helping with the washing up' where the helper reduces the task by doing some of it, or, as seems more likely, does Mary give the kind of support which enables Sasha to do the task for himself? What Sasha identifies as 'just' helping could well be the kind of 'assisted performance' that Tharp and Gallimore (1988:21) see as virtually synonymous with teaching. Further research into classroom interactions would help illuminate these questions.

References

DfEE (1998) *The National Literacy Strategy: A framework for teaching*. London: DfEE.

DfES (1999) *Additional Literacy Support*. London: DfES.

DfES (2002) *Time for Standards: Reforming the school workforce*. London: DfES.

DfES (2003) *Raising Standards and Tackling Workload: A national agreement*. London: DfES.

Doddington, C., Bearne, E., Demetriou, H. and Flutter, J. (2002) *Sustaining Children's Progress in Learning at Year 3*. Cambridge: Homerton College.

Hancock, R., Swann, W., Marr, A., Turner, J. & Cable, C. (2002) *Classroom Assistants in Primary Schools: Employment and deployment, project dissemination report*. The Open University, Faculty of Education and Language Studies.

Moyles, J., with Suschitzky, W. (1997) *Jills of all Trades? Classroom assistants in KS1 classes*. London: Association of Teachers and Lecturers.

Tharp, R.G. and Gallimore, R. (1988) *Rousing Minds to Life*. Cambridge: Cambridge University Press.

Chapter 27

Child voice and cue cards

Ann Lewis, Helen Newton and Susan Vials

Policy makers and researchers do sometimes consult children. However, such consultations can become difficult when children have disabilities and learning difficulties. This chapter by Helen Newton from Ash Field School, Leicester, and Ann Lewis and Susan Vials from the University of Birmingham, reviews a technique that uses eight 'cue cards' to prompt children's thoughts and ideas. The authors suggest that the cards have important applications in both teaching and assessment.

Hearing children's views, particularly in relation to children with special needs or disabilities, presents significant challenges (Lewis and Porter, 2004, 2007). First, there are indications that commentators and professionals are beginning to express some disquiet about what is possible and reasonable in this context (Hart, 2002). For example, Felce (2002), with reference to people with learning difficulties, has raised concerns:

> 'Obtaining the views of people with learning difficulties – even those with severe or profound intellectual impairment – is becoming a ubiquitous imperative'. We should, he suggested, be much more cautious than we usually are about assuming the validity of views passed on via proxies or facilitators.
>
> (Ware, 2004)

Second, there is a danger that the pressure arising from the welter of policy initiatives leads to an over-formalising and/or an over-pressurising of the process of hearing the views of children, perhaps particularly those with disabilities or difficulties. The presence of assigned support workers, signers or

Source: An edited version of Lewis, A., Newton, H. and Vials, S. (2008) 'Realising child voice: the development of cue cards' *Support for Learning*, 23 (1), 26–31. Reprinted with permission from Blackwell Publishing.

translators may (despite good intentions) be, or be seen by the child, as making obligatory a response of some kind. (See Alderson and Morrow, 2004; Clegg, 2004; Lewis and Lindsay, 2000; for reviews of ethics and consulting with children.) There has also been a wide range of questionnaires aimed at ascertaining the pupil view, for example the 'Pupil Attitude to School and Self Survey' (P.A.S.S.), but these highly structured approaches may distort pupil views through the nature and phrasing of the questions.

Ways to hear children's views

In the light of these challenges, this paper reports work on the use of cue cards which, drawing on extensive UK-based development, has been found to be highly effective in facilitating the eliciting of views from a broad spectrum of children including many whom (through emotional, behavioural, cognitive or sensory factors) adults may not have expected to give such full information. The cards also provide a structure which, while scaffolding elicitation processes and responses, do not constrain or bias. The approach accords with the underlying principles in work on child 'voice', of authenticity, credibility and trustworthiness (Lewis, 2002, 2005). It is a positive and practical response to the challenges noted above and complements more open-ended approaches. It accords well with accounts of visual methods to mediate communication with children with autism. Preis (2007), for example, notes the value of the non-transience of iconic picture systems for these children. More widely, and beyond the scope of this paper, underlying issues concerning methods of eliciting views resonate with debates concerning visual methodologies (including art, photographs and video) (Wall and Higgins, 2006; Wall et al., 2005; Rose, 2007).

In Leicester City Local Authority a group of teachers and teaching assistants with a shared interest in supporting pupils with SEN worked together as the Cue Cards Working Group. Two years of development work (2004–6) by this working group resulted in the refinement of the cue card approach and in examples of the successful use of cue cards across a range of contexts. The working group based their approach on the premise that if pupils learned to use the cards in a wider context this would improve their spoken and written language and it would also mean that those pupils had developed the skills to use the cards for the expression of more sensitive or personal views. The group did not explore the use of the cards to elicit sensitive views and concerns from the pupils; the members explored how to teach and use the cards in a more generalised fashion. The examples included below show how the spoken and written language of some pupils improved through the use of cue cards.

The cue card approach

Cue cards provide highly specific structured visual prompts, ideally free of verbal leads from the interviewer, when eliciting children's versions of events. The cards were originally used by psychotherapists investigating cases of suspected child abuse; hence the stress on full and truthful responses. The initial set of cue cards comprised six cards (representing triggers for ideas about place, people, feelings, talk, actions and consequences). Each card depicted a simple black and white symbol, designed to avoid any leading material (Lewis, 2002, 2005). The rationale was derived from Fivush's script theory (cited in Lewis, 2002) concerning consistent key elements in a narrative.

Three aspects of the approach are important from both theoretical and practical perspectives. First, all potentially important aspects of the event were addressed (place, feelings, actions, etc.); second, this was done systematically; and third, the way in which this was done encouraged as full and as truthful an account as possible. The theoretical literature on interviewing children indicated that recurrent questioning, adult intervention and distracting details all hamper children from giving their views. Hence the simplified and focused approach behind cue cards.

The revised set of eight Leicester cue cards developed by the working group varied slightly from the original six-card set described above. First, for the Leicester cue cards, only one version of the place card was used (the original version had both an indoor and an outdoor cue card picture on separate cards). Second, pilot work with the original set indicated that it would be helpful to have an additional card showing time (interestingly, this was omitted completely in the original set). Third, the consequences card in the original set (a broken window) was found to be very difficult for many children (particularly those with learning difficulties) to interpret. After trying out various alternatives with a range of children, the working group arrived at two cards ('end' and 'consequence'; see below) as a more effective alternative.

The Leicester cue cards are;

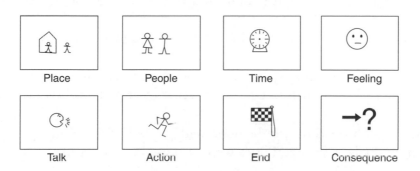

Using the cards

In using the cards, two key principles in order to use the cards successfully
became apparent to the working group. Firstly children needed to be taught
systematically how to use the cards and each card needed to be carefully
explained and practised. There is good evidence that children will give
fuller responses if their narrative is not interrupted; therefore they must be
confident in the independent use and manipulation of the cards. Secondly,
the presentation of the cue card must give the child an unspoken prompt;
therefore adults working with the children have to demonstrate a
willingness to listen and an understanding of the importance of reducing
adult talk to an absolute minimum. This principle is paramount in a move
away from the rigid and limiting question–answer–response format of much
adult–child talk.

   The working group found that the preliminary work spent teaching
children how to use the cards was essential to their success but they found
that it was neither possible nor desirable to script, or to prescribe exactly,
how the cards are taught; effective use will respond to the needs and
responses of the group or individual. It is not possible to be specific about
the correct way to use the cards but the working group identified
a number of useful pointers for teaching children how to use them.
These include:

* Introduce the cards one at a time.
* Allow children the opportunity to handle the cards.
* Encourage talk about what children think the cards may mean.
* Work with a limited selection for a period of time, for example, people, action, and feeling cards only.
* Allow children thinking time.
* Frequently remind the children, and the adult leading the activity, that the adult is there to support the use of the cards (not to ask questions!).
* Use non–verbal prompts (a nod towards a card or gentle point) as soon as possible.
* Model using the cards to recount a story or to give information to the class.
* As the children gain experience, allow them to choose cards from the selection about which to talk (so creating their preferred sequence).

This work with the cards can be done with a whole class, with a group or
with individuals. Starter activities were also used by the group, including

lotto games using the card images and 'passing the card' in circle time, e.g., pass the action card and each child thinks of an action, etc.

Once pupils understand the cards then there are different ways in which to use them. The use of the cards with individuals, groups or whole classes was not constrained by a rigid format but whatever method was used was always shared with the pupils and then used consistently. When working with an individual or small group, the method could be to:

- place all the cards on the table and ask the pupil to pick up each card and then use it as a prompt;
- place the cards on the table one at a time;
- give the cards to the pupil to hold and encourage them to put the card on the table as they use it to prompt talk;
- display the cards on a laptop computer.

For individual or small group work, the cards were either A5 or A6 in size. When working with a large group or whole class, the method could be to:

- display the cards and encourage pupils to use them as a visual rather than tactile prompt;
- display large cards on the wall and point to the one about which the child will talk;
- scan the cards and use them on an interactive white board.

For whole-class work, the cards were A4 or larger.

Much of the evidence from the working group was formative and qualitative as the group worked in a developmental way rather than following a rigid research design. The following four examples demonstrate the effectiveness of the Leicester City cue cards. These show:

1) the difference between a child's spoken language without and then with the use of cue cards;
2) how a child has used the cards to sustain a narrative;
3) the difference in a seven-year-old child's written work without and then with the use of cue cards;
4) how the use of the cards elicited a significantly improved written output from a Key Stage 1 child.

Example 1

The teacher worked with one Year 2 child, Kim, and sat opposite him at a small table. The teacher asked the child to 'tell me what you did at the weekend'. Without cue cards, Kim responded:

I went to the Circus. I gone on a donkey and on the park . . . that's it.

The teacher then laid the cue cards on the table in front of Kim and asked the same question again. Kim picked up the cards (which he had used before) and talked to each card in turn. The cards he chose are shown in parentheses.

I went to the Circus with Rick and Mary. (People card) *Then I went (with) Mary and Rick and me.* (Time card) *Quarter past eight.* (Feelings card) *Sad and happy. I was happy. Running to the Circus and Mary think we miss it. We weren't late. We watched all of it. We didn't feed the tigers or the lions.* (Talk card) (Action card) *Now I told you something. I said thank you and please so I could go on the donkey and the pony. And you know they don't walk properly the donkeys. They go like that [wobble action] they wobble a bit like that.* (End card) *I gone home and played on my computer.* (Consequence card) *I went home, sat down a minute and played on my computer. That's it.*

This example shows the extended and enriched talk that resulted from the use of the cue card prompts.

Example 2

Here the cue cards were used to support talk, this time with a small group of children in a special school context. The group included a Year 3 child (X) who had severe communication difficulties and was on the autism spectrum. The teacher held up the following cards in turn: people, place, time, action, say, feeling, end, consequence. X was the first child in the group to be invited to tell a story to the rest of the group. The cards are shown in parentheses in the transcript below.

Once upon a time, there was a boy and a girl (People card) *and they just loved school* (Place card) *because it made them brainy (like fish fingers). It was 1/2 past 4* (Time card) *and then their work time was over. They ran* (Action card) *round a little bit and went back inside to get more brainy. When the teacher gave the questions* (Talk card) *they gave the correct answers to the maths problem and they were different answers. They were happy* (Feelings card). *And when school was out they went home and asked mum the question* (End card). *And they asked the question to mum and they got brainy again* (Consequence card).

The class teacher reported that when X used the cards he surprised her by sequencing a story, sustaining the narrative and moving away from the literal. He used vocabulary which she did not know he knew.

Example 3

Children who have difficulty with writing are often those for whom talk is also difficult. Therefore, for some members of the working group, it seemed like a natural progression to use the cards to support the written word. Examples 3 and 4 show this. Here a Year 2 child is retelling a story in writing, firstly without the use of Cue Cards.

Without cue cards:

Anancy and Drybone

Mr Drybone lived on top of a hill and wanted to marry Miss Louise. Anancy lived on the foot of the hill and wanted to marry Miss Louise too. Mr Drybone went to see Miss Louise and knocked on her door. I've brought a conjuring trick and I'm going to make you laugh. Miss Louise said 'This I've got to see'.

On the next occasion when the child was asked to retell a story the cue cards were spread on the table in front of him for reference. The resulting writing was as follows:

With cue cards:

Once upon a time in a big fur tree lived a rabit coled peter and his three sisters and his mother one day mrs rabit was going to the shop to buy some bread and buns the three sisters went to pick berys and peter hoe was a naughty rabit went, stayt to Mr. mgregors gardn and sqeasd under the gate. He eat some radishes lettuce and some French beans and after that he felt sick so he went to find some parsly when he a found a qcumber house behind it he found Mr mggregor Mr mgregor chasd him saying stop theaf and he ran into the tool shed.

The second piece of writing includes time, feeling, consequence and end. The cards gave the child confidence through structure and resulted in a more varied and less restrained piece.

Example 4

In this last example a child (E) was asked to recount a school outing. The child was given the following cue cards: action, time, place, talk, consequence, end.

Our steam train trip

On Thusday I went on a steam train. We got on the bus at ten a cock. When we got there we went to the wtroom. Then the train cem. Athet that we got on the train. Aahet we sur llodewis. ten we got of the train and et gor lush, ten we went to the miniature ten we sur the livur. Ten we got on the train and went back to school my fefut bit was wen we went to the miniature, my fetfht bit was gawin to the museum.

The child has used all the cards given except for 'talk'. The child's teacher commented that E made a significant improvement, was much more focused and was able to do much more writing. Perhaps the teacher's most significant comment was that E didn't panic when asked to write. The support of the cards had given E confidence.

Questions about the cue card approach

The above examples were ones which were brought to the working group and discussed. As the working group became more experienced and their application of the cue card approach developed, some important questions arose about using cue cards. These included:

Does it matter that the cards are open ended?

One issue that had to be dealt with by the working group was the relationship between the symbols on the cards and commonly used symbol systems. The cue cards differed from other symbol systems in that the cards are designed to be open ended. In contrast, many other approaches using Picture Communication Symbols (PCS), Makaton and Rebus (such as Widgit Writing with Symbols) deliberately have a specific meaning and are intended to lead to a more closed response. Consequently cue cards, as described here, may not be suitable for a child who has a limited symbol vocabulary and is concurrently learning a different (i.e. closed) symbol system.

Can the cards be used if children have a limited spoken vocabulary?

The use of the cards does not, in itself, increase a child's vocabulary. Therefore supporting (extension) activities may need to be used alongside or before the cue card work (particularly for 'feelings', 'action' and 'time') in order to maximise the child's response. Otherwise the child may understand the 'cue' and have ideas to express but not be able to put these into words.

How should the cards be presented?

Children's talk in response to the cards may result in rather disjointed and poorly structured talk. To help children to structure their talk more fluently, once they were confident with the cards, the working group found it useful to give children time to handle the cards. Providing children with more than one copy of each card also helped some to talk about, for example, feelings more than once in their dialogue.

   Presentation of the cards varied by adult and by child; different approaches worked best in different situations. Sometimes cards were presented singly in turn and in the pre-specified sequence as in the original cue card work (because then the more comfortable aspects came first, e.g., place preceded feelings). At other times, and when children were very familiar with the cards, it was helpful to present these as an array. This gave the child control over which elements to talk about and in what order. However, this may mean that some elements are omitted and so generate a less full response. (We found that if all the cards were shown in an array, the children used them all!)

Is it useful to have several sets of cards?

For some children, it was particularly helpful to have several sets of cards which they could handle. This enabled them to return (e.g., to the 'feelings' element). This may be too distracting for children with moderate or severe learning difficulties.

Will the cards work well across various disabilities and special needs?

The working group found that the cards worked well with a range of pupils who could understand that one symbol might cue a number of responses. Children ranging from Year 1 in one of the most deprived wards in England to secondary aged pupils and those in a school for moderate and severe learning difficulties used the cards effectively with dramatically good results. Using the cards challenged teachers' expectations of limited language from some children. Most notably one teacher had great success with a child with autism who, in common with other children on the autistic spectrum, found it difficult to move away from a particular response to a particular card. (So, for example, if in one session the action card was associated with football in the playground, this same feature was triggered when the actions card was shown later in other contexts.) Using the cards, this child produced language which was more advanced than anything he had previously been heard to say in school.

Conclusion

The work described here has shown how the generalised use of cue cards can be used successfully to support spoken and written language. The account also illustrates that when more personal or sensitive views or issues are sought or discussed, the cue cards provided a tool without the restrictions and disadvantages of adult questioning. They complement other approaches which may be more open-ended but which, in combination, enable all children to share their views (Lewis, Parsons and Robertson, 2007; Lewis, Robertson and Parsons, 2005).

This account is intended not only to share information about the cue card approach and its effectiveness but also to highlight the creative potential for exciting and productive university–service/local authority relationships. The drive was the strong motivation of all those involved to improve practice around child 'voice'.

References

Alderson, P. and Morrow, G. (2004) *Ethics, Social Research and Consulting with Children and Young People*, London: Barnardo's.

Clegg, J. (2004) Practice in focus: a hermeneutic approach to research ethics. *British Journal of Learning Disabilities*, 32, 4, 186–190.

Felce, D. (2002) Gaining views from people with learning disabilities: authenticity, validity and reliability, *Presentation at ESRC seminar series; Methodological issues in interviewing children and young people with learning difficulties*. School of Education, University of Birmingham, March.

Hart, S. N. (2002) Making Sure The Child's Voice is Heard. *International Review of Education*, 48(3–4), 251–258.

Lewis, A. (2005) Researching a marginalized population: methodological issues, in P. Clough, P. Garner, J. T. Pardeck, and F. K. O. Yuen (eds.), *Handbook of Emotional and Behavioural Difficulties*, pp 385–398. London: Sage.

Lewis, A. (2002) Accessing, through research interviews, the views of children with difficulties in learning. *Support for Learning*, 17, 3, 110–116.

Lewis, A. and Lindsay, G. (eds.) (2000) *Researching Children's Perspectives*. Buckingham: Open University Press.

Lewis, A., Parsons, S. and Robertson, C. (2007) *My school, my family, my life: telling it like it is. A study drawing on the experiences of disabled children, young people and their families in Great Britain in 2006*. London: Disability Rights Commission/Birmingham: University of Birmingham, School of Education, http://www.drc.org.uk/library/research/ education/my_school_my_family_my_life.aspx

Lewis, A. and Porter, J. (2004) Interviewing children and young people with learning disabilities*: guidelines for researchers and multi-professional practice. *British Journal of Learning Disabilities*, 32, 191–197.

Lewis, A. and Porter, J. (2007) Research and pupil voice. In L. Florian (ed.), *Handbook of Special Education*, pp 222–235, London: Sage.

Lewis, A., Robertson, C. and Parsons, S. (2005) *Experiences of Disabled Students and their Families. Phase 1* Research report to Disability Rights Commission, June 2005. Birmingham: University of Birmingham, School of Education. Full report on DRC website http:// www.drc.org.uk/library/research/education/experiences_of_disabled. aspx

Preis, J. (2007) Strategies to promote adaptive competence for students on the autism spectrum. *Support for Learning*, 22, 1, 17–23.

Rose, G. (2007) *Visual Methodologies: An Introduction to the Interpretation of Visual Methods*. London: Sage.

Wall, K. and Higgins, S. (2006) Facilitating metacognitive talk: a research and learning tool. *International Journal of Research and Method in Education*, 29, 1, 39–53.

Wall, K., Higgins, S. and Smith, H. (2005) 'The visual helps me understand the complicated things': pupil views of teaching and learning with interactive whiteboards. *British Journal of Educational Technology*, 36, 5, 851–867.

Ware, J. (2004) Ascertaining the views of people with profound and multiple learning disabilities. *British Journal of Learning Disabilities*, 32, 4, 175–179.

Chapter 28

From one professional to another

Jonathan Rix

Jonathan Rix is a father and senior lecturer at The Open University. In this chapter he provides a poignant account of how it is to be a parent receiving information and advice from professionals about the development and education of his son, Robbie. Managing and implementing such advice can be a challenge for families even though professionals are, in the main, well meaning. Parents have important insider knowledge and understandings, of course, and this needs to be fully respected and taken into account when discussions take place and 'interventions' are proposed.

I do not think that my expectations on becoming a parent of a child with Down syndrome were the same as many parents, because my sister, Shelley, had prepared the ground for me. Growing up as a sibling of a person with Down syndrome allowed me to understand that people really are people first regardless of the labels we give them. This head start meant that I knew from the word go that I would be as proud of my son, Robbie, as any other child I might have been given (for example his fab older sister, Isabel). This did not prepare me for what a parent has to go through with professionals however; neither did many years of working in education.

Professionals give parents a huge amount of work to do. This has a wide range of practical, emotional and psychological consequences. Explaining this impact to other people, whether they be professionals or parents of typically developing children is difficult, but it is immediately recognised by other parents of children with an impairment. We all have our own versions of the tale, of course, but I'm going to try and explain mine.

It begins with the diagnosis. No one really wants to tell you what it is they have identified; and can you blame them? They know that it is going to upset you; that it is going to turn your life upside down. But of course,

Source: Rix, J. (2006) 'From one professional to another', in B. Rix *All About Us: The Story of People with a Learning Disability and MENCAP* (London: MENCAP).

every baby does that. It is the social construction about what a baby should be that makes it different. We learn our notions of normality from our earliest days. We throw away a doll that has lost an arm or a leg. We are told not to stare or to ask questions. A baby is an image of perfection. It is meant to make us smile and feel protective. So when one comes along that does not fit this model we get in a tizz. Suddenly, the mid-wife who knows perfectly well that a child has an impairment is not allowed to talk to the parents about this. Someone in authority has to take on this role. We knew that our lovely lad had Down syndrome the second time we looked at him. Robbie was sticking his tongue out at us. We had to ask if people agreed. No one would say, of course. Not until Caroline and I got the mid-wife to ourselves and finally she told us that we were probably right, though we weren't to tell anyone that she had told us. When the consultant paediatrician visited the next day, he sat very nervously at the end of my wife's bed and told her the news. He didn't do a bad job. He didn't say anything truly insensitive . . . well, apart from saying she could take Robbie to the United States to have plastic surgery on his eyes . . . but everything about the way he did it, made it clear that this was bad news. And so it was again the next day, when he ran through all the medical problems that might be stored up for Robbie, and the ways in which his development might be impaired. Of course, his discomfort and his lists just played into the fears we had about having a baby that didn't fit in with everyone's idea of perfection. It did not help us reach the obvious view that our baby was a human being who would develop in his own way. It encouraged a vision of our child as a baby who needed to be assessed and measured and treated differently from the rest. It encouraged a sense of sadness and loss.

Over the next few days, the medical staff did their best to be positive. They were always popping in to say something cheerful:

'He doesn't look very Downs.'

'Well at least he can get a job in Sainsbury's nowadays.'

'He's not a bad one, is he?'

Hardly surprisingly, none of this really helped. Neither did the constant comparison of our son to the norms and averages that fill the medical discourse. But after a week or so we had Robbie at home. Our lives together as a family could begin. This life now required us to visit doctors and therapists on a weekly basis, of course, or to have them come into our homes. We have spent hundreds of hours answering their questions, describing Robbie and our lives, coming up with strategies and plans, making decisions based on possible outcomes and norm-based goals. Over the years the frequency of these visits has decreased but the impact of them has not.

Lots of these people we have met have been very kind to us. All of them have been overworked. Most of them have been underpaid. We have had some arguments and complaints, but we have also shared many valuable moments with them. We have met paediatricians, various other types of doctors, various types of nurses, hearing specialists, speech and language therapists, portage workers, physiotherapists, Sure Start advisors, health visitors and educational psychologists. Robbie has had heart tests, thyroid tests, blood tests, hearing and sight tests, and has been constantly measured (sometimes discreetly, sometimes openly) against developmental norms. We have been encouraged by this process to focus less on what Robbie can do now, and much more on what we want him to do next. Our lives with our son have been filled with exercises and games that are designed to move him forward, to overcome those delays in development that the consultant paediatrician first mapped out for us on that hospital bed. It has been made absolutely clear to us, that if we carry out these interventions then Robbie will develop as fast as he possibly can, and by implication that if we don't carry them out then he will not.

So let's talk about guilt and a sense of failure. We are given a target for our son, one among many, for example to say the sound 'S'. With the professional we come up with some possible strategies to get him to say or hear this sound. Sometimes it goes brilliantly. You have a hoot. Your morning is energised because you had such a successful session. But the next time you see this person, Robbie is not yet saying "S". Nor is he for the next five visits. We are not achieving the targets set for us. We have failed. Robbie has failed. There must another strategy out there to make him say the sound. We have to try harder, but Robbie isn't interested in the strategies we come up with. He loathes sound cards, he won't collect objects together that begin with S, he doesn't like me singing Sing a Song of Sixpence . . . well, he just doesn't like me singing . . . the list goes on. We are aware of errorless learning techniques, using small steps, mirroring, scaffolding, slow, passive modelling, and we are totally up on avoidance tactics and the need for consistency to develop appropriate behaviour. But none of this seems to . . . HELP!

And then you are told that because he can't do this it means he must have dyspraxia. A new label; a new bad bit of news. And whose fault is that? Quite possibly, it is the fault of the research community. Quite possibly it is because we have a tradition of giving a label to a child on the basis of what they cannot do. Quite possibly it is because we are fixated by the search for symptoms. That's how you can make someone better. But it takes a while to reach that realisation. In the meantime, you look into the black hole of uselessness and feel like shit.

Our measure of effectiveness as parents of Robbie is in so many ways fundamentally different to our effectiveness as parents of Isabel. Generally speaking, we avoid forcing Isabel to do things just because we believe it will be good for her in the end. We are firm believers in discipline, we make her eat a couple of sprouts, we expect her to go to bed at a particular time, we tell her she is going to go on that walk with us, but we would never make her play a game she did not want to play nor come up with cunning strategies to keep her standing up for longer. But with Robbie we are faced with confrontations about all kinds of things that we would let come naturally with Isabel. They come out of trying to teach him the sounds he should be saying, the way that his body should be moving, how he should doing a jigsaw, or insisting that he makes himself understood. Throughout the day, there are possible points of conflict not because of the person you would typically be with your child, but because you have become a person 'delivering' a programme in conjunction with a professional. And to make it worse, you know that the professional would hate to think that they were the cause of even the slightest bit of conflict. They are good people. People you like. But because of the relationship you have built with them, you now judge the effectiveness of your parenting against their targets, not your child's.

This change in our way of thinking is a surreptitious process, of course. It does not come about as a result of witnessing huge changes in Robbie because of these activities. We could not put our hands on our hearts and say that any of the interventions have had a clear-cut impact on Robbie and who he is now. The change in thinking comes about through learning the language of the professionals, and through the routine nature of carrying out the process. We get used to finding moments to fit in the activities, and gradually it becomes second nature to think of new ways to carry them out, of creating situations in which the activities become play. We don't notice what has happened until we lapse in this role. And, of course, all parents lapse. There are periods of time when life is too busy to properly carry out what we and the professionals are expecting of us, or when we lack the wherewithal they require. So, for example, I remember very clearly spending a weekend with Robbie when I had carried out none of the activities, and waking up on Monday morning, lying there at 6 am, thinking to myself, 'I'm a useless father', then realising what I was doing to myself. So, I went back over the past week and realised that I had played with him quite a lot . . . just played with him . . . and I thought, 'What's wrong with that? Aren't I allowed some time off? Isn't he?'

Of course, life moves you on. And so in his fifth year, Robbie started attending the local primary school, and we were no longer responsible for carrying out his learning programme. Now, like every other parent we just had to support his school and encourage him to engage with all they offer. But, of course, it was not quite as simple as that. Legally, Robbie only has special educational needs if he is provided with additional support, but it is largely up to us, his parents, to make sure the school receives the appropriate resources from the local authority so that they can provide that additional support. We had to make sure that Robbie had a suitable Statement of special educational needs or else everyone would suffer.

Robbie had his first Statement when he was two and a half. We were told by all the professionals that we spoke to, that Robbie was too young to have anything in his Statement except for the most general outline of his educational needs and how these should be met. It was explained that at this age things change so fast it is hardly worth getting things in writing. What really mattered was having the hours of support guaranteed by the local authority. Maybe they were right. But in hindsight I doubt it. What it actually meant was that they were able to get away with woolly targets and woolly descriptions of practice, which gave us no insight into how our son should be supported in his early years settings and no leverage when they patently failed to carry out strategies recommended by other professionals – strategies which were not included on the Statement, of course.

When it came to reviewing Robbie's Statement for the start of primary school, we were slightly more wary. We received the reports from various professionals and wondered if we had enough to work with. Surely, across all these reports were enough details for a suitable description and set of strategies to be mapped out. What is surprising is that we were surprised when the proposed Statement arrived from the local authority – outside the timelines required in the Code of Practice. Why were we expecting anything but the vague and woolly document that we were presented with, and one which offered too little support? Maybe it was our naivety. Maybe it is that faith in authority and the professionals who represent authority that has been drummed into all of us in our early years.

Of course, the reason that they do it is because they can.

So, on receiving the Statement we kicked up a stink. We contacted people with contacts, we obtained a report from the Down Syndrome Educational Trust, we went through the literature on Down syndrome; we rewrote their proposed Statement. And they ignored the lot. They told us that detail about how to work with Robbie should go in an Individual Education Plan, not a Statement. Again they wanted us to place our trust in the professionals, to trust our son's teachers to know what to do and to carry it out. Now as it happens we did trust our son's teachers. They had spent a year preparing for his arrival. But teachers move on, pupils change classes, new problems and opportunities emerge. Without a clear Statement we have no control, and the school has no guarantees or guidelines. So we had to take the local authority to a Tribunal. And on the day before it was due they agreed to our requests. And what was it all about . . . just three pages of clear description of how to support Robbie; a request that they specify how many times a year the different professionals visit; and our need for the Statement to state that the short activities recommended by the professionals are carried out daily, activities of the sort that we spent so many hours carrying out in our home.

The irony of it all was not lost on us, of course. We had become the professionals now. We were the ones driving them to list our son's needs, to create their checklists; we have to make sure that they get on with it. In the early days, it felt as if we were just passing through the lives of these professionals. We were in transit. Now, after so many of them have passed through our lives, we realise that they are the transient ones. We are the long-term providers and Robbie is the only constant. We are Robbie's mum and dad. That's all.

And now, Robbie is 10. Understanding him is still a great struggle, particularly for those who do not spent much time with him. As a consequence, much of the world is still immensely frustrating to him. Yet, we are preparing for the transition to secondary; he has chosen where he wants to go. We are meeting the next set of practitioners; and preparing to deal with government changes to the funding arrangement around our child. And we have so many other tales to tell – of hundreds of formal and informal meetings. Of all those issues we have discussed; about staffing and resources within our local authority; about changing relationships and attitudes; about home and school. We have explored our failure to transition Robbie effectively to a new class, the struggles of a teacher to creatively resolve issues, the ill health of a head teacher, and the accidental breaking of a teaching assistant's finger. We have discussed which class he should be in; who should come to his birthday party; how hard teachers find it to deal with Robbie and their expectations of what he can achieve.

We have put up with suggestions that he should go to a special school, that we can't really expect him to learn how to spell C–V–C words, and that having to teach him was 'a big ask'. We have heard about the training needs of staff; how he has been the best continuing professional development they have ever had and how he has reinvigorated a love of teaching. We have wept when he won the junior school science prize, stared aghast at a video of him turning a horse left and right on instruction after a week in the saddle, and sighed over how in Year 5 he still chooses to play repetitively with leaves in the playground. And so on and so forth. Strategies, policies, practices, tales, views and beliefs have been shared and considered.

It has been a long journey to here from the day when that first professional sat on our bed and began to make us doubt our ability to cope as parents. Along the way we have met many good people, many lazy ones, and many who really need to be a bit more reflective. Some have had an essential humanity, others have not. They have challenged us and changed our ways of thinking. They have damaged us at times and supported us at others. They have made this a very public experience and yet one that has turned us inward and become intensely private. Of course, many parents of typically developing children will see echoes of their own struggles with their offspring in this tale. They will feel that they have been as much concerned with the schooling of their children as we have, that they too struggle to get them to the next stage of learning. Many will feel they have given as many hours to swimming lessons, reading and writing and the learning of a musical instrument, and so on, as we have to Robbie. They too will see themselves as just as much revealed to the world by bringing up kids. Once I might have argued with them about this. Now I am not so sure. After all, we are all just parents. Robbie is just another child. But, when I look at my peers and at my early relationship with Isabel, I do feel there is a small difference that is worth noting. And as with all things this difference is both a blessing and a curse. The difference is that with Robbie everything is just a bit more. Life with Robbie involves just a bit more planning, more patience, more determination, more frustration, more reward, more extremes, more learning – more professionals.

So what, after a decade of being in the company of these trained individuals would I wish them to do differently? Well, I think I wish that they were better at encouraging us all to value our children for whom they are, rather than worrying quite so much about who they could be. I wish they would look less for the barriers to be overcome and more for the opportunities that are presented. After all, when all is said and done, Robbie is just a red-headed kid with a life of his own.

Chapter 29

Bangladeshi women and their children's reading

Adrian Blackledge

It has long been recognized that children can benefit greatly from their parents' involvement in learning to read. Adrian Blackledge's study of Bangladeshi families found that mothers were very keen to support their children's reading at home, but were frustrated by the gap between home and school literacy and by schools' lack of understanding of home literacy practices. Blackledge concludes the chapter with six recommendations to help bridge this cultural divide.

This study initially developed from questions about what happens when young, minority-language schoolchildren take home reading books which they are expected to read with their parents. Interviews with the mothers of young Bangladeshi children in Birmingham revealed that the home–school reading process reflected structural relations of power between minority and majority groups in society. In Bangladeshi families home and community literacies were associated with cultural identity, cultural transmission and symbolic power. School literacy, on the other hand, was a source of frustration and disempowerment.

Literacy as a social process

Different families and communities have different literacies (Street 1993). Cultural groups may differ in what they consider to be their 'texts' and in the values they attach to these, and may also differ in what they regard as literate behaviour. The same person may be regarded as 'illiterate' in one culture, while appearing to be quite literate in another. Often, 'school literacy' tends to define what counts as literacy, and this may construct the lack of school literacy in deficit terms (Street and Street 1991). That is,

Source: Blackledge, A. (1999) 'Literacy, power and social justice: Bangladeshi women and their children's reading' *Primary Practice: The Journal of the National Primary Trust,* 21 (September).

those who are not literate in the terms prescribed by the school may be seen as illiterate and therefore lacking essential skills.

When literacy is transferred from a dominant culture to a minority culture which has not historically been literate, majority culture values may be transmitted as part of the 'package' of literacy. In order to acquire literacy in the majority language it may be necessary for the learner to adopt some of the cultural behaviours and values of the majority, and risk sacrificing cultural group identity (Ferdman 1990). It was in the context of this theoretical framework that literacies in a Bangladeshi community in Birmingham made visible relations of power between the dominant and minority group.

Method

The initial stage of data collection was to record reading interactions between 18 six-year-old Bangladeshi children and family members as they attempted to read school books at home. The same children were recorded reading in school with their teachers. These data, reported elsewhere (Blackledge 1999), revealed that the children usually read with their siblings, who used a narrower range of support strategies than did the teachers. Several days after each recording was made, I interviewed the children's mothers, and their teachers. A bilingual/bicultural interpreter who lived in the local community assisted with the interviews, which were conducted in Sylheti (a spoken, but not literate, language of north-east Bangladesh). The interviews took place in the women's homes.

The women had migrated to Britain between seven and seventeen years earlier. Most of them had attended school for five or six years in Bangladesh, although three had never been to school. All of the women were able to read and write Bengali (the standard language of Bangladesh), except the three who had not attended school. None of the 18 reported that she was a confident reader or writer of English, or a confident speaker of English. All of the women reported that Sylheti was the only language used by them in the home. They said that their children spoke English to each other, and Sylheti when speaking to parents and other adults at home.

The 18 Bangladeshi women were interviewed about their children's reading, and their attempts to support their children's literacy learning. In addition to questions about their children's home reading practices, the women were asked about their interactions with the school as they attempted to find out about their children's academic progress. The children's teachers were interviewed about the process of teaching literacy, and their attempts to involve Bangladeshi parents in their children's school-related learning.

The women's attitudes to their children's English learning

The 18 women were asked about their attitudes to their children's language learning. All of them were positive about their children learning English at school. A common response was the following: 'It is very important that the children learn English, because this is where they live. They need to learn English to do well at school.'

The women's aspirations for their children's educational attainment were high, and they wished to do everything possible to support their progress. However, they found difficulties in contributing to this process.

Almost all of the women said that siblings were the main providers of English reading support. One of the women said that she did attempt to help her child to read English, and two said that their husbands sometimes helped. There was no evidence that the women's lack of reading support for their children was due to lack of interest. Rather, it seemed to be due to a feeling of powerlessness: 'It's very hard to teach the children at home because I don't speak English. I am trying my very best.'

Some of the women indicated that the reason they were unable to support their children's reading was not a deficiency in them, but the fact that the reading resources sent from school were in a language in which they were not literate: 'I would like the story books to be in English and Bengali, because I could explain the stories to the children. I can't read the English books.'

Some of the women said that nursery-age children brought home dual-text books, in Bengali and English. They welcomed these books, and read them to their young children. For the most part, however, books taken home by children were in English only.

School support for home literacy learning

The women were asked whether they had ever received explicit advice from the school about how to support their child's reading at home. Seven of them replied that they had received such advice, while eleven said that they had not. The women typically described the advice they had been given as follows: 'The teacher has told me that if I can't understand a book,

I can talk about the pictures. But if the book was in Bengali and English I could read the story myself.'

The teachers had given advice to these women which correctly assumed that they were unable to read English. However, the women's responses clearly demonstrated that although they could not read English, they were literate in Bengali, and they could have used this literacy to support their children's reading.

Most of the women said they would like more advice about how to support their child's reading, but they found it difficult to approach the teachers at the school: 'I did ask the teacher for advice about how to help Shanaz to read, but because I didn't know the language, or read and write, I felt embarrassed and couldn't understand. I don't really say anything to the teachers now.'

Although the problem of approaching teachers about children's reading is not confined to minority-language speakers, these mothers clearly identified the home–school language divide as the main reason that they had difficulties communicating with their children's teachers. The teachers had responded to this need by planning a strategy for educating the parents in home reading support: 'There are a lot of parents, particularly younger parents who have been educated in this country, they have some understanding of the system, and they do ask a lot of questions . . . we think they might be quite a captive audience.'

This positive step may not have solved the difficulties of the group in this study, however, as none of them had been educated in Britain. In fact, in targeting those parents who already had some understanding of the education system in Britain, the school potentially increased inequality (Toomey 1989), as those parents in most need of support were excluded. Those who were already relatively able to relate to the school had the opportunity to become further empowered if they could play by the rules of the school and 'understand the system', while also using and comprehending the language of the school. Those who either were unable, or refused, to adopt the cultural and linguistic norms of the school remained outsiders.

The women's attitudes to the cultural value of Sylheti

All of the women believed that maintenance of Sylheti was important for their children. Their main reason for this was that they wanted to be able to communicate with the children. However, the home language also seemed to have a symbolic importance for the women, as they indicated that Sylheti transmitted aspects of their cultural identity. This positive attitude to the cultural role of Sylheti was evident in responses to questions about storytelling in the home. Fifteen of the women said that they told stories to their children in the home language. These stories were told regularly, and were in a variety of traditions: 'I tell the children stories in Sylheti, traditional stories, Islamic stories, and stories I make up myself. I do this two or three times a week.' 'I make up stories for my three boys, like "there were once three princes who became kings", and so on.'

These responses make it clear that home-language storytelling was thriving in the homes of these families. This 'oral literacy' (Delgado-Gaitan 1990) activity was used to reinforce religious and cultural traditions. Teachers were aware of home-language storytelling as a valuable learning opportunity, but they had been unable to realise its potential in the classroom. The cultural and linguistic resources of the families remained in the private domain of the home, as the women were reluctant to enter the public domain of the school.

The women's attitudes to their children's Bengali literacy learning

The women were also asked about their attitude to their children's Bengali literacy learning. Bengali was the standard language of community literacy for these families, and different from Sylheti, the spoken language of the home. The women's responses made explicit the links between the community language and cultural identity. Most of the women either taught their children to read and write Bengali, or sent them to a local community class to learn. Although they spoke of the importance of Bengali for reading letters from the home country, the language had a significance beyond its function as a means of communication. It represented the group's identification as Bengalis, and their difference from the majority culture, and from other minority cultures: 'It is very important to me that he learns the language because we are Bengali. It is good that he has English as a second language.'

Twelve of the eighteen women took steps to directly support their children's Bengali literacy learning: 'As often as I can I will spend twenty minutes teaching them Bengali. I sit with the children for two hours on Saturdays and Sundays, and I teach them Bengali and Arabic.'

Those women who did not offer support at home for the children to read Bengali said that they would send their children to a tutor for this purpose when they were eight years old. The women's active support for the children's Bengali literacy learning made visible the symbolic association between language and cultural identity. They were able to offer Bengali literacy support to their children without having to acquire a new language, and without having to adopt aspects of the majority culture. Bengali literacy had a symbolic significance beyond its use as a means of communication.

For these women, to learn to read and write Bengali was to be Bengali. Teaching their children to be literate in Bengali represented a symbol of solidarity with their cultural group. Economic power was not likely to accrue from their children learning to be literate in Bengali. Yet the women invested considerable resources in Bengali literacy instruction. Far from being 'illiterate', the women organised their homes so that they actively taught their children to become literate in the community language.

Communication with their children's teachers

The Bangladeshi women had opportunities to talk to their children's teachers in formal and informal settings, including parents' evenings, parents' workshops and day-to-day contact when bringing children to, or collecting children from school. However, despite these opportunities, the women largely said that they found communication with teachers difficult because they were unable to speak English. There were rarely bilingual Sylheti-English school staff available on a day-to-day basis, and at parents' evenings interpreters were spread so thinly that young children often took on the role. For this reason some of the women had stopped going to parents' evenings.

The school had recently developed an initiative to involve parents in the school curriculum by inviting them to come into school to share in parents' workshops, which demonstrated aspects of the curriculum. Although a Sylheti interpreter was present, some of the women said that she was inappropriate for the role, as she was too young. Some of the women found these workshops useful, while others spoke of their 'embarrassment' at going to the school site, as they could not speak English. So although this school was doing more than most to communicate with this marginalised group of parents, the Bangladeshi women were still frustrated in their attempts to support their children's school work, and in their efforts to find out information about their children's progress.

Summary

These Bangladeshi women had a clear sense of the value of their languages and literacies. They operated successfully in their home and community linguistic domains, where their languages were accepted and valued. Both the spoken Sylheti language and the literate language of Bengali were important features of their cultural identity, and had a symbolic significance beyond their functional use. The women's languages represented solidarity with their cultural group.

The school seemed to consider that they were unable to contribute to their children's literacy learning, because their home and community literacies did not fit with the literacy of the school. The teachers did not incorporate the families' languages in the education of their children, or provide advice or resources to enable the women to become involved in their children's schooling. In dictating that the language of interaction in, and with, the school was solely English, the teachers demanded that the Bangladeshi mothers play by the cultural and linguistic rules of the dominant majority, or put at risk their children's academic progress. If they were willing and able to acquire the language and literacy of the school, they were able to gain access to information about their children's education. If not, they remained disempowered in their attempts to support their children's education.

Implications for policy and practice

Each time people are required to learn another language in order to participate in society, an act of injustice occurs (Tollefson 1991). In the study presented here, a group of women was effectively prevented from finding out about, or contributing to, their children's education. The main reason for this was that the school required that the women become proficient readers, writers and speakers of English in order to participate in the educational process. Schools in similar contexts can take steps to redress the balance of injustice by:

- Sending reading books home with children; these should be high-quality, dual-language texts. Where possible, these should be texts which originate in the heritage country of the family.
- Talking to parents about their literacies, including 'oral literacies' such as storytelling. Plan for the parents' languages and literacies to be authentically incorporated in the curriculum. All children will benefit from seeing that teachers give high status to minority languages.
- Offering parents practical, comprehensible advice about how to use school reading books at home. If parents will not come into the school (many parents perceive the school as the domain of the teachers), other

sites can be used – libraries, community centres, etc. There is much evidence (Toomey 1993) that home visits to parents can make a significant difference to their confidence and competence as home literacy tutors.

- Ensuring that appropriate, trained interpreters are available at all times, including the beginning and end of the school day, parents' evenings, parents' workshops, women's groups, coffee morning, etc. Ask parents' permission to use individual interpreters for particular situations, and try to offer alternatives – for example, should a neighbour be involved in a sensitive conversation about a child's behaviour or attainment?
- Recruiting teachers who speak the language(s) of the community served by the school, and encouraging them to use their languages where appropriate. Of course this does not mean simply helping young children until they are able to speak English, but is about valuing the languages of the school community at all levels. The study presented here makes it clear that languages are very much associated with cultural identity.
- Involving minority parents in policy-making and planning. Schools may have the best intentions in developing policy for all children, but they may be unaware of the needs and resources of the community. Only a local community can really know what is necessary for its children (Corson 1994).

At a time when the management of learning in English primary schools has become increasingly controlled from the centre, it is important to develop language and literacy policy and practice at the local level, to meet the needs of local communities. In this way the teaching of literacy in minority communities can become the site of renegotiation rather than reproduction of power, and the balance of injustice can be redressed.

References

Blackledge, A. (1999) *Literacy, Power and Social Justice*. Stoke-on-Trent: Trentham Books.

Corson, D. (1994) 'Bilingual education policy and social justice', in: A. Blackledge (ed.), *Teaching Bilingual Children*. Stoke-on-Trent: Trentham Books.

Delgado-Gaitan, C. (1990) *Literacy for Empowerment*. London: Falmer Press.

Ferdman, B.M. (1990) 'Literacy and cultural identity'. *Harvard Educational Review*, 60, 181–204.

Street, B. (1993) 'Introduction: The new literacy studies', in: B. Street (ed.), *Cross-Cultural Approaches to Literacy*. Cambridge: Cambridge University Press.

Street, B. and Street, J. (1991) 'The schooling of literacy', in: D. Barton and R. Ivanic (eds.), *Writing in the Community*. London: Sage.

Tollefson, J. (1991) *Planning Language, Planning Inequality*. Harlow: Longman.

Toomey, D. (1989) 'How home–school relations policies can increase educational inequality'. *Australian Journal of Education*, 33 (3), 284–98.

Toomey, D. (1993) 'Parents hearing their children read: a review. Rethinking the lessons of the Haringey Project'. *Educational Research*, 35, 223–6.

Chapter 30

Breaking the taboo

Ruth Pooley

In this chapter, Ruth Pooley, a teaching assistant and psychotherapist, urges us all to be alert to the possible signs of children's unhappiness and abuse. She lays out the evidence in no uncertain way, arguing that adults in schools must be vigilant and prepared to share and formally report any concerns that they may have about some children. Her dual work involvements make her well placed to provide insights into this essential aspect of school practice.

I have two careers; in one there are intimate and reflective moments spent as a psychotherapist, then in the other I work in noisy, busy, classrooms filled with young children where I am a teaching assistant. I find these roles complement each other but at times I can't help wondering if any of the children engaging with me in a classroom might be tomorrow's clients; and if there is anything I can do now to prevent future needs for psychotherapeutic assistance. Many of my clients, in my work as a psychotherapist, were sexually abused when young so I do think about what I can do, as a teaching assistant, to prevent this apparent cycle. This leads me to think about child protection policies and how effective in practice they really are.

The people I work with, like most teaching assistants, continually implement the child protection policy ensuring the children's and their own boundaries are respected and protected. As carers in a professional role we balance the needs of children who sometimes seek attention, or even parenting, with professional conduct. I see this administered skilfully every day. A more subtle part of child protection is to inform our managers if we are worried about a child's behaviour, especially if we have concerns about the origin of that behaviour.

Not all unusual behaviour indicates abuse, so how can we know which of the children will have been abused? That's the thing, of course, we don't

Source: Commissioned by The Open University for this volume.

know. 'Child abuse is usually hidden from view and the children may be too young, too scared or too ashamed to tell anyone about what is happening to them' (NSPCC, 2011a: 1).

We know that according to NSPCC research 'One in nine young adults (11.3%) experienced contact sexual abuse during childhood' (NSPCC, 2011b: 1). There aren't 'bad' areas of the country where it happens more; it can be present in all schools wherever they are. A Cross Government Action Plan on Sexual Violence and Abuse stated 'it's much more common than people think' (p. iii), giving figures that 1 in 5 girls and 1 in 10 boys experience some sort of child sexual abuse (Home Office, 2007).

In May 2011 the NSPCC released new figures, obtained from police forces, stating that 'At least 64 children are sexually abused every day in England and Wales' (BBC, 2011). These figures can be broken down to show that a quarter of the abusers are children themselves and the NSPCC are launching a programme to work with these children to prevent them perpetrating the cycle of abuse. 'Staff in schools . . . are uniquely placed to be someone to turn to for children . . . requiring support and advice, and to help protect them from harm' (NSPCC, 2011c: 1). And that's why I do want to urge you to be especially aware in the classroom, seriously considering (when your interactions with children cause you concern) if some of those pupils around you are being exposed to abusive behaviour. This is a fundamental contribution to the prevention of abuse.

It is important, of course, to log worrying behaviour and to do this thoroughly. It is also essential to talk to the '*Designated Teacher for Child Protection*', required in every school according to the Education Act (2002). Those children who are being abused (or at serious risk of being abused) must get protection. That's part of child protection. Noticing and reporting incidences concerning children that, perhaps, seem out of sorts in some little way, may mean you could eventually be protecting them from the unimaginable but very real incidence of being sexually abused. Of course, it is quite plausible that a troubled child has something else bothering them from friendship issues to perhaps parents getting divorced. Careful observations and sensitive interactions with children that identify and better understand these types of life event are also good practices in schools.

To be fully aware and prepared it is important to be familiar with a school's child protection policy and procedures that will contain information about promoting well-being as well as child protection. It is important to know exactly who to talk to and remember that any suspicion of child abuse may become a police matter and therefore a teaching assistant cannot have interrogated or questioned the child in any way. If we do feel a child has suffered some form of abuse it is paramount to remember the child's specific needs and the need for reassurance. You would be unlikely to gain a whole story or, for that matter, an entirely truthful story due to the fear of reprisals. That is another reason to keep logging small incidences in writing and sharing these notes with the designated teacher so that she/he can pass these on if deemed significant. Insignificant details, if recorded, can sometimes add to a picture in hindsight, but those finer details tend to be easily forgotten unless noted. The balance is to reassure a child while remaining professional and not promising confidentiality. It is also important to stay very aware of national and local changes in policies and practices.

On The Open University module 'Supporting learning in primary schools' (E111) there is a study topic on observation that looks at the benefits of watching children with a specific focus. When practising this, a teaching assistant could also bear in mind the dynamics of the class or a certain child. I was fascinated when I started using observation; we can learn so much during a short time of simple yet careful watching. Once practised, such skills can be used, even in a relaxed way, when observing in the playground. It is interesting to notice what we focus on when observing a large group of children; for instance, we may be familiar with spotting a dangerous playground incident. However, try asking your mind to watch other types of behaviour; who is left out, lonely, awkward, or despondent? It is surprising how much we can start to see when we really stop and look.

In my work as a psychotherapist I facilitate a support group for women who have been sexually abused. These women have been violated in the most awful and taboo way imaginable. They haven't just been hurt, brutally and physically, they have been manipulated and lied to and terrorised into not telling. When a child falls over in your school don't they want to tell you about it? So why do abused children keep quiet? Because they might have been told their mum will die (or something similarly terrifying) if they talk about what is being done to them. They aren't just harmed but their rights to trusting adult-to-child relationships have been violated and broken. Many abused children are also told it's their fault, 'they asked for it'. Their self-respect is thus stolen alongside losing their trust in adults. No wonder it's hard for them to talk about abuse. To even get to the support group most of the women I work with have an intense feeling that they would be rubbished. One of them said to me 'Sexual abuse violates the sanctity of a person. Their personality is reached and damaged' (L.W., 2011) With children the sense of breaking a threat is even more present.

'Children usually find some way of expressing their distress or crying out for help even though they cannot ask for help directly' (Ainscough and Toon, 2000: 170) This may include behaviour that is withdrawn or bullying, clinging, or disruptive and also eating disorders.

As teaching assistants we have a unique role to support children with their journey through the education system. Our relationship can affect their academic achievement, their understanding of appropriate behaviour and values and we can support them to gain their personal independence. Sometimes we are mediators between the education system and the child and I see many of my colleagues working in ways that embody commitment and professionalism. We are also mediators between the wider society and the children and occasionally that might mean acting on their behalf. Breaking the taboo, speaking out when necessary, about child sexual abuse, will mean we can play a part in exposing the perpetrators who prey, not only on children, but on all of our good natures.

References

Ainscough, C., and Toon, K. (2000) *Breaking Free Workbook: Practical Help for Survivors of Child Sexual Abuse*. London: Sheldon Press.

BBC (British Broadcasting Corporation) (2011) 'NSPCC urges action on child abuse'. Accessed 25 September 2011, from BBC News UK, http://www.bbc.co.uk/news/uk-13558164

Home Office (2007) *Cross Government Action Plan on Sexual Violence and Abuse*. Accessed 25 September 2011, from http://webarchive.nationalarchives.gov.uk/20100413151441/http://crimereduction.homeoffice.gov.uk/violentcrime/finalsvaap.pdf

NSPCC (National Society for the Prevention of Cruelty to Children) (2011a) 'How to find, understand and use statistics about child abuse'. Accessed 25 September 2011, from http://www.nspcc.org.uk/Inform/research/statistics/introduction to child abuse statistics_wda68935.html

NSPCC (National Society for the Prevention of Cruelty to Children) (2011b) 'Statistics on sexual abuse'. Accessed 25 September 2011, from http://www.nspcc.org.uk/Inform/resourcesforprofessionals/sexual_abuse_statistics_wda80204.html

NSPCC (National Society for the Prevention of Cruelty to Children) (2011c) 'Safety in learning'. Accessed 25 September 2011, from http://www.nspcc.org.uk/Inform/trainingandconsultancy/learningresources/safetyinlearning_wda51474.html

Acknowledgement

With thanks to LW for her quote from a private conversation on 6 March 2011.

Chapter 31

Common sense has much to learn from moonshine

Philip Pullman

Philip Pullman is able to write about learning to read and write from the perspective both of a former middle school teacher and author. Rather than teaching children about grammar rules, he argues that the main concern of schools should be with the picture books, stories, poems and songs which are the full realisation of the powers of language. The confidence children need to become readers and writers comes from playing, speculating, and 'fooling about' rather than 'drilling and testing . . . and correcting'.

The report published by the University of York (2004) on its research into the teaching of grammar will hardly surprise anyone who has thought about the subject. The question being examined was whether instruction in grammar had any effect on pupils' writing. It included the largest systematic review yet of research on this topic; and the conclusion the authors came to was that there was no evidence at all that the teaching of grammar had any beneficial effect on the quality of writing done by pupils.

Needless to say, this goes against common sense. That particular quality of mind, the exclusive property of those on the political right, enables its possessors to know without the trouble of thinking that of course teaching children about syntax and the parts of speech will result in better writing, as well as making them politer, more patriotic and less likely to become pregnant.

For once, however, common sense seems to have been routed by the facts. If we want children to write well, giving them formal instruction in grammar turns out not to be any use; getting them actually writing seems to help a great deal more. Teaching techniques that do work well, the study discovered, are those that include combining short sentences into longer ones, and embedding elements into simple sentences to make them more complex: in other words, using the language to say something.

Source: Pullman, P. (2005) 'Common sense has much to learn from moonshine', *Guardian* 22 January. Copyright Guardian Newspapers Limited 2005.

A word often flourished in this context by the common sense brigade is 'basics'. It's always seemed curious to me that commentators and journalists – people who write every day and who presumably know something about the practice of putting words on paper – should make such an elementary error as to think that spelling and punctuation and other such surface elements of language are 'the basics'. These, and deeper features of language such as grammar, are things you can correct at proof stage, at the very last minute, and we all do that very thing, every day. But how can something you can alter or correct at that late point possibly be basic? What's truly basic is something that has to be in place much earlier on: an attitude to the language, to work, to the world itself.

And there are many possible attitudes to take up. There are some that are confident and generous and fruitful, and others that are marked by fear and suspicion and hostility. We instill these attitudes in children by the way we talk to them, or the fact that we don't, and by means of the activities we give them to do, and the environments we create to surround them, and the games and TV programmes and stories we provide them with. The most valuable attitude we can help children adopt – the one that, among other things, helps them to write and read with most fluency and effectiveness and enjoyment – I can best characterise by the word playful.

It begins with nursery rhymes and nonsense poems, with clapping games and finger play and simple songs and picture books. It goes on to consist of fooling about with the stuff the world is made of: with sounds, and with shapes and colours, and with clay and paper and wood and metal, and with language. Fooling about, playing with it, pushing it this way and that, turning it sideways, painting it different colours, looking at it from the back, putting one thing on top of another, asking silly questions, mixing things up, making absurd comparisons, discovering unexpected similarities, making pretty patterns, and all the time saying 'Supposing . . . I wonder . . . What if . . .'

The confidence to do this, the happy and open curiosity about the world that results from it, can develop only in an atmosphere free from the drilling and testing and examining and correcting and measuring and ranking in tables that characterises so much of the government's approach, the 'common sense' attitude to education.

And the crazy thing is that the common sense brigade think that they're the practical ones, and that approaches like the one I'm advocating here are sentimental moonshine. They could hardly be more wrong. It's when we do this foolish, time-consuming, romantic, quixotic, childlike thing called play that we are most practical, most useful, and most firmly grounded in reality, because the world itself is the most unlikely of places, and it works in the oddest of ways, and we won't make any sense of it by doing what everybody else has done before us. It's when we fool about with the stuff the world is made of that we make the most valuable discoveries, we create the most lasting beauty, we discover the most profound truths. The youngest children can do it, and the greatest artists, the greatest scientists do it all the time. Everything else is proofreading.

Take the National Curriculum. The authors of the York study remind us that it lays down that children aged five to seven 'should be taught to consider: a) how word choice and order are crucial to meaning, b) the nature and use of nouns, verbs and pronouns' and so on; that children aged seven to eleven 'should be taught word classes and the grammatical functions of words, including nouns, adjectives, adverbs, pronouns, prepositions, conjunctions, articles', as well as 'the grammar of complex sentences, including clauses, phrases and connectives . . .' Think of the age of those children, and weep. It simply doesn't work.

What does work, the York study maintains, is writing in a meaningful context: writing as a practical hands-on craft activity. One of the implications of this is that teachers have to be confident about writing – about play, about delight. Too many are not, because they haven't had to be; and the result is the dismal misery of the 'creative writing' drills tested in the SATS, where children are instructed to plan, draft, edit, revise, rewrite, always in the same order, always in the same proportions, always in the same way. If teachers knew something about the joy of fooling about with words, their pupils would write with much greater fluency and effectiveness. Teachers and pupils alike would see that the only reason for writing is to produce something true and beautiful; that they were on the same side, with the teacher as mentor, as editor, not as instructor and measurer, critic and judge.

And they'd see when they looked at a piece of work together that some passages were so good already that they didn't need rewriting, that some parts needed clarifying, others needed to be cut down, others would be more effective in a different order, and so on. They'd see the point of the proofreading, at last; and they'd be ready, because they were interested, to know about subordinate clauses and conjunctions and the rest. The study of grammar is intensely fascinating: but only when we're ready for it.

True education flowers at the point when delight falls in love with responsibility. If you love something, you want to look after it. Common sense has much to learn from moonshine.

Reference

Andrews, R., Torgerson, C., Beverton, S., Freeman, A., Locke, T., Law, G., Robinson, A. and Zhu, D. (2004) *The effect of grammar teaching (sentence combining) in English on 5 to 16 year olds' accuracy and quality in written composition*, Department of Education Studies, University of York, UK.

Chapter 32

Children and spelling

Marsha Bell

Such is the complexity of written English, argues Marsha Bell, an author, that in 1953 there was a private member's 'Spelling Reform Bill' which gave rise to the idea of an 'initial teaching alphabet' (ITA). Reading books were made available to schools during the 1960s which used ITA to simplify the relationship between letters and their sounds thus better enabling children's early reading and writing. The project was not sustained, however. Children in schools today, of course, continue to encounter the many irregularities of the English spelling system and this chapter argues for a greater understanding of the difficulties faced by children and their teachers.

Irregular English spelling

Most teachers realise that many pupils find learning to read and write English difficult because of the endless error correcting they have to do. There is research evidence for this too. A cross-European study (Seymour, 2003), found that English-speaking pupils take three times longer to master the basics of reading and writing than the European average of just one year.

They found that speed of literacy learning correlated with the consistency of spelling systems. English spelling was judged to be the most irregular and English literacy acquisition was found to be the most time consuming. Finnish, by contrast, beats all other European writing systems for simplicity and regularity. The study found that Finnish children learned to read and write much faster than in any other of the 12 languages which the project included.

The impact of English spelling on literacy learning was first thoroughly investigated in England in 1963–4, in a large-scale study conducted by The

Source: An edited version of Bell, M. (2010) 'Supporting children with spelling problems', in *Special Children*, August, 34–38.

London Institute of Education and the National Foundation for Educational Research. This compared the literacy learning and general educational progress of 873 English children who learned to read and write with traditional English spelling and an equal number who were taught with the more regular spellings of the initial teaching alphabet (ITA – see www.omniglot.com/writing/ita.htm). This research was carried out because in 1953 the House of Commons had passed all three stages of a private member's Spelling Reform Bill and the government of the day had consequently agreed to ascertain if English spelling irregularities really impeded literacy progress.

The study proved very clearly that they did. It left no doubt that if English spelling were simplified, we would reduce the literacy problems that so many children continue to exhibit to this day. Children using ITA learned to read English far more easily and much faster. They also read more fluently, made fewer errors and gained higher comprehension scores. No children in the ITA groups made the very poor progress recorded for several children learning with traditional spelling. The writing of children on ITA was also superior. Their compositions were longer and contained a much wider vocabulary. They also showed more enthusiasm for learning all subjects, not just reading and writing.

For native speakers of English it is not easy to appreciate how much English spelling differs from other alphabetic writing systems or the way in which it makes both learning to read and write uniquely difficult. Literate adults nearly all began to become acquainted with English spelling at a very young age, on their parents' laps, and they have generally taken quite a long time to master it. They were usually also never made deliberately aware of how much more time and effort, in comparison to other languages, English literacy acquisition takes.

To me the uniqueness of English spelling was made more obvious, because I did not begin to learn the language until the age of 14, before starting German the following year. My first languages were Lithuanian and Russian. I could therefore not help but notice that the three others were all spelt much more consistently and so reading and writing could be mastered much more quickly. Over the past 12 years I have spent much time investigating the English spelling system by analysing the 6,800 most used English words and establishing how many of them have regular or irregular spellings, and hope that I can now explain quite clearly how the English writing system differs from all other alphabetic ones.

The English spelling system

Most languages have around 40 sounds. English has 43½. (The half sound is any unstressed vowel, as in 'cert*ai*n, flatt*e*n, *a*band*o*n'. It is never clearly audible, because only stressed English vowels can be heard properly (c*er*tain, fl*a*tten, ab*a*ndon). Of those there is usually only one per word.

All alphabetic writing systems start by obeying the basic alphabetic principle of using a grapheme (a single letter or letter string like *sh*) to spell one sound only and to spell a sound with just one grapheme. Quite a few European languages still conform to this principle entirely (Finnish) or fairly closely (Italian and Spanish). Finnish uses just 38 spellings for its 38 sounds. Other European languages have an average of 50 graphemes. The Finnish orthography exemplifies alphabetic perfection. English spelling lies at the extreme end of alphabetic imperfection. It uses 185 spellings for its 43½ sounds. This is why Professor Seymour and his colleagues ranked it as the most irregular and hardest-to-master of the 13 European languages that they compared.

One reason for the larger number of English spellings is that 19 of its sounds are spelt with more than one grapheme. This can depend on whether a sound is in the middle of a word (s*au*ce, l*a*te) or at the end (s*aw*, l*ay*); or on the sounds which follow (**c**/at/ot/ut, **k**ite/kept) or precede (pi**ck**, see**k**). This gives English 81 basic spelling rules for its 43½ sounds. In addition to those, there are also nine patterns for endings and prefixes (love*able*, vertic*al*, ordin*ary*, fast*en*, abs*ent*, fath*er*, sing*le*; *de*cide, *in*dulge), and the consonant doubling rule ([d*i*ne – d*inn*er), making 91 basic spelling rules in all.

Unfortunately, only 11 of the 91 basic English spelling rules have no exceptions (**b**ed, **j**ug/jog/jab, gor**ge**, ri**ng**, sing**le**, **p**in, musi**ci**an, **th**is, *th*ing, **v**an, televi**si**on). The other 80 all get broken in at least one word (eg last – *ll*ama). Some patterns get broken in so many different ways, and by so many words, that they cannot really be said to have any rule or pattern at all.

The ee-sound, for example, is spelt with **ea** in 152 common words (beach, bead, beak. .), but **ee** in another 133 (beef, beer, bleed. . .), e-e in 86 (eve, even, here. . .) and an assortment of other spellings in a further 81 words (s**ei**ze, s**ie**ge, pol**i**ce, b**e**, k**ey**, sk**i**. . .). This means that all the spellings for the ee-sound have to be individually memorised for each of the 452 words.

Even if English spelling were entirely consistent, mastering its 91 rules would already take a little longer than the mere 38 totally reliable sound-to-letter correspondences of Finnish spelling. Having to learn a much smaller number of sound-to-letter rules, and the sounds for far fewer spellings inevitably enables children to learn to read and write faster.

When spelling and decoding rules are entirely one-to-one, as in Finnish, reading and writing also have a reversible and mutually highly supportive relationship. If the English ai-sound, for example, was always spelt ai, as in 'main rain drain', learning to read the ai grapheme would help with spelling the ai-sound too. With positional spellings (m**ai**n m**ay**; g**oa**t g**o**) learning to spell immediately becomes more complex.

Basic English literacy acquisition is made even more difficult by the use of the rather complex 'open' method for some of its vowels (cr**ane**; h**idi**ng; h**ole**; t**ubu**lar) which is linked to the use of doubled consonants for keeping vowels short (cr**ann**y, h**idd**en, h**oll**y, t**ubb**y).

The main retardants of progress

Despite being relatively complex, the basic English spelling system would cause far fewer learning difficulties than it does, if it really were a 'system' – if it was applied consistently. The main retardants of English literacy progress are English spelling inconsistencies. The fairly difficult 'open' and 'closed' method for spelling long and short vowels, for example, is made much harder to grasp by many words with short vowels left 'open'-looking, without the consonants after them being doubled: pane – p**a**n*el*, line – l*inen*, cone – *conif*er, student – st*udy*.

Consonant doubling happens to be the very worst English spelling problem. Its irregularities create the longest word-by-word memorisation list: 372 common words of more than one syllable use a doubled consonant to keep a stressed vowel short (poppy, berry), 384 don't (copy, very) and 158 have doubled letters for unfathomable reasons (afoot, arise – *afford*, arrive). The 452 words with unpredictable spellings for ee create the second-longest rote-learning burden. See www.englishspellingproblems.co.uk for tables about spelling patterns.

Lack of consistency in the application of its spelling rules and patterns is what makes learning to read and write English much harder than any other alphabetic language. (Chinese is quite difficult too, but is not really comparable because it uses pictograms, which give a clue to meaning, instead of representing sounds with letters.) The endless need to keep having to memorise exceptions is the hardest part of learning to read and write English.

Altogether, at least 3,695 common words (as listed at the English Spelling Problems website, above) contain one or more spelling irregularities which have to be learned word-by-word. Most English words with spelling abnormalities have only one redundant letter (fr*i*end, he*a*d, b*u*ild] or irregular spelling (pr*e*tty, M*o*nday, so*u*p), but several hundred have more (b*ea*utiful, m*a*ny, r*ough* – cf. d*u*tiful, pe**nn**y, st**uff**).

Some patterns have very few exceptions and are much more teachable than others. The a-sound of 'cat, bad' and 'rang', for example has just three exceptions (plait, plaid, meringue); the initial ch-sound of 'chat' and 'check' just one (cello).

Most consonant spelling patterns have very few exceptions, but the rules for spelling the k-sound are quite tricky (**c**at, **ki**ck, comi**c**, sti**ck**, **c**lever, an**kl**e), and have quite a few exceptions too (*ch*ara**c**ter, ka*y*ak, mos*q*ue, un*c*le).

Most other European languages also have *some* words with irregular spellings, but they number just dozens or at most a few hundred. In Finnish, only a handful of recently imported words from other languages have not entirely regular spellings. Italian and Spanish each have around 300 words with minor spelling abnormalities. German has around 800. The memorisation burdens they create for learners are miniscule compared to the minimum of 3,695 common English words with one or more unpredictably spelt letters. The much heavier load of word-by-word memorisation inevitably makes literacy progress in English considerably harder and slower than in other languages.

Reading difficulties

English differs from other alphabetic languages even more, by posing reading as well as spelling difficulties. It is the only European language that has wide-spread use of identical letters for different sounds in addition to having a much greater number of variably spelt sounds. Apart from a few very rare exceptions, such as regional differences for a couple of letters in Spanish, other spelling systems don't pose pronunciation problems, only spelling ones.

The German graphemes 'ir','ier' and 'ihr', for example, all spell the English 'eer' sound and make learning to spell some words with that sound (wir, hier, ihr – Eng. 'we, here, to her') slower than it would be without this irregularity. The pronunciation of 'ir', 'ier' and 'ihr', however, is never in doubt: Once children have learned to pronounce them, they can decode those graphemes thereafter in any word they meet. The same applies to the French spellings for the English long 'oo' sound (**ou, nous,**

tout, ch**oux**). Learning to write such words takes time, but learning to read them is easy.

In English, variable pronunciations for identical single letters or letter strings (s**ou**nd, s**ou**p, to**u**ch; **ear**, *ear*ly, w*ear*) are not a rare exception. They are common.

Sixty-nine of the 91 basic English graphemes can have more than one pronunciation. Because the phonic unreliability of some graphemes, such as 'o' (on, only, once), 'ea' (treat, great, threat) and 'ou' (count, country, groups), makes several dozen words not entirely decodable, the total number of common English words with some tricky-to-read letters is 2,031. This is why English-speaking children need several years just to learn to read, never mind spell; and why other European children with their reliable 50 or so graphemes all learn to read and write much faster.

How understanding can help

I recently explained how English spelling differs from other writing systems at the annual conference of NATE (National Association for Teachers of English). And although my audience seemed to find my presentation enlightening, several attendees asked how a better understanding of the complexities of English spelling helped in the classroom.

The main benefit of appreciating the complexities of English spelling is probably that it enables teachers to make struggling readers and spellers feel better about their literacy problems. Making struggling pupils aware that their difficulties are due mainly to the irregularities of English spelling tends to be a great morale booster.

Most learners with reading and writing problems tend to believe that these are unique to them, that they are somehow 'failing to get' what everyone else finds easy. They don't know that over half of all students regularly misspell many common words, and that one in four find learning to read English extremely difficult. Few of them know that many very bright people, from Darwin and Edison to Einstein and Richard Branson, found English spelling very difficult too. Even quite a few well known writers are or were poor spellers: Ben Elton, Agatha Christie, John Steinbeck, for example.

The best spellers are almost invariably ones who are blessed with an above-average visual memory, like people with exceptional musical or artistic talent. This makes learning to read and write English much easier for them than for the majority. Because those skills come easily to them, they also find reading and writing more enjoyable, they therefore read and write more, and stay ahead of everyone else.

My daughter has always been an above-average speller, but I cannot remember her ever revising for a spelling test or being anxious about one. She seemed to be able to spell without trying, but she did start to read and write at a very young age. She asked to be helped to learn to read and then just took off. My son, by contrast, found both learning to read and write difficult, was reluctant to do either for a worryingly long time, then had to work hard at both skills and made lots of spelling mistakes throughout his educational career, even beyond graduation.

Most people learn to spell well enough for their needs, in the end, but it can take a long time. Nobody can memorise the various spelling quirks in 3,695 common words in just a couple of years. Even the best spellers can only spell the majority of English words correctly after roughly 10 years in education.

Poor spellers are not lazy. Their brain wiring is just less suited to coping with the inconsistencies of English spelling. Italians with similar neural connections have no literacy problems in their own more regularly spelt language. They only discover that they have dyslexia when they begin to learn English.

A better understanding of what makes learning to read and write English difficult also makes teachers more able to evaluate proposed changes in teaching methods which are invariably hailed as a sure cure for literacy problems. Debbie Hepplewhite, the passionate advocate of synthetic phonics claimed in an interview for the last issue of *Special Children* that 'it is sometimes the case that teachers simply don't know what they don't know' and therefore many 'can be teaching their hearts out but with flawed methods'.

Nearly everyone blames poor literacy standards on poor or wrong teaching. The current education secretary Michael Gove believes that literacy standards started going downhill with the abandonment of systematic synthetic phonics in the 1960s and 70s. He fails to appreciate that this happened only because the earlier approaches were consistently leaving too many pupils failing to learn to read and write. The Moser survey of 1999 concluded that 22%, or seven million adults, across the whole age range, were 'functionally illiterate' (Moser, 1999). The percentage of schoolchildren and adults with severe literacy problems has hovered around 20 for as long as it has been measured.

Practicalities

Anyone who takes a closer look at English spelling really cannot fail to see that the inconsistencies of English spelling are responsible for making learning to read and write slow and difficult. If one examines the words that young children regularly stumble over in reading [eg could, bought, touched) and the spelling errors that they commit in writing (granmar, lernt, scool) one finds that, apart from the occasional inexplicable slip, they are all due to irregular spellings.

Teaching children to read English is not nearly as difficult as to spell, mainly because the number of words with unreliable letters (a, man, can – *any, many*) is only just over 2,000; for spelling it's nearly double that amount. Many unpredictable spellings have regular pronunciations: 'main, rain, drain' – 'crane, lane, plane'. Learning when to use which in writing is much harder and takes longer.

Individual children's ability to learn to spell is also more variable. They differ greatly in their capacity for rote learning. This makes the use of whole-class spelling tests of very limited value. They are a nice ego booster for naturally good spellers, but a nightmare for really weak ones, and not even of much help to middling ones. The best approach is to encourage pupils to take note of their particular errors and to learn from those, by the well proven 'look, say, cover, write and check' method. The main part of learning to spell English is 'just a bunch of memorisation', as the winner of the 2008 US national spelling bee put it.

It is simply not possible to learn to spell English merely by learning 'to apply the English alphabet code', as current advocates of more rigorous phonics teaching claim. Teaching pupils that the ee-sound can be spelt with 'ea, ee, e-e, ie, ei, i-e, e, ey', and some rarer graphemes (people, ski, quay) is really teaching them that spellings for the ee sound obey no code. The hard part is learning which words use which.

It is, however, not just English spelling which requires substantial amounts of word-by-word work. Learning to read words like 'ghost', 'woman', or 'beautiful' does too, and involves much more than simple phonic decoding. They are learnt mainly by the nowadays much despised whole-word method.

Finding the balance

Given the inconsistencies of English spelling, learning to read and write English requires a mixture of phonics and word-by-word memorisation, for both reading and writing. The only thing that makes a difference to literacy progress is lots of teaching. English-speaking children simply need much more of it than speakers of other languages.

It is best administered in daily, short, well-planned and lively bouts, and the weakest pupils do best with one-to-one sessions that address their particular problems. On closer examination, that is also all that synthetic phonics really advocates too.

Unless we get round to reducing at least some of the most learner-unfriendly English spelling irregularities, it will remain thus, and around one in five children will continue to have difficulties with reading and writing, even if 'teachers teach their hearts out', by whatever method. For some pupils, the current English literacy-learning burden is just too overwhelming, comparable to trying to teach the violin to a tone-deaf child. It is unfair to keep blaming teachers for failing to perform miracles, if the rest of society does not think it's worth putting up with some changes to English spelling in order to enable more children to learn to read and write, and to give them access to the many benefits which this brings.

Reference

Moser, C. (1999) *A fresh start: Improving literacy and numeracy*. London: National Literacy Trust.

Chapter 33

Learning in a breakfast club

Peter Woolston with Roger Hancock

In many UK primary schools, breakfast clubs have become an integral part of an extended school day. This arises from concerns that a substantial number of children arrive at school without having had breakfast and this, understandably, can impact on their ability to learn and behave as required in the classroom. Teaching assistants can play a central role in facilitating and running such clubs. Here, Peter Woolston provides an insight of how he helped set up a club at Herbert Thompson Primary School, South Wales.

I helped in the initial set up, in conjunction with the head teacher and another teaching assistant. In the first year the children were asked to pay 10p an item for cereal, toast and jam, or a drink of fruit juice or milk .We used to have to buy our supplies from a local cash and carry, which was quite hard work, loading and unloading stock.

For the last seven years we have been Welsh Assembly funded and all children are entitled to a free breakfast. Supplies are regulated by the county and I have to order through their approved suppliers, which are then delivered weekly. Currently we have an average of 90 children having breakfast, often peaking at more than 100 in an even mix of Key Stages 1 and 2.

Parents who wish their child to attend fill in a simple form giving any dietary or medical conditions and emergency contact numbers. We have some children with lactose intolerance but we use soya milk for them.

The club is staffed by me, as the co-ordinator, and six other teaching assistants, who supervise the children in our two interlinked areas in the school canteen building. There are also four serving assistants, who happen to be mothers of some of our children. They prepare and serve toast, cereals, and drinks and clean up the area when all the children have gone to class.

Source: Commissioned by The Open University for this volume.

The club is very hands on and we have to be adaptable in terms of covering absence through illness and being able to take on any of the roles in the club, work well in both the Key Stage 1 and 2 breakfast areas and even in the kitchen.

The sessions begin at 08.00 and we serve breakfasts till 08.40 when we encourage the children to clean and tidy up. The Key Stage 2 children then go out onto the yard and are supervised playing games until the bell goes for all at 08.55 when school begins. The Key Stage 1 children also tidy up but are then engaged in a story or singing with the teaching assistants in that area. At the moment we are teaching them to sing the school song, 'Find your talents and let them grow'. This does tend to settle them so they're more ready for the school day.

We try to make the club relaxing for the children by facilitating activities such as listening to our local radio station, Capital FM, playing chess, reading magazines, playing dominoes, playing cards and the latest favourite games. Draughts is popular in the Key Stage 2 area and building with bricks or cards in Key Stage 1 area.

We try to develop some physical skills by taking groups out on the playground, weather permitting, where they are encouraged to run or walk as many laps of the yard as they want to, approximately 300 metres a lap. This is recorded and a certificate given for doing 1500 metres, for instance.

The children seem to like attending a club before school and often just sit and chat amongst themselves before the formal curriculum of school begins. We also organise seasonal activities like, for instance, an Easter Egg Drawing competition, and a Mother's Day card. However nothing is forced on the children and they can choose to join in or not.

The whole club environment is a continual flux of children arriving, eating, playing games, and talking together. Children come in at various times to eat breakfast and are moving back and forth to get food and a drink. So, it is difficult to sit them all down and engage in one formal activity as in a classroom environment. We believe that the way we organise the club does prepare them for the more formal learning experiences of school. Because we don't have a captive audience, we suit the selected activities to a moving population and their shifting interests.

The children are all encouraged in good eating habits, talking together, and clearing away, especially the younger ones in Key Stage 1, some of whom find it hard to clear away or are even not very adept at using a spoon or knife. With our guidance most children, whatever their age, soon learn what is expected of them at the breakfast tables.

As a context for learning I think the club is somewhere between a classroom and playground. It does enable children to develop important educational and social skills in a non-classroom environment. In addition, we find we can do a lot of friendly nurturing during the club time.

There are, of course, rules that are based on the school rules and occasionally we have to remind the children of these. We expect and maintain a good code of language and behaviour, but we try to be more informal than we might be in a classroom situation. Sometimes a child may misbehave but normally they will respond to me, or one of the other teaching assistants, as we are all familiar with the children in our care. If we have constant disruption from a child then I will take them to talk it through with his or her class teacher and usually things will improve. However, if not, then we might talk to the parent and, as a last resort, the child might be excluded from the club for a while until the parent and teacher feel the child can go along with our rules. But this is a very rare step in my experience.

Sometimes we can sense there is a problem when younger children are brought in by parents, and as we are the first contact we sensitively chat with the parent and attempt to resolve the situation, if necessary, mentioning it later to the child's teacher. There was one occasion when a father was being quite sharp with his child and I was able to talk tactfully with him. It was because the mother and father had a big argument before coming in and this was carried over between the child and father into club. I was able to calm him and arrange a meeting with our head-teacher so he was able to resolve his family situation with a little help from us.

At 08.55 am we are responsible for ensuring all children in our care arrive safely at their classrooms ready for the beginning of lessons.

This is achieved by the Key Stage 1 staff walking the children across from breakfast club to the appropriate school entrance and handing them over to their class teacher. The Key Stage 2 children are usually out at play and they are supervised lining up ready for their teacher to lead them into school to begin the day's lessons.

My role, as co-ordinator, is to overview the entire operation from start to finish ensuring the smooth running of the breakfast club. I'm responsible for staffing and job allocation. Also I do the food ordering, where I contact our suppliers to arrange orders through our county approved suppliers and subsequent invoice delivery to our catering office. Recently we had a problem with milk deliveries so we now need to use a particular dairy that has been checked for the provenance of its product.

We are accountable to our funders, the Welsh Assembly, and have to take a register of all the children attending every day, which is used for funding allocation purposes.

I have been involved with the breakfast club from its start 8 years ago and have been co-ordinator for the last 2 years, which has been a new challenge for me. I have introduced many of the activities and continue to try out new ideas from the staff or the children. My own background was working in the chemical industry as a technician and I was able to take early retirement and begin a totally different career. I was a governor and parent-teacher association member at my son's school and I used to help occasionally as a volunteer in the school where my wife was a teacher.

Because I enjoyed this involvement I thought that I would like to do this work so I applied for a few positions in Cardiff schools and was lucky enough to get a position as a teaching assistant at Herbert Thompson Primary School. I was encouraged to do an NVQ3 and sent on numeracy and literacy courses to enable me to be a special educational needs teaching assistant.

Music is a particular interest of mine and once a week I assist with a visiting group of peripatetic musicians, teaching two Year 4 classes. The percussion tutor encouraged me to join in and guided me to a 'Samba' band group, where I have learnt to play an instrument and now enjoy playing at various functions in the area.

My teaching assistant role at Herbert Thompson is very different from my previous working life and I wish I could have made the career change earlier. It is something I really enjoy; especially working with the children and helping them develop their life skills and also mine too. For them and myself I do think it's all about lifelong learning.

Chapter 34

Enriched curriculum to the foundation stage curriculum

Dympna Meikleham with Roger Hancock

Dympna Meikleham is an outreach support assistant based at Harberton Special School, South Belfast, and Roger Hancock is a senior lecturer at The Open University. The account that follows makes conceptual and practice links between two curricula – the play-based, enriched curriculum, which was mainly adopted for children in the early years by Belfast primary schools and the foundation stage curriculum which with statutory backing is being adopted by all primaries in Northern Ireland.

Enriched curriculum

The enriched curriculum was a 'play-based' or 'doing-based' curriculum. It arose in early 2000 (see Sproule *et al.* 2002), out of the activities and collaborations between a number of Belfast primary and special schools, the Northern Ireland Council for Curriculum Assessment and Examinations, and members of the Belfast Education and Library Board.

The traditional curriculum at that time was very similar to the English National Curriculum assuming children would learn through formal class teaching quite early in their school careers. A different 'enriched' curriculum and less formal pedagogic approach was seen to be essential given the difficulties that many Key Stage 1 children were experiencing with a formal curriculum, especially rising five-year-old children in Primary 1 classes. The need for it grew out of the political and social difficulties within Belfast that many inner city families were caught up in. An additional consideration was that many children in Northern Ireland start school a little earlier than their English counterparts and they had been expected to start formal learning within the first term.

Source: A revised version of Meikleham, D. and Hancock, R. (2004) 'Learning through the enriched curriculum', commissioned by The Open University for *Primary Teaching Assistants: Curriculum in Context* (London: Routledge). Reprinted by permission of The Open University and Taylor & Francis Ltd.

Since that time, the enriched curriculum – in terms of its attention to children's interests and their wish to play as well as learn – has greatly influence practice in many Belfast schools and beyond even though it wasn't statutory. Its effect was most realised in Primary 1 but also, to some extent, as far up as Primary 4, the end of Key Stage 1. It's possible too that this approach to organising the curriculum and teaching it influenced practice into early stages of Key Stage 2.

Many teachers too have had to change their practice. For instance, you don't see so many teachers sitting at their desks, they are much more amongst the children and their desks are mostly used for storing papers and resources. The teacher is therefore more an integrated part of the class now, not someone who is positioned away from the class so to speak.

After a number of years of its implementation, the general feeling from practitioners was that the enriched curriculum worked for children and for them. Moreover, it was endorsed as best early years/early primary years practice by the Curriculum Authority and, to a certain extent, by the Education and Training Inspectorate (ETI). As for parents, there were mixed feelings. Those whose children went to inner city Belfast schools appeared mainly for it; those from more affluent and higher achieving areas were less so. Many parents in these areas felt they wanted their children to be moved forward academically as soon as possible – in short, to have a reading book and to be writing from day one.

Foundation stage curriculum

The current foundation curriculum arose out of the experience and success of the enriched curriculum. The purpose of the foundation stage:

> '. . . is to concentrate on developing a child's dispositions and readiness to learn, rather than to force the pace with children who are not sufficiently prepared for formal learning.'
>
> (BBC, 2007, p. 1)

The foundation curriculum became statutory in 2009–10 and, in many ways it is very similar to its forerunner. It's slightly more formal in that there were at first six areas of learning – language and literacy, mathematics and numeracy, the arts, personal development and mutual understanding, physical development and movement, and the world around us. Later, religious education was included as an area of learning.

The enriched curriculum was, right from the beginning, seen as a play based curriculum; the foundation stage curriculum is being seen as skills based. It differs from the old Key Stage 1 curriculum in that it's not content based. Therefore, we don't now say, for example, you're in Primary 4 now and in this class we study World War 2. It's much more skills based and child led. Imagine the children in a class develop a big interest in, say, weather for perhaps for half a term, they might study weather patterns and extreme weather on the internet, search out books in the library, make and paint volcano models, make their own musical instruments to produce weather sounds and so on. The new curriculum has few statutory requirements relating to subject content. This enables staff to choose the most relevant content for the children they are teaching.

With regard to possible repetition of such themes across classes, it's important to make sure that different aspects of the weather topic above are introduced to enable skills to progress. So, there has to be good communication between parallel classes and year groups, and where similar topics have been chosen you need to focus on how these can be extended so that new content is covered by the children. So, the emphasis is on the required skills like information management, thinking skills, personal capabilities, problem solving and creativity. How we teach such skills involved in researching and studying weather is up to those professionals who work with the children.

A further difference between the foundation curriculum and our old Key Stage 1 curriculum is that the former has no formal assessment. We do this in an ongoing way mainly through observation. Every classroom in my base school, Harberton Special School, for example, has a 'WALT' board, i.e. 'what we are learning today' and a 'WILF' board, i.e. 'what I'm looking for'. At the start of a lesson, the children will know what it is we're looking for in terms of specific skills that we are hoping to achieve in a particular activity and also what we are learning to do. This is explicit and shared with them.

In Primary 1 or 2, we would never, for instance, report to a parent that a child is working at 'Level 1' in the foundation stage. We would be looking at the child as an individual and assessing what skills are needed and how these can be developed through teaching and learning. Because I had worked within the enriched curriculum this approach isn't a great change for me. However, for those who had no experience of the enriched curriculum it would be quite a big change and this is so for a large number of staff in primary schools away from Belfast.

The new curriculum also places a great emphasis on talking and listening. For example, last year I worked in a Primary 1 class in a mainstream school and every session started with ten minutes together on the mat. This would be a talking and listening activity perhaps in literacy or maths and it involves listening carefully to what others are saying. Each session finishes with a plenary session when the children are asked to go over what they have been listening to and talking about. The teacher and the classroom assistant would themselves be listening carefully to this as part of their observation of children's learning: and they will note which children need more help to achieve the skills and concepts identified on the WALT board. Worksheets are not part of this new curriculum.

Of course it's not easy to observe and teach at the same time. One of the really good things that has come out of the foundation stage curriculum is that the teacher and classroom assistant must be working closely together in order that teaching and assessment can be effectively integrated. So there has to be close collaboration. Often, the teacher is going to be relying on the classroom assistant to be observing and taking notes as to which child isn't getting the hang of it and feeding this information back. This shared way of working and the way that all classroom staff need to be communicating with each other are highlighted in the foundation stage curriculum document. There's an emphasis on classroom teams. As the Introduction to the Foundation Stage Document (CCEA, 2006) states:

> A culture of mutual respect is based on open communication and positive relationships, with each individual participating as a team member.
>
> (p. 7)

As with the enriched curriculum at first, there were schools that found implementing the foundation stage a challenge. These schools, maybe through parental pressure to be 'academic', and especially pressures related to transfer to grammar schools, had become quite academic. They would have had children mainly sitting at desks writing and doing a lot of listening to teachers and other adults. Schools that initially engaged with the enriched curriculum did not find this observational way of working and implementing the foundation stage difficult.

Many parents wish schools to adopt early academic approaches to teaching because of our transfer system which still involves a form of eleven plus examination. So, for them, the day a child starts school, they see them as working towards a grammar school. Most areas in Northern Ireland still operate this system of transfer despite a move for change. The transfer test was once carried out in schools when children reached Primary 7 but now it's done on a Saturday morning in the grammar schools themselves which is meant to take the pressure away from the schools. Schools are not suppose to be teaching for transfer, however, the expectation is still there as many parents become anxious that their children should do well and want the kind of teaching that gets children into a grammar school.

In Primary 3 and 4, learning becomes more formal; but if progression through the foundation stage has been done well then there should not be a big difference for children moving their way through a primary school. It will, of course, be more pencil and paper work than other kinds of practical skills work and the content is certainly more laid out.

My role

I work in nursery schools in an outreach support role and I support children who have emotional and behaviour difficulties. When they come to the end of nursery I will go with them for the first one or two months, or whatever it takes, into a primary school to ease the child's transition. After that, when I withdraw, further measures may be put into place to support them in that primary school. I provide personal support and help them get used to the routines of primary school, and help them deal with the changes in ways of teaching and the more structured activities they do there. The classrooms in Primary 1 and 2 will be a little like those of a nursery school in terms of resources and the way the furniture is set out. However, children will sometimes be expected to sit at a table on a specific activity more often and for a longer period of time. With regard to being outside, they need to get used to a much bigger playground space with many more children playing. This can be a particular difficulty for the children I support.

The foundation stage, however, requires that children have a certain amount of their school day outside. This means, apart from being in a large playground, they will have access to some of the equipment like bikes and scooters, large climbing frames, possibly sand and gardening areas for digging as they would have had in a nursery.

One of the big things about the foundation stage is the idea that children should be involved in planning their own learning activities. In a Primary 1 class where I support a child they became interested in hairdressing because they had been looking at a shared reading book which was about a child going to the hairdressers. That had led on to role play. We had a hairdresser's set up in the classroom with a computer for the receptionist to book in appointments. The children printed out signs and pictures of different hairstyles. It went into number work in terms of the cost of a hairstyle and the times of the appointment. The children matched each customer with a towel, a hairbrush, a bottle of shampoo, and they counted out the money. They were therefore very involved right from the start in terms of planning and decisions about what should be in a hairdressers and how it might successfully run.

The child that I support really got into this whole theme. Her uncle actually had a hairdressers and she could hardly contain herself with enthusiasm. I found myself drawing her back a bit because everyone needed an opportunity to come up with ideas. Although her ideas were really good and informed by her experience, she could take over at times. She therefore needed to listen to others much more and to let them have their say. It was this social, interactional side of her development that I found I needed to focus on. And yet this was a child with great potential to be challenging in school but she was really into this topic.

For her, it was therefore about finding a balance between contributing and listening. It helped to have her very close to me and, if she had an idea, I encouraged her to whisper it in my ear. Then, after a while, when there was a lull in the discussion, I would say to the teacher Jenny's had a very good idea can she say it now. So, with my help she was able to manage her hastiness. Interestingly, the teacher in her class had not had experience of working with another adult in this way but she valued me taking care of Jenny as this enabled her to lead the whole class discussion without lots of interruptions or indeed temper tantrums.

This kind of learning needed to continue for Jenny as the topic unfolded. For instance, I had to help her to understand that she couldn't always be the hairdresser, sometimes had to be a customer or the receptionist. Such strong desires can cause a lot of friction in a class group and take a lot of teacher time – it's about children learning to turn-take and co-operate with the other children, of course. I interested Jenny by having pictures of various roles within the hairdressers. Each time she took on one role we discarded a picture and she had to choose another role (a sort of play schedule but for one activity). When in the nursery she had the same temperament but wasn't able to respond to opportunities to do well in this way. I spent every minute of every day with her during her transition period of around two months.

It's the same with all children I support until they've become accustomed to the change so there's a cyclical aspect to my role. It's work that I greatly enjoy because I'm supporting them through a transition and I learn a lot about what they are experiencing and the difficulties that confront them during this time. I often find that when they first move up they do regress a little but then, with appropriate help, can come around quite quickly.

The children I support are definitely more suited to the foundation curriculum than they were to the previous Key Stage 1 curriculum. I think the newer curriculum takes an awful lot of pressure off them, and I think I have more scope for support as I'm involved in talking to the child, establishing their interests and listening to their feelings. I'm not sitting at a table with them helping them to do worksheet-related activities. I'm helping them to work things out for themselves so there's a lot of two-way communication. Also because the foundation stage curriculum requires the classroom assistant to be fully involved in the class I find I can support the child whilst making it less obvious that I am there for a particular child. He or she can be in my small group, or I will be quietly reminding all of the children of the rules for good talking, good listening or good sharing – thus letting the target child know that the same rules apply to everyone. But at the same time I'm there and can intervene quickly should the need arise. It's a role that enables me to feel I make a difference in a very specific but also in a more general way.

References

BBC (2007) Northern Ireland Curriculum: Overview, Teacher's Resources. Accessed: http://www.bbc.co.uk/northernireland/schools/pdf/NIschools_curriculumOverview. pdf (accessed 03/07/11)

CCEA (Council for the Curriculum, Examinations and Assessment) (2006) Understanding the Foundation Stage, CCEA/Multimedia, Belfast.

Sproule, L., Trew, K., Rafferty, H., Walsh, G., McGuinness, C., Sheehy, N. and O'Neill, B. (2002) *The Early Years Enriched Curriculum Evaluation Project*: Second Year Report. Report produced privately for Northern Ireland Council for Curriculum Examinations and Assessment (CCEA).

Index